PULPIT & POLITICS

PULPIT & POLITICS

Separation of Church & State in the Black Church

MARVIN A. McMICKLE

Foreword by Rev. Dr. W. Wilson Goode Sr.

JUDSON PRESS
PUBLISHERS SINCE 1824
VALLEY FORGE, PA

Pulpit & Politics: Separation of Church & State in the Black Church
© 2014 by Judson Press, Valley Forge, PA 19482-0851
All rights reserved.

No part of this publication may be reproduced, stored in a retrieval system, or transmitted in any form or by any means, electronic, mechanical, photocopying, recording, or otherwise, without the prior permission of the copyright owner, except for brief quotations included in a review of the book.

Judson Press has made every effort to trace the ownership of all quotes. In the event of a question arising from the use of a quote, we regret any error made and will be pleased to make the necessary correction in future printings and editions of this book.

Interior design by Crystal Devine, Devine Design.
Cover design by Wendy Ronga and Hampton Design Group.

Library of Congress Cataloging-in-Publication data
McMickle, Marvin Andrew.
  Pulpit & politics : separation of church & state in the Black church / Marvin A. McMickle. -- first [edition].
      pages cm
     ISBN 978-0-8170-1751-4 (pbk. : alk. paper) 1. African American Baptists. 2. Baptists--Doctrines. 3. Church and state--United States. 4. African American preaching. I. Title. II. Title: Pulpit and politics.
  BX6447.M36 2014
  261.7089'96073--dc23
                    2014008417

Printed in the U.S.A.
First printing, 2014.

CONTENTS

Foreword by Rev. Dr. W. Wilson Goode Sr.   vii
Introduction   1

PART I:
The Preacher/Politician: A Model of Clergy Leadership

1. Preachers Have a Place in Politics   9
2. My Own Experiences in Politics   23
3. "Politics Is a Dirty Business"   41

PART II:
The Evolution of Religious Liberty and the Separation of Church and State

4. The Quest for Religious Liberty   57
5. The United States as a Secular Society   79
6. What the U.S. Constitution Actually Says   96

PART III:
The Rise and the Role of the Black Preacher/Politician

7. Moral Conflict in the New United States of America   109
8. Four Models of Black Clergy Leadership for the Twenty-First Century   129
9. Black Preacher/Politicians as Public Theologians   150

PART IV:
The Black Church and Political Activism

10. The Dos and Don'ts That Every Church Should Know   163
11. The Marks of a Politicized Congregation   175
12. Political Churches and Campaign Finance Laws   195

A Concluding Word: Calling All Interested Persons!   211
Recommended Bibliography   215

FOREWORD

Marvin A. McMickle has given a gift to church leaders, especially to pastors who need guidance in engaging the political system. This book is a road map for those who are unsure about their involvement in elected office while remaining active in a leadership role in their congregation.

I remember running for the office of mayor in 1983. At that time I was chairman of the board of deacons at my church, the First Baptist Church of Paschall. Many would ask me the same question—how can you profess to be a Christian and at the same time be an effective politician? It was a common question but one that I felt could easily be answered.

I believe people of faith with a deep sense of purpose are perfect for public offices. People would often ask me, Would you rather have in office a person of faith with deep-seated principles or have someone with no faith and no principles? To me the answer to that question is very easy and very simple. It is a person of faith. It was my faith and the principles by which I live that enabled me while mayor to develop socially innovative programs. During my administration, I created the first program for the homeless in any city in the country, the first innovative AIDS program, and the first program on literacy. As a person of faith I was able to look through different lenses and develop initiatives that specifically targeted the less fortunate.

In doing all that I did while Mayor of the City of Philadelphia, at no time did I feel conflicted about what I ought to do. I understood clearly my legal responsibility as mayor, but I also understood the spiritual framework that was working within that enabled me to make sound decisions. These decisions were not based just upon my legal responsibility as mayor, but on my spiritual responsibility to help those in the most need. When I left office in 1992, one of the reporters who covered me during my administration wrote an assessment of my time in office and concluded that I probably would have been a better politician if I had had the mindset of a ward politician rather than that of a Baptist deacon. He meant it as a form of criticism, but I wear it today as a badge of honor. Preachers have a special role to play in politics, and that role is not the same as the professional politician. The preacher/politician brings a unique perspective that looks beyond the game that mere politicians play to perceive the humanity of the city.

This book explores this topic of **pulpit and politics** in a candid and informational way. McMickle skillfully traces thoughts of religion, liberty, and separation of church and state, and rightfully concludes there is nothing in these concepts that should dissuade preachers from involvement in politics. Moreover, I would add that those who seek to improve the lives of people beyond that of the congregation can best do so by using an elected office to bring about fundamental change to the myriad social problems facing urban and rural areas. McMickle paints a clear picture of the uniqueness of the African American church and culture in our society and the need for leaders in those churches to be more than a Sunday morning preacher if they are to confront the social ills and enact change in public policy that disproportionally impacts the African American community. The preacher/politician can be a major voice in bringing about change.

McMickle has provided the nation a useful and practical tool for creating a merger of faith and the public square. If its insights are heeded, it will educate a new group of leaders in government that will result in a public awareness not seen in decades. In *Pulpit & Politics*, McMickle has provided a classic of how preachers/politicians can function in a society without violating the law of God or the law of government. The church and society have suffered in the past because of the lack of intellectual leadership that this book pursues. McMickle has written a blueprint for the way forward—we all should take the journey!

Rev. Dr. W. Wilson Goode Sr.
President and CEO, Amachi, Inc.
Mayor, 1984–1992, City of Philadelphia

INTRODUCTION

A man in this State cannot do his whole duty as a minister except he looks out for the political interests of his people.[1]
—Rev. Charles H. Pearce

These are the words of an African Methodist Episcopal pastor from Florida spoken during the Reconstruction era (1865–1877). It was his view then, and it is my view today, that it is essential that black preachers be engaged in the political process of this country, not so they can simply accumulate more and more power and influence, but so that such power and influence as they may accumulate can be used for the empowerment of other people and the betterment of our society.

I address my concerns toward black preachers and black churches for a particular reason. As will be pointed out repeatedly in this book, the white population majority of the United States has never needed its clergy to serve as its political and spiritual leaders. There has always been a full supply of white citizens from a wide array of professions who could serve as the political leaders of their community. As Peter Dobkin Hall points out, in the seventeenth century ministers were the only members of a learned profession to constitute a significant group in New England. However, by the eighteenth century things had changed significantly in regard to clergy leadership in any area of white society was concerned. He writes,

> By the early decades of the eighteenth century, clerical authority and the status of clergymen in their communities could only be maintained by actions that made clergymen dependent either on the legislature or on powerful mercantile interests. Where once

clergymen, as the only highly educated translocal group, had led the colonists, forming their opinions and serving as advisors and sometimes masters of the magistrates, by the mid-eighteenth century they were struggling for survival.[2]

On the other hand, the history of black people in the United States created circumstances under which the black church quickly became the most important institution among black people, and the preacher quickly emerged as the leader within that institution. That leadership resulted in the black preacher being far more than a spiritual leader dealing only with matters of church doctrine and discipline. The black preacher quickly emerged in the role of the preacher/politician.

Eric Foner, in *A Short History of Reconstruction*, notes how the role of the black preacher as politician emerged:

> Even those preachers who lacked ambition for political positions sometimes found it thrust upon them. Often among the few literate blacks in a community, they were called upon to serve as election registrars and candidates for office. Over 100 black ministers ... would be elected to legislative seats during Reconstruction.[3]

This does not mean that all of the black elected officials during the Reconstruction era were preacher/politicians. Foner estimates that the total number of black politicians serving at every level of government in the country between 1865 and 1877 may have been close to two thousand.[4] Thus, in terms of proportion, the number of black preacher/politicians was about 5 percent of the total number of black officeholders. What I am arguing here is not that black preachers ever did or ever should comprise the statistical majority of officeholders in the black community, but rather that there always has been and always should be room for those black preachers who want to shape their ministry in a way that blends religion and politics, church and state, or in terms of being black preacher/politicians.

What may have been forgotten by many people in this country, even by people intimately familiar with various aspects of the history of the black church, is the important role played by black preacher/politicians over the last 150 years. This book is an attempt to reintroduce that history and to take a careful look at many of the black preachers who have served in political positions at various levels of government over that period of time. However, this book intends to do more than offer a historical reflection on the role that black preacher/politicians have played in the past. It is my hope that this book will also result in the emergence of a new generation of black preacher/politicians who will step forward and, in the words of Anthony Pinn, "use their religious sensibilities as a way of shaping governmental policies for the welfare of the underprivileged."[5]

WHAT ABOUT THE SEPARATION OF CHURCH AND STATE?

As soon as someone joins the words "preacher" and "politics," there will likely be the response that what is being proposed is a violation of the principle of the separation of church and state. Surely, according to the views of some, there is a constitutional prohibition against the active involvement of members of the clergy in the political process in general and in holding elective office in particular. As will be discussed at length later, I ran for a seat in the U.S. House of Representatives in 1998. Within minutes of the announcement of my candidacy I was confronted with this charge. "It is against the U.S. Constitution for ministers to be involved in politics as officeholders" was the view of some. "A preacher seeking or holding political office is a violation of the principle of the separation of church and state" was the response of others.

Those responses have troubled me in the intervening years since I sought to win election to Congress. To a very great degree, this book also intends to make the case that the involvement of black preachers or any other members of the clergy in the political process is in no way a violation of the separation of church and state. Such involvement has been going on since Rev. John Witherspoon of New Jersey was appointed to the First Continental Congress and signed the Declaration of Independence in 1776, and also since Hiram Revels, an African Methodist Episcopal preacher from Mississippi, was elevated to one of two vacant seats in the U.S. Senate in 1870. This book offers a review of the concept of the separation of church and state, as well as a careful study of the long and well-documented history of black preacher/politicians. The conclusion will be that what I was undertaking in 1998 may have been politically naïve in terms of breaking into the world of electoral politics at the age of fifty, but it was in no way a violation of any law or constitutional prohibition.

The fact is that the words "separation of church and state" appear nowhere in the Constitution of the United States. What the Constitution does prohibit is found in the First Amendment, which speaks about the establishment of, or the granting of preferential treatment or taxpayer support for one religious group over all others. In addition to that, the Constitution says that government shall not interfere in the free exercise of religion, or the right of citizens to worship God or to disavow any belief in God according to their own conscience. Thus, when it comes to the matter of church and state, the greater intent is to limit if not eliminate any government involvement in the matter of religious institutions, beliefs, and practices. What was never intended as far as church and state issues are concerned was to limit or eliminate the involvement of people of religious faith, including members of the clergy, from active involvement in the political life of this country.

Something else that the Constitution prohibits is found in Article 6, which says in part, "No religious test shall ever be required as a qualification to any office or public trust under the United States." That phrase carries two levels of meaning. First, it means that political office is not reserved only for those who belong to the state-sanctioned church, as was so often the case in Europe during those years. Second, it means that a person's existing religious views or practices should not serve to exclude a person from holding political office. Religious affiliation should not be a factor, one way or another, in deciding who is qualified to hold public office in this country. People who are quick to argue for the separation of church and state, which does not appear in the Constitution, as the basis upon which clergy should not be engaged in political activity, are usually completely unaware of Article 6, in the main body of the document ratified in 1787, which refutes their argument altogether.

Not only is political involvement by black churches and black clergy leaders allowed by the Constitution, but also it should be seen as a significant part of black church history and practice. In fact, political involvement in one form or another should also be viewed as an essential part of the role of black churches and black clergy in the twenty-first century. If black churches and black preachers are to do their full duty as shepherds of the flock of God and as interpreters of the present time, they will have to provide leadership in areas beyond prayer and spiritual formation. They will also have to find ways to engage the political process of this country on behalf of the people who look to them for leadership.

Notes

1. Quoted in Eric Foner, *A Short History of Reconstruction, 1863–1877* (New York: Harper & Row, 1990), 41.
2. Peter Dobkin Hall, *The Organization of American Culture, 1700–1900: Private Institutions, Elites, and the Origins of American Nationality* (New York: New York University Press, 1984), 30.
3. Foner, *Short History of Reconstruction*, 41.
4. Eric Foner, "Rooted in Reconstruction: The First Wave of Black Congressmen," *The Nation*, November 3, 2008, 10.
5. Anthony B. Pinn, *The Black Church in the Post–Civil Rights Era* (Maryknoll, NY: Orbis Books, 2002), 76.

Part I

THE PREACHER/POLITICIAN: A MODEL OF CLERGY LEADERSHIP

1

PREACHERS HAVE A PLACE IN POLITICS

I am aware that there are likely to be many people, including many black clergy, who will not immediately agree with my insistence upon political involvement as an essential aspect of the work of the church and the clergy. They will likely be inclined to say, "Render unto Caesar that which is Caesar's, and unto God that which is God's" (see Matthew 22:21), or, "Be in the world but not of the world" (see John 15:19; 17:14; Romans 12:2). I honor those who see it as their chief vocational task to serve in a priestly or pastoral role with spiritual formation as their primary objective. However, I want to call attention to the claim by Peter Paris that over the years that black people have been living in the United States and its colonial predecessors, black clergy have functioned within four distinct leadership models: priestly, prophetic, nationalist, and political.[1]

Most black preachers have always gravitated to the more sheltered and less controversial role of priestly leaders working almost exclusively within the church and within church-based or church-affiliated organizations. It should not be forgotten that while the priestly role may have been the most frequently chosen role for black preachers, it was by no means the only role chosen by all black preachers. Readers of this book will be reminded of the other three models of leadership mentioned by Paris, including the political model of clergy leadership within the black church that has functioned with great effectiveness over the last 150 years, and that can and, hopefully, will continue to play an important role in the twenty-first century.

It should be noted that a separate attempt at defining the leadership models of the black preacher in America is offered by Tamelyn Tucker-Worgs in her book *The Black Mega-Church: Theology, Gender, and the Politics of Public Engagement*. That book looks at the public engagement models of 149 black congregations with an average weekly attendance of two thousand persons or more. The author states, "The repertoire of black church public engagement activities comprises three broad categories: protest politics, electoral politics, and community development."[2]

For Tucker-Worgs, the protest aspect of black church leadership is typified by the Civil Rights era and would match up well with Paris's reference to the prophetic model of leadership. The community development model, which is a new designation, relates specifically to the capacity of megachurches to leverage their resources into 501(c)(3) organizations that can seek grants and engage in not-for-profit efforts that range from housing rehabilitation, to retail and commercial outlets, to other forms of physical redevelopment in hard-hit urban centers. However, she also points to the electoral politics focus of many black megachurches when she says, "As African Americans gained greater access to the electoral sphere, activist black churches in post–civil rights America hold candidate forums and distribute voter guides, and in more than a few cases their ministers have run for public office."[3]

Tucker-Worgs suggests that this kind of political activism has been present in black churches since African Americans "gained greater access to the electoral sphere." What she does not suggest, but what is central to the argument in this book, is that black people first gained such access with the passage of the Fifteenth Amendment to the Constitution in 1870 during the Reconstruction era, not with the Voting Rights Act of 1965. Thus, the involvement of black churches and black ministers in electoral politics does not come on the heels of the Civil Rights era of the 1950s and 1960s; rather, political involvement greatly precedes that era by nearly one hundred years, then runs parallel to it, and continues into the twenty-first century well beyond the time of what she calls protest politics.

The central point is this: both Peter Paris and Tamelyn Tucker-Worgs recognize that there are several legitimate and long-standing models for leadership and activity among black churches and black clergy, and that one of those models involves electoral politics. Neither author offers even a hint of concern that this political involvement is a violation of the idea of the separation of church and state. In fact, both of them would agree that it was the separation of black people from the mainstream of American society with the sanction and support of the state that created the conditions that gave birth first to the black church, then to the black preacher, and finally to the black preacher/politician.

If political leadership for black communities in the nineteenth century could have arisen unobstructed by racism and the lingering effects of centuries of slavery, the political model of black clergy leadership might not have been necessary. Such leadership could have arisen from within any number of professional groups in which black people normally would have been engaged. This was the experience of the white church community, which never had to look to its clergy for political leadership because persons could be found within the fields of law, education, business, and the military to fill those electoral positions.

That is only now becoming true in the black community. Thus, the issue here is not upholding the separation of church and state when black preacher/politicians emerge; rather, the issue is what many black preachers and black churches had to do and chose to do because the masses of black people had been intentionally and systematically denied access to power or influence within the United States.

This point bears repeating for the sake of added emphasis. If "liberty and justice for all" had included black Americans from the founding of this country, it is very likely that black preacher/politicians would never have emerged. Like their white counterparts, there would have been more than an ample supply of potential political leaders rising up from all the various professions to which black people would have had unfettered access. It was in response to the absence of liberty and justice for their people that black preacher/politicians began to emerge. It was because so many professions were closed to black Americans from which civic leaders and political leaders could have emerged that a disproportionate number of persons from this particular profession began to emerge as soon as the burdens and limitations of slavery were lifted. This point must be kept in mind when someone seeks to challenge the presence of black preacher/politicians in the political process by referring to "the separation of church and state," a phrase that does not appear in the Constitution.

A THEOLOGICAL POINT OF DEPARTURE

The case that I want to make about the preacher/politician focuses primarily upon the black churches of the United States, but I want to begin by setting forth a theological claim about the link between religion and politics that transcends race or denomination. In order to preempt being criticized for offering only a liberal or progressive theological perspective on this issue, I will draw from the writings of two theologians of great standing within their respective theological traditions: Robert McAfee Brown and Carl F. H. Henry. We begin with the words of Robert McAfee Brown:

> Any Christian worth his salt knows that in this day and age there is an imperative laid upon him to be politically responsible. When one considers the fateful decisions which lie in the hands of the politicians, and the impact which these decisions will have for good or ill upon the destinies of millions of people, it becomes apparent that in terms of trying to implement the will of God, however fragmentarily, politics can be a means of grace. Christians may not retreat behind the specious excuse that politics is too messy. Politics has become an arena where the most fastidious Christian must act responsibly and decisively if he is not to be derelict in his duties.[4]

These words from Robert McAfee Brown about acting responsibly and decisively in the political arena were written some sixty years ago, and they came forth in the context of his own involvement in the reelection campaign of Eugene McCarthy as a member of Congress from Minnesota. Brown, himself an ordained Presbyterian minister, wrote them while serving on the faculty of Macalester College, a college affiliated with the Presbyterian Church, prior to his move to Stanford, where he taught from 1962 to 1976. He was cofounder of Clergy and Laity Concerned about Vietnam. He was also arrested in 1961 during his participation as a Freedom Rider in Florida.

These words were instructive to me in 1998, when I ran for a seat in the U.S. House of Representatives, and they are instructive in today's political environment. Is it appropriate for members of the clergy to be involved in the political process, and to what degree? Should clergy speak about and advocate for specific political issues? Should they write editorials and opinion pieces for the local newspaper on political questions? Should they actively support and even personally endorse persons who are running for political office? Should members of the clergy themselves seek and serve in elective office? If politics can be a means of grace, then why should members of the clergy not seek to engage in what can be essentially another form of ministry?

It is important to begin a discussion about religion and politics and about the involvement of preachers and pastors in the political process by offering a philosophy upon which that involvement can be understood. That is where this statement from Robert McAfee Brown comes in, since he talks about politics as having the potential to be "a means of grace." For most people, these words do not describe their understanding of the political process. Most people likely see politics as divisive, contentious, intrusive, bureaucratic, and corrupt or corrupting. For all of these reasons, many people want nothing to do with politics as it is being practiced in the United States at the present time.

Their point is well taken. As these words were being written, the federal government of the United States was shut down by members of Congress, who were embroiled in a war for and against the Affordable Care Act, which some refer to as "Obamacare." This is a law that was voted on and passed by both houses of Congress; it was endorsed by the reelection of Barack Obama in a campaign against Mitt Romney in 2012 in which the health care law was the central item of contention; and it was upheld as constitutional by the U.S. Supreme Court. Nevertheless, those who have opposed the health care law all along intended to prevent it from taking effect by refusing to provide funding for its operation.

When Congress failed to vote in 2013 on a federal budget that would include funding for the Affordable Care Act, more than 800,000 federal workers were laid off for sixteen days, and the national economy incurred a loss of more than $24 billion. All of this was the result of the inaction of a minority of the 585 members of Congress, all of whom continued to draw their salaries. This is the politics that left Congress with a 13 percent approval rating by the American people. This is the kind of partisan bickering that has turned so many Americans off in regard to the political process.

POLITICS CAN BE A MEANS OF GRACE

This is not how politics was meant to work in this country, and according to Brown, this is not how politics has to work in this country. Politics can be a means of grace. Political institutions, along with other agencies in our society, can be one of the vehicles by which a more just and humane society can be shaped. Brown is correct when he observes that the decisions made by political leaders impact the lives of millions of people for good or for ill. Our society has allowed for the use of mass incarceration as a way to marginalize black and brown people, as has been powerfully pointed out by Michelle Alexander in *The New Jim Crow: Mass Incarceration in the Age of Colorblindness*.[5] Will we allow this to continue? That is a political decision made by persons who hold in their hands the fate of millions of people.

Will we have meaningful immigration reform, a minimum wage that can lift working people from the ranks of the working poor, a foreign policy that prefers diplomacy over missile strikes, and a respect for the rights and value of every person, including persons in the LGBT community? These are political decisions, and when they are made by people who possess a passion for justice and equal opportunity, politics can become a means of grace because it becomes the means by which these outcomes are brought to pass. Surely the idea of politics as a means of grace was what President John F. Kennedy had in mind in his inaugural address in 1961 when he said,

> With a good conscience our only sure reward, with history the final judge of our deeds, let us go forth to lead the land we love, asking His blessing and His help, but knowing that here on earth God's work must truly be our own.[6]

This is not the message of a preacher aspiring to be involved in politics and looking to insert the word "God" into the national conversation. This is the thirty-fifth president of the United States reminding us that politics can be a means of grace through which the broad values of human dignity and mutual respect for all people can be advanced. When politics is viewed from this angle, it makes perfect sense that people of faith in general and members of the clergy in particular might want to be involved in such an enterprise.

This is not the petty bickering and ideological stalemates currently on display among so many of our political leaders. This is a new understanding of what politics can be and what politicians can accomplish when faced with a more promising philosophy and purpose—politics as a means of grace.

AVOIDING DERELICTION OF DUTY

A second challenge comes from those words of Robert McAfee Brown that have informed my ministry and now inform this book: Christians must act responsibly and decisively within the political arena if they are not to be derelict in their duties. If the phrase "politics as a means of grace" puts a positive spin on involvement of Christians and other faith communities in terms of the good that can be accomplished through the political process, then the phrase "derelict in [their] duties" points to the negative consequences of failing to be involved in the political process. If a church or a pastor focuses only on the sanctuary, the hospital bedside, the support of grieving families at a grave site, and the instruction of children and adults in the doctrines of their denomination, they may still be charged with dereliction of duty for failing to engage the process that could, with a single vote, transform for the better the lives of millions of people, including people in that very congregation.

Again, I recognize that there will be many Christians, both lay and clergy, who will not initially embrace the idea of political activity being an essential aspect of the work of the church and its clergy. Some Christians from the holiness/sanctified faith traditions will state that politics can only lead to corruption and a loss of focus on spiritual matters. It is not my intention to refute those views or to demean or declare as unfaithful those who hold them. It is simply my intention to offer an alternative understanding of the link between religion and politics, and to suggest how many opportunities exist to advance the very values that we teach in our churches when we avail ourselves of the influence and resources that reside within the political process.

THE CHURCH DOES BELONG IN POLITICS

The second understanding of the link between religion and politics that has informed my ministry and that now informs this book comes from Carl F. H. Henry, who was a leader within the conservative evangelical movement in the United States largely through his role as the founder and former editor of *Christianity Today*. In his book *Christian Countermoves in a Decadent Culture* he says,

> Does the church belong in politics? Since God wills the state as an instrumentality for preserving justice and restraining disorder, the church should urge members to engage in political affairs to their utmost competence and ability, to vote faithfully and intelligently, to engage in the public process at all levels, and to seek and hold public office.[7]

Notice the positive tone with which Henry speaks about the link between church and state. He says that the church "should urge members" to be politically engaged. He goes beyond the step of urging people to cast their votes and states that Christians should "engage in the public process at all levels" and should "seek and hold public office." This is no cry to keep church and state as far removed from one another as possible. This is an invitation for Christians to be as diligent and determined in the performance of their civic duties as any other segment of society. Christians should be informed voters. Christians should be conversant in the political issues of their time and region of the country. And when called upon or inclined to do so, Christians should seek and hold public office as well. This call to action does not say "Christian lay people, but not their clergy." Henry does not draw a line around one segment of the church and say that his invitation to be politically engaged does not refer to them. What we hear in the words of both Robert McAfee Brown and Carl F. H. Henry is that all Christians, clergy included, can and should be active in politics even to the point of holding elective office.

Notice that Henry offers a rationale for the involvement of church people in politics as did Brown with his reference to politics as a means of grace. Henry talks about "preserving justice and restraining disorder." This theological position does not focus on the quest simply to amass power and influence, but rather on what can be accomplished for good when that power and influence is in the hands of people who want to use it to accomplish things that expand opportunity for all citizens and prevent things that result in disadvantage or discrimination directed toward any segment of the society.

As I listen to the current political debates in this country, these concepts seem totally absent from the agenda of so many lawmakers. The discussions seem to be about how much money can be cut from food stamp programs, or how many children can be removed from Head Start programs, or how many people with preexisting medical conditions can be kept away from affordable medical insurance, or how many college students can be priced out of the market because of a sharp increase in the interest rates for federally funded student loans. I remember watching a Tea Party convention on C-Span a few years ago at which a woman was weeping as she cried out, "I want my America back." Since this gathering was occurring the day after Barack Obama had nominated Sonya Sotomayor to a seat on the Supreme Court, I knew exactly which America it was that she wanted back. It was an America where there would not be an African American president who could nominate a Hispanic woman to the nation's highest court. And so, we indeed do need people at every level of government who see it as their duty to preserve justice and restrain disorder.

POLITICS SHOULD NEVER BE USED TO PROSELYTIZE OR EVANGELIZE

The only caution that Henry offers as it involves Christians and the political process is this: the church must not "use the mechanisms of government to legally impose upon society at large her theological commitments."[8] This is the principle of "no establishment of religion" found in the First Amendment to the Constitution. This is the principle of religious liberty that is central to the reason why this nation was founded. This is the reason why the founders of the nation and several Supreme Court rulings focused on the principle of the separation of church and state. This is a view with which I am fully in accord. Politics and government should never be in the business of endorsing, advancing, funding, or even favoring any religious group or ideology over any other.

The objective of being involved in politics is not that we transform the society into a church or, more narrowly, transform society according to the social agenda of a particular segment of the faith community. This is precisely where the issue of the separation of church and state must be engaged. The issue is not and never was a matter of keeping people of religious faith from being involved in political activities. The issue is far more nuanced: first, to prevent government from favoring one religious group over another; second, to prevent religious groups from using the political process to impose their particular theology or social agenda.

The caution issued by Carl F. H. Henry puts him in full agreement with my former seminary president, John Bennett, who wrote,

> The churches in America should not use their members as political pressure groups to get special ecclesiastical privileges for themselves as against other religious bodies. They should not seek legislation ... which interferes with the religious liberty of minorities and they should be thankful that the courts stand guard at this point.[9]

Bennett continues,

> No church, no matter how powerful, should bring pressure on the state to enact laws which are based upon principles that depend for their validity on its own doctrine or ethos. ... It is wrong to make the ethos of one part of the community the basis of law.[10]

The best way to avoid the issue of separation of church and state is to steer clear of linking any matters of individual church doctrine or dogma, such as the forms of baptism, the ordination of women, the authority of Scripture, or the divinity of Jesus. All of these and many more are matters to be worked out within and between church bodies, not imposed by the coercive power of government. Let us look at two examples.

First, the Supreme Court ruling in *Roe v. Wade* is a highly contentious issue in this country. This 1973 court ruling deals not only with a woman's right to have an abortion, but also with the right of poor women to have access to federal funding that can pay for a legal procedure that women who have personal financial resources or access to private insurance can fund without reliance on the government. The hook being used by many to oppose *Roe v. Wade* is not just a personal opposition to abortion, but also the use of "their tax dollars" to fund a medical procedure that they find morally objectionable.

The same objections are being made to provisions within the Affordable Care Act that require employers to provide medical insurance that would include coverage for birth control and forms and methods of abortion. Privately owned companies such as Chick-fil-A and Hobby Lobby are seeking a waiver from that provision because their owners are devout Christians who are strongly opposed to all forms of abortion. The issues of religion and politics are so tightly entwined in the debate over abortion that is it difficult to tell where one ends and the other begins.

Is this a religious question based upon the views of some people about abortion as an act of murder or at what stage in the nine-month process a fetus becomes a human being? Or is this a Fourteenth Amendment "equal protection under the law" issue, whereby the government works to ensure that legal resources and services available to some persons in society are equally available to all who might benefit from that service? Should the views of some members of the church prevail over the voted actions of the highest court in the nation? Or should religious communities use their maximum influence to create a climate in which future nominees to the Supreme Court will be inclined to share the view that abortions should be banned and that *Roe v. Wade* be overturned? There is no common agreement within the Christian world about abortion, much less within the secularized American society. This is one instance where the separation of church and state makes sense! It is wrong and extremely divisive to attempt, as Bennett put it, "to make the ethos of one part of the community the basis of law."

Second, this same challenge exists where the practice of capital punishment is concerned. People within the faith communities of this country hold contrasting views on whether or not it is right for the state to put to death, by one method or another, persons found guilty of a certain level of criminal conduct. Some argue through the use of certain texts in the Bible that those who take the life of another person should pay by having their own life taken away. Others respond with other parts of the same Bible that it is no more right for the state to end a human life than it is for one person to end the life of another. That argument usually is reinforced by the observation that DNA evidence often has later determined that innocent persons were executed for crimes that they did not commit, or that people of a lower economic level or of certain ethnic groups are more frequently charged with crimes that could result in the death penalty than are persons of higher income levels or other ethnic groups.

When the church makes it its business to impose its view upon the whole of society, no matter how narrowly that view might be held, it is time to talk about the separation of church and state. No single sermon or sermon series, no statement of concern issued by a denominational gathering, and no papal encyclical can, will, or should impose that religious understanding of the issue upon the whole of American society. It is time for us to take a reminder from Stephen Prothero: "Thanks to the establishment clause, the

US government is secular by law; thanks to the free exercise clause, American society is religious by choice."[11]

The British essayist G. K. Chesterton once described the United States as "a nation with the soul of a church."[12] This is not surprising, since the issue of the role of government in the matter of religion was one of the questions around which the nation was birthed and around which the First Amendment to the Constitution was deeply concerned. How does a nation allow some of its citizens to have the right to exercise their religious beliefs according to their own conscience, while at the same time protecting other citizens from having to live by religious values that they do not share and may fervently oppose? Government ought not be the mediator of religious disputes that rely not upon legal precedent but rather upon scriptural interpretation. That is what the principle of the separation of church and state seeks to clarify.

HOW DO WE CARE FOR THE "LEAST OF THESE"?

How should people of faith in general and preacher/politicians in particular seek to navigate the politics of a nation that has the soul of a church? For me, the answer lies with those broad moral and ethical issues that all Christians and persons of other faith groups hold dear. They are found in biblical texts, but they can be and often have been advanced and enabled by political action. When Jesus speaks in Matthew 25:31-46 about the hungry, the thirsty, the naked, the sick, the stranger, and the imprisoned, he is pointing toward things that can be addressed at a macrolevel through progressive social policies enacted by a legislative body that benefit the whole of society. This only augments what is done in these areas by well-meaning Christians and their congregations operating at a microlevel as they seek to advance these same issues through one family or person at a time.

Politics can sometimes appear to be about rather mundane things such as paving roads and picking up trash. However, as Leonard Pitts Jr. pointed out recently in his syndicated column, the question is often whose roads will be paved, whose trash will be picked up, and whose neighborhoods will be protected against toxic waste dumping. He described a situation in Miami, Florida, that involved two adjacent communities, Coconut Grove, with "side streets lined with cozy bungalows," and West Grove, "the hardscrabble, historically black area that abuts Coconut Grove. I had driven less than a mile—and ended up on the other side of the world."[13]

Pitts points out that when toxins were found in the soil in a park in Coconut Grove, the residents were alerted, the park was closed, and the toxic soil was removed within a few days. However, when the very same conditions were found in the soil in West Grove, the city of Miami was given sixty days to address the problem, a deadline that the city missed twice. After several months had passed by, the city of Miami declared that the soil that required immediate removal from Coconut Grove was deemed "not a health risk" in West Grove.

This was a political decision by people who obviously do not see it as their responsibility to look out for the ones whom Jesus calls "the least of these my little ones." Pitts denounces the mindset of those who made this judgment in Miami when he writes, "These inequities exist because we allow them, because we condone by our silence the second-class citizenship of those who are not us. People have the right to expect they will be treated as if they matter. Even if they live on the other side of the world."[14]

This is what it means to have a politics that is a means of grace—a politics that protects the rights and hears the voices of all people regardless of income, ethnicity, or region. This is how the power of politics and the broad values of religious faith can and should work together, treating all people as if they matter. There is a place for people of religious faith, including clergy, in the political process, to make sure that politics works to care for the least of these and not just for the richest and wealthiest among us.

EVERYBODY TALKING ABOUT HEAVEN AIN'T GOING THERE

I am not saying that people with no religious foundation are incapable of using political power with a sense of moral conviction and with a desire to achieve a more just and equitable society. There are undoubtedly many people at work at every level of government who serve our society quite well without claiming any religious faith as the basis for their motivation or their choices. I am also quite aware that religious faith, or at least the claim of having it, is not a guarantee that a person will work for a just society once elected or appointed to political office. It is likely that most of the politicians who worked and voted to maintain slavery in this country were persons of religious faith. The same can be said about those political leaders who denied human rights and land rights to Native Americans, who sought to prevent women from gaining the right to vote, and who refuse at this present moment in history to enact equitable immigration policies for the more than twelve million undocumented workers (or "illegal immigrants" as they are called by some) currently living in the United States.

What I am suggesting is that our society has been well served by a steady stream of black religious leaders who, in addition to their duties in the sphere of the sacred, have also made great contributions in the sphere of politics. They have used political office as a means of grace (Robert McAfee Brown). They have used political office as a way to preserve justice and restrain disorder (Carl F. H. Henry). They have used their religious sensibilities to shape public policy that has aided the disadvantaged (Anthony Pinn). Along with the priestly, prophetic, and nationalist models of leadership that have emerged within the life of the black church, there is another model that has operated since the days of the Reconstruction: the black preacher/politician.

Notes

1. Peter J. Paris, *Black Religious Leaders: Conflict in Unity*, 2nd ed. (Louisville: Westminster/John Knox Press, 1991), 17.
2. Tamelyn N. Tucker-Worgs, *The Black Mega-Church: Theology, Gender, and the Politics of Public Engagement* (Waco, TX: Baylor University Press, 2011), 103.
3. Ibid.
4. Robert McAfee Brown, "Confessions of a Political Neophyte," *Christianity and Crisis*, December 24, 1953, 186.
5. Michelle Alexander, *The New Jim Crow: Mass Incarceration in the Age of Colorblindness* (New York: New Press: 2012).
6. Gregory R. Suriano, ed., *Great American Speeches* (New York: Gramercy Books, 1993), 220.
7. Carl F. H. Henry, *Christian Countermoves in a Decadent Culture* (Portland, OR: Multnomah Press, 1986), 118.
8. Ibid.
9. John C. Bennett, *Christians and the State* (New York: Scribner, 1958), 207.
10. Ibid.
11. Stephen Prothero, *Religious Literacy: What Every American Needs to Know— And Doesn't* (New York: Harper One, 2007), 22.
12. G. K. Chesterton, *The Collected Works of G. K. Chesterton*, vol. 21 (San Francisco: Ignatius Press, 1990), 41–45.
13. Leonard Pitts Jr., "Shame on Systemic Inequity," *Democrat & Chronicle*, October 1, 2013, A9.
14. Ibid.

2

MY OWN EXPERIENCES IN POLITICS

I am drawn to the topic of this book not merely out of curiosity or scholarly objectivity. I am drawn to it because for most of my forty years in ministry I have also been actively involved in the political process either as an officeholder, a candidate, or an active member of countywide Democratic Party organizations. Whenever I or my church was called upon by others to assist them in their pursuit of a political office, there was no problem. However, as soon as I ran for an office and later held an elective office, the topic of the separation of church and state suddenly popped up. I have been a preacher/politician for several decades. I have witnessed firsthand how politics can be used to bring about outcomes that are perfectly consistent with the values of Scripture, and I did so without turning a political office into a platform for evangelization. What I want to examine in the pages that follow is why, at least in many black churches and black communities across the country, being a preacher/politician is not in conflict with the separation of church and state.

MY ROOTS AS A BAPTIST

I am well aware of the strong emphasis that Baptists, especially American Baptists, have placed on the issue of the separation of church and state. In a pamphlet entitled "10 Facts You Should Know About American Baptists," fact number 6 says,

> As a people whose forbears came together in response to intolerance, American Baptists have cherished freedom and pursued

it for millions around the world. Manifestations of that ideal include supporting separation of church and state, advocating for people everywhere to be guaranteed the right to worship free from discrimination, and lifting up respectful dialog as a healthy means of understanding.[1]

Baptists, as much as any other Protestant denomination, have valued and sought to safeguard the separation of church and state because of their own history of being oppressed, discriminated against, and even physically assaulted in the seventeenth and eighteenth centuries both in Europe and later in colonial America. As much as anyone else, I want to be sure that no level of government—local, county, state, federal—ever uses its power to tax or to harass any citizens because of the way they choose to express and exercise their religious faith. How and even whether or not a person chooses to engage with religion in any form should be a matter of personal conscience, not something that is coerced or condemned by the government.

However, I also write this book to take a fresh look at the issue of religious liberty and the separation of church and state to clarify what those two principles do and do not intend to prevent in the interface between religion and politics. For instance, does the separation of church and state mean that people of faith in general and members of the clergy in particular should not be involved in politics beyond the simple act of voting or attending a political rally? Should people of faith, including members of the clergy, not participate in the political dialogues going on in their nation and in the communities in which they live?

As a Baptist, I am committed to the principle of religious liberty and the separation of church and state as a safeguard against the government favoring or supporting one religious group over all others. That being said, I remain convinced that Christians in general and clergy in particular can and should be politically active, and I will argue here that such involvement is in no way unconstitutional, illegal, or improper.

PROMINENT BLACK CLERGY ACTIVE IN POLITICS

One of my daily disciplines, in addition to prayer and Bible study, is to carve out the time Monday through Friday, 6 to 7 p.m., to watch *Politics Nation* with Rev. Al Sharpton on MSNBC. Over the course of that hour he and his guest commentators discuss various political issues being currently debated by Congress as well as by state legislatures around the country. Most of his guests are political commentators, such as Dana Milbank and E. J. Dionne of the *Washington Post*, former Pennsylvania governor Ed Rendell, and Melissa Harris Perry and others who also host programs at other times on MSNBC.

I find it especially interesting in those conversations how those guests refer to Al Sharpton. Few if any of them refer to him simply by his first name, even though that is how he invariably refers to all of them—except those currently or formerly in political office, whom he addresses with their official title: governor, representative, mayor, and so on. In referring to him, they say "Rev. Sharpton" or "Rev. Al" or just use the title "Rev." These conversations between reporters from the *Washington Post* and the Reverend Al Sharpton are not about religious topics. Instead, they are discussing hot-button political issues such as voter suppression, political gridlock in Congress, gun control legislation, immigration reform, "stand your ground" laws spreading across the country, and the deep resentment that many in the United States feel toward Barack and Michelle Obama as the country's first black president and first lady.

What I find most interesting is when Al Sharpton invites Representative Emanuel Cleaver to be a guest on the program, which happens at least once every week. Not only is Emanuel Cleaver a member of Congress from a district that represents Kansas City, Missouri, and also a former two-term mayor of Kansas City; add to that the fact that he is an ordained United Methodist pastor who served congregations in Kansas City for more than twenty years, and you end up with two ordained Christian clergymen discussing political and public policy topics on national television at the prime time news hour in the United States.

This is not two black preachers on the Word Network engaging in some convoluted debate about whether or not women should be ordained into Christian ministry or why they are opposed to same-sex marriage. This is two progressive black clergypersons, both of whom have long since endorsed women in ministry and favor marriage equality, but in this instance they are spending their time and energy discussing the political issues that impact the lives of every single person living in this country.

What I have never encountered is anyone who responds to a conversation between Sharpton and Cleaver by invoking the separation of church and state. NBC, the parent company of MSNBC, obviously knows that Al Sharpton is a Christian clergyman, yet the network has not asked him to limit his comments to matters of theology or occasional topics of religious interest. What is it that allows Al Sharpton to host a program entitled *Politics Nation*?

It has to do with the role that black clergy and black churches have played in the American political process for the last 150 years. It has to do with Sharpton's own long history of activism and involvement in social and political issues over the last thirty years. In addition to being an ordained clergyman in the Church of God in Christ, he was also a compelling and articulate candidate for the Democratic Party nomination for president of the United States in 2004. Sharpton twice ran for the Senate, in 1992 and again in 1994. In his second race he garnered 18 percent of the vote statewide, 21 percent of the vote in New York City, and 70 percent of the African American vote.[2]

How is it that Emanuel Cleaver can move from being a local pastor in Kansas City to becoming first its mayor and then its congressional representative? Why did the principle of the separation of church and state not work to prevent that from happening? It is impossible that the people of Kansas City did not know that Emanuel Cleaver is an ordained clergyman. It may well be that one of his political opponents tried to use the principle of the separation of church and state as an argument against his election. If so, that argument was obviously unsuccessful both for a local and a national political office.

And then there are the political activities of the Reverend Jesse Jackson, who also ran two campaigns for the nomination of the Democratic Party for president of the United States, in 1984 and again in 1988. In the 1988 campaign he actually won several state primaries and one-third of the delegates present at the national convention that year. In 1988 Jackson garnered 6.9 million votes in the various state primaries across the country, winning outright in Virginia, Louisiana, Georgia, Mississippi, Alabama, Delaware, Vermont, Alaska, Michigan, South Carolina, Washington DC, Puerto Rico, and a caucus in Texas. Jackson won 12.5 percent of the white vote and a phenomenal 92 percent of the black vote in 1988.[3]

MY FORTY-YEAR INVOLVEMENT IN POLITICS

My interest in the intersection between religion and politics and of the role of black preachers in the political process is fueled not solely by the activities of Al Sharpton, Emanuel Cleaver, Jesse Jackson, and the other black preacher/politicians who have held elective office in this country over the last nearly 150 years, but also by my own experiences over the last forty years.

CANDIDACY FOR THE U.S. HOUSE OF REPRESENTATIVES IN 1998

I served as senior pastor of the Antioch Baptist Church in Cleveland, Ohio, from 1987 to 2011. In the summer and fall of 1998, more than a decade into my ministry in Cleveland, I became a candidate in the race to represent the 11th Congressional District of Ohio in the U.S. House of Representatives. That district covers the east side of the city of Cleveland and many of the eastern suburbs as well. For the preceding thirty years, that seat had been held by Louis Stokes, the older brother of Carl Stokes, who was the first African American to be elected mayor of a major American city (Cleveland, in 1967). Louis Stokes was a legendary legislator who ran virtually unchallenged for most of the years he served in Congress. He was a founding member of the Congressional Black Caucus. He served as a member of the Appropriations and Intelligence Committees. He was on the special committee that investigated the assassinations of President John F. Kennedy and Dr. Martin Luther King Jr.

However, in 1994, after years of serving with the party that held the majority of seats and committee chairs in the House of Representatives, Louis Stokes found himself in the minority party in the House when the Republican Party took the majority of seats. In view of the stalemate in the legislative process that he foresaw then (and that is fully apparent today), he announced in 1998 that he would not seek reelection. As surprising as that announcement was to the people of the 11th Congressional District of Ohio, even more surprising was that he made no mention of any person who he hoped would succeed him in that office. There may have been private conversations about his successor, but there was no public announcement either on the day he announced his decision to retire from the Congress or in the days immediately following.

As the weeks went by with no one announcing an intention to run for that vacant seat in Congress, I first visited with Stokes and then made the announcement that I would enter the race and become a candidate for that office. There were two immediate reactions to my decision to enter a political campaign. The first reaction was that other candidates very quickly made the announcement that they, too, were entering the race. It was as if other interested persons were waiting to see who else might be seeking that seat before they revealed their intentions. However, once I made my announcement and became the first candidate to declare and to seek the requisite number of signatures on my petition to appear on the ballot, four other candidates entered the campaign. Included in that number were two well-established and highly regarded political officeholders. One was a common pleas court judge and the other was a state senator. The three of us would run a very spirited campaign for the next several months, with the judge becoming the eventual winner. All of us had been friends for years, and that friendship carried over into the campaign, so there was never a hint of negative campaigning or character assassination by any one of the three of us or by any of our supporters.

The second reaction was the question raised by some, and the firm conviction held by others, both in the faith community and within the political establishment, that it was inappropriate and perhaps even unconstitutional for an active member of the clergy to run for and serve in political office. People who were not constitutional scholars or experts in American history seemed absolutely certain of two things. First, it was their belief that the First Amendment of the U.S. Constitution included the phrase "separation of church and state." Second, it was their belief that implicit within the notion of the separation of church and state was the clear assumption that to have a member of the clergy serving in a political office was a violation of that principle.

POLITICAL INVOLVEMENT AS A NON-CANDIDATE FROM 1987 TO 1998

It should be noted, as I did several times during that campaign, that during my eleven years as pastor of Antioch Baptist Church, from 1987 to 1998, I had agreed to host numerous political rallies and debates inside the church, many of them on behalf of people who were now saying how inappropriate it is for clergy to be involved in politics. Over those eleven years I was approached by scores of political candidates who wanted either my personal endorsement in their quest for elective office or the chance to address or at least be introduced by me to the Antioch congregation, preferably during a Sunday morning worship service. Included among those who spoke before that congregation on a Sunday morning were U.S. Representatives Louis Stokes and John Lewis, as well as U.S. Senators Howard Metzenbaum and John Glenn.

In 1994, at the request of Representative Stokes, President Bill Clinton spoke from the pulpit of Antioch Baptist Church about the dangers of the upcoming Contract With America, then being proposed by Newt Gingrich and the Republican Party. In preparation for that visit, the entire church staff and the members of my immediate family had to undergo a Secret Service background check, since we would have direct contact with the current president of the United States. The entire church was searched and then secured by the Secret Service. My office became a temporary Oval Office, complete with the installation of a telephone line that allowed for the famous "hotline" to be installed in case the president had to make any secure calls while on site at the church. President Clinton gave that address before an audience of more than eight hundred that included political and clergy leaders from across the state of Ohio and also the entire national press corps, not one of whom whispered a word about the separation of church and state.

My fondest memory of that visit actually does not involve meeting or sitting next to the president (who, by the way, sang all three verses of "Lift Every Voice and Sing" from memory). Instead, it involves the fact that the church staff and my family were given lapel pins to wear to indicate to the Secret Service that we had the highest level of clearance for that event. Those who did not wear such a pin were kept outside of a two-block perimeter, and they could enter the church only by passing through a screening booth, staffed by uniformed Secret Service officers, with a metal detector. People stood in that line for at least an hour to enter the church. Those with the pin could enter and leave at will.

At one point in the afternoon, before the president arrived but after the perimeter had been set up, my fourteen-year-old son, Aaron, decided to walk to a nearby fast-food restaurant for a snack.

Of course, leaving the area was no problem. However, when he attempted to return and get past the perimeter, he was stopped by a member of the Secret Service and told that he could not go beyond that point. Without saying a word, he pulled back his overcoat and displayed his lapel pin granting him unlimited access to the President of the United States. The Secret Service agent never said another word. He removed the barricade, wished my son a good day, and left a fourteen-year-old-boy with the memory of a lifetime.

In 1992, while serving as president of the Cleveland chapter of the NAACP, I organized and served as moderator for a televised debate between the two African American candidates then running for the office of mayor of Cleveland, Michael White and George Forbes. That was the first and only time the NAACP in Cleveland ever served in that capacity, with television sponsorship for the hour-long debate on an ABC affiliate underwritten by a local bank. The event was held before a live audience in a packed auditorium on the campus of the local community college. It was a major political event in Cleveland, attended by every political leader in the city and the surrounding suburbs. Interestingly, at no point before, during, or after that event was it ever hinted by the television station, the bank that sponsored the event, the candidates who agreed to participate, or the people who watched the event live or on television that my involvement as the organizer and moderator of that political debate was a violation of the separation of church and state.

There was another act of political hypocrisy that I found most interesting after I announced that I was running for a seat in Congress. Many of the political leaders who saw my attempt to run for public office as a violation of the separation of church and state did not seem bothered by that principle when they asked me to make radio and television commercials endorsing their candidacy, or when they asked me to sign on to newspaper ads that would serve the same purpose. There was never a political season when I was not approached by candidates at the city, county, state, and federal levels seeking my verbal or written endorsement of their candidacy. However, when I sought something similar from them, I was almost universally refused on the grounds that my involvement in politics at that level would have been a violation of the principle of the separation of church and state.

In other words, everything that I had been doing in the political sphere for the preceding eleven years was deemed appropriate and allowable. My views were sought after, my support and endorsement were actively solicited, and my presence at political rallies and fundraisers was always welcomed. However, when I decided to become an active candidate myself, everything changed. I was suddenly told that clergy should not be involved in politics, and that now I was violating the principle of the separation of church and state. In fact, one female state senator who had regularly sought my help and advice on matters of importance to her at the state capitol in Columbus told me following one of several candidate forums in the 1998 campaign, "You should stay in the pulpit, where you belong." Those comments resulted in my campaign chairman, Rev. Dr. Otis Moss Jr., observing this strange logic. He noted that there are some politicians who say, "Pastor, we want you to give up your democratic, constitutional, and inalienable right to seek political office. However, we want you to be available to help us get elected."

EXTERNAL ANALYSIS OF THE 1998 HOUSE CAMPAIGN

That 1998 campaign was extensively covered by Mittie Olion Chandler in a book entitled *Black Churches and Local Politics*.[4] That book made two crucial observations concerning clergy involvement in politics and the issue of the separation of church and state. First, Chandler states, "What the election revealed most was that the black religious community in Cleveland was not ready for a clergy member as politician."[5] On the other hand, says Chandler, "If the electorate was troubled by ministers running for office as a potential violation of church and state, the sentiment was riddled with contradictions. Black churches were so integral to the primary race that the *Plain Dealer* declared that the primary 'Was played out largely in black churches.'"[6]

In fact, I received the endorsement of the *Plain Dealer* in that race, and the editorial board of what was then the largest daily newspaper in Ohio made no reference to the issue of the separation of church and state.

THE ROLE OF CLERGY AND CHURCHES IN POLITICS

What is the appropriate role that clergy and churches should play in the political process? What is the line drawn beyond which the principle of the separation of church and state can rightfully be invoked? Can the clergy be involved in politics at all levels as long as they do not become active candidates? Can churches host political events, such as rallies and candidate forums, and serve as polling places on Election Day? Is it acceptable for the clergy to endorse other persons for political office as long as they themselves never seek to become a candidate for elected office? Why was the Cleveland community so accepting of the overtly political activities I had been engaged in between 1987 and 1998 but suddenly resistant to the idea of my candidacy for the congressional seat on the grounds of the separation of church and state? That is the question that I had to consider then, and that is the question that still haunts me today.

CANDIDACY FOR THE U.S. SENATE IN 2000

There was another interesting contradiction on the issue of the clergy and politics, in addition to the one mentioned earlier concerning the 1998 campaign being "played out in black churches."[7] Remarkably, two years later I was approached by many of the people who opposed my congressional candidacy in 1998 to become a Democratic candidate for the U.S. Senate. Former representative Louis Stokes, Representative Stephanie Tubbs Jones (who won the election in which I ran in 1998), and retiring senator Howard Metzenbaum endorsed me for that office. In fact, Metzenbaum even appeared in my first statewide television commercial. Representative Jones agreed to travel with me to campaign events across the state of Ohio. I was endorsed by newspaper editorial boards in major cities such as Youngstown, Lorain, Akron, and Toledo. I was endorsed by county Democratic Party organizations in Bowling Green, Cleveland, Cincinnati, and Dayton. I received nearly unanimous support from the Cleveland-based labor organizations.

In the Democratic primary I received nearly 450,000 votes statewide and raised in excess of $500,000. I polled second in that race; losing to a man whose brother had been the former governor of Ohio. His name recognition was well established, while mine was barely known outside of my home county of Cuyahoga. Most of his campaign material simply used his last name in bold letters with his first name in much smaller print. Many people may have thought that the campaign material referred to his brother. However, at no point during that 2000 campaign did I hear any objections to my involvement based upon the issue of the separation of church and state. I would like to think that was because of the way I had tried to address that objection two years earlier.

A DELEGATE FOR BARACK OBAMA

My political involvement extended well beyond my two campaigns for federal elective office in 1998 and again in 2000. In 2008 I was elected by persons in the 11th Congressional District of Ohio to be a delegate for Barack Obama at the Democratic National Convention, held in Denver. I met every day with the statewide Ohio delegation. I sat every night in the convention center, where the nomination process played out. I sat with my son on the night when the roll call of states took place to determine whether Barack Obama or Hillary Clinton would be awarded that nomination. We listened as the roll call came to the state of New York, and we experienced a combination of joy and amazement as Hillary Clinton announced her decision to drop out of the race and throw her support behind Barack Obama.

I was trailed by Byron Pitts of CBS News throughout the convention, and I was interviewed by him after the convention voted for Barack Obama by acclamation. I was an eyewitness to history, as the way was paved for the first African American to be elected President of the United States. I would subsequently edit a collection of essays about the eventual election of Barack Obama as the nation's forty-fourth president entitled *The Audacity of Faith*.[8] At no point in the process that stretched from my election in January of 2008 through the convention in August of 2008 did anyone raise the question of my involvement on the basis of the separation of church and state.

WHY I CHOSE TO RUN IN 1998

Four things informed me during my 1998 congressional campaign despite the sometimes vociferous cries of those who thought I should drop out of the race.

POLITICAL PASTORS

First, I ran for a seat in Congress because I had spent four years on the ministerial staff of Abyssinian Baptist Church of New York City. I served under the leadership of Rev. Dr. Samuel DeWitt Proctor, from 1972 to 1976. From 1937 to 1972 the pastor of that church was Rev. Adam Clayton Powell Jr. In addition to serving as pastor, Powell was elected to serve as a member of the New York City Council from 1941 to 1944. Then, in 1945, he was elected to the first of eleven terms in the U.S. House of Representatives. Powell became chairman of the House Education and Labor Committee in 1961 and during his six years in that position (1961–1967) that committee passed more than sixty pieces of progressive legislation signed into law by Presidents John F. Kennedy and Lyndon Baines Johnson. Among those bills, copies of which were on display in the Powell Room at Abyssinian Baptist Church, were the authorizations for the Head Start Program, Job Corps, workplace safety regulations, hot-lunch programs for public schools, the antipoverty program, and federal aid to education.[9]

I understood, taking Powell and numerous other black clergy who have served in political office as examples, that the justice agenda of Isaiah 58 and Isaiah 61 and the gospel mandate in Matthew 25:31-46 to care for the hungry, the homeless, the sick, the imprisoned, and the poor can be powerfully addressed by those who occupy positions of political power and influence. The entire country was better off as a result of Powell's stewardship over that committee. Between 1972 and 1976 my basic understanding of pastoral ministry was being shaped and formed in the very church where that clergyman/congressman served for twenty-two years. It was with that sense of history informing me that I offered myself as a candidate in the hope of continuing the very kind of work that had been done so well by Adam Clayton Powell Jr.

CLERGY IN THE U.S. CONGRESS

Second, I ran for elective office because I was fully aware of the fact that many other members of the clergy had served in the House of Representatives in recent years, some of them doing so at the very time my candidacy was being criticized as a violation of the separation of church and state. There was Andrew Young from Georgia, who went on to be a two-term mayor of Atlanta and U.S. ambassador to the United Nations under President Jimmy Carter. William Gray of Pennsylvania became chairman of the House Budget Committee. Floyd Flake of New York and Walter Fauntroy of the District of Columbia were the other African American clergy who served in Congress in recent years. Interestingly, Gray, Flake, and Fauntroy continued to serve as pastors of local churches while serving in Congress.

At the same time, three white members of the clergy were also serving in Congress. First, there was Robert Edgar, an ordained United Methodist minister who served in the U.S. House of Representatives from 1975 to 1987. Following his congressional career, he went on to be president of Claremont School of Theology in California, then general secretary of the National Council of Churches, and finally president of the social-advocacy group Common Cause. The second person was Father Robert Drinan of Massachusetts, a Jesuit priest who served in the House from 1971 to 1983, when the Vatican had determined that no priest could hold a legislative office. Prior to that, he served as dean of the Boston College Law School from 1956 to 1970. During his time in Congress, Father Drinan was a member of the House Judiciary Committee when the famous Watergate investigation was underway, which eventually resulted in the resignation of President Richard M. Nixon. Then there was Senator John Danforth of Missouri, who was also an ordained priest in the Episcopal Church. Senator Danforth served as attorney general of Missouri and as ambassador to the United Nations.

As I stated earlier, that tradition of ordained clergy serving in Congress continues to this day, with Emanuel Cleaver of Missouri, who formerly served as mayor of Kansas City. And this is to say nothing about the more than one-hundred-year-old legacy of African American clergy serving in political offices at every level since the era of Reconstruction. (That history will be reviewed later in this book.) Suffice it to say, however, that anyone who is aware of just the contemporary instances of clergy who have served in Congress is unlikely to be easily persuaded that such service to the nation is a violation of the principle of the separation of church and state. That is especially true because most of those who make the claim about the separation of church and state have been unfamiliar both with the actual historical meaning of that concept and with the history of the black preacher as politician stretching back to the Reconstruction era. Whatever the phrase "separation of church and state" was designed to protect (and we will come to that later), it was never meant to prevent members of the clergy from running for and serving in elective office.

A written exchange between Thomas Jefferson and James Madison supports the claim that clergy were never meant to be excluded from active involvement in politics, including holding elective office. Writing in *Religious Freedom: Jefferson's Legacy, America's Creed*, John Ragosta points out that Jefferson was "initially insisting that ministers should be ineligible for public office, reasoning that history demonstrates that clergy's political influence resulted in 'too many atrocities not to merit a proscription from meddling with government.'"[10] However, Jefferson was convinced to alter his views on that subject by an equally influential architect of religious liberty in America, James Madison. It was Madison who told Jefferson that "exclusion of ministers would be a violation of their rights (and that the Constitution forbids only an institutional role for religion or any special privileges or positions, not the participation of individual clergy in politics)."[11]

Jefferson himself seems to have come to that same conclusion when he wrote this in the 1789 Virginia Statute for Religious Freedom:

> ... that our civil rights have no dependence on our religious opinions, more than our opinions in physics or geometry, that therefore the proscribing any citizen as unworthy the public confidence, by laying upon him an incapacity of being called to offices of trust and emolument, unless he profess or renounce this or that religious opinion, is depriving him injuriously of those privileges and advantages, to which, in common with his fellow citizens, he has a natural right.[12]

Is it not injurious of those rightful "privileges and advantages" that belong to all citizens to deny a member of the clergy the opportunity to serve in a position of "trust and emolument" simply because of his or her vocation, especially when no evidence exists that such a person would use that office to advance any particular sectarian agenda? Perhaps Jefferson recalled the diligence and integrity with which Rev. John Witherspoon of New Jersey served with him in the Second Continental Congress, which ratified and signed the Declaration of Independence in 1776. Witherspoon was a Scottish-born Presbyterian clergyman. He was the first moderator of the Presbyterian Church in the United States. He was twice elected to the New Jersey state legislature. He also served as president of the College of New Jersey (now Princeton University) from 1768 to 1782. There is no record that any member of the Continental Congress objected to the presence of John Witherspoon on the grounds that he was a member of the clergy.

PERSONAL EXPERIENCE IN POLITICS

Third, I ran for public office because I understood that this was not my first attempt to be elected to political office. I served eight years (two full terms), from 1992 to 2000, as an elected member of the

Board of Education in Shaker Heights, Ohio. I had also served as an appointed member of the Board of Education in Montclair, New Jersey, from 1982 to 1986. I had organized political campaigns, raised money for campaign needs, garnered endorsements, participated in debates, served on committees, responded to constituent needs, and won reelection in Shaker Heights with the most votes ever cast for any candidate for any office in the history of that city.

When I ran the first time for the school board in Shaker Heights, there was some concern about a member of the clergy serving in that position. There was a sizable Jewish population in that community, and that election was taking place when the so-called Religious Right was coming to power behind leaders such as Pat Robertson and Jerry Falwell. The suspicion about my candidacy was that I might use my seat on the school board to "Christianize" the curriculum, or promote mandatory school prayer, or push for explicit Christmas observances that non-Christian students would be required to attend. Those concerns seemed to greatly outweigh any interest that those who held them might have had in my views on school funding based upon property taxes, the low academic achievement of so many minority students, or the impact of charter schools on the future of public education. The big concern for many seemed to be that I would use a political office to advance a theological agenda.

I was extremely sympathetic to those concerns, recognizing that those were among the legitimate issues that would result in the concept of the separation of church and state becoming such an important part of American social and political life. While I completely dismiss the notion that clergy should not serve in political office solely on the basis of their vocation, I completely embrace the idea that clergy serving in political office should never use their office to advance or give preference to any religious group or denominational doctrine. A member of the clergy can use a political office to advance those core principles that are at the heart of many religions: justice, compassion, care for the needy, defending the powerless, and affirming the worth and value of all persons. Clergy should not, however, use a political office to seek funding or special privileges for any religious group, mandatory attendance at religious services or programs, or compulsory confession or conversion to any religious tradition under penalty of law. That was the threshold test I knew I would have to pass.

I understood the history of this country coming out of eighteenth-century Europe, where established churches existed in almost every country. I understood how the apparatus of government even in colonial America had been used to protect and prefer one Christian tradition (Roman Catholic, Anglican, Lutheran, Presbyterian, Congregational) above another. As will be discussed at length in the next chapter, there was a good reason why the founders of this country said in the First Amendment to the Constitution, "Congress shall pass no law regarding the establishment of religion or the free exercise thereof." Political power was not to be used in this country to impose or advance any religion, nor to prefer one religious tradition over all others. Although the expression "separation of church and state" does not actually appear anywhere in the Constitution, the spirit and intention of that phrase certainly is alive in the First Amendment.

I seem to have passed that test of not using my political office to advance or impose any religious agenda, since I ran unopposed for reelection. I was then elected by my peers on that board to serve as president of the Board of Education for the next four years. That allowed me the great honor of signing the high school diploma for four classes of graduates from Shaker Heights High School, including my own son, Aaron, in 1998.

It was while serving in that elected position that I announced my candidacy for the congressional seat. All that notwithstanding, the issue about the separation of church and state persisted throughout that campaign. Was it appropriate for a member of the clergy to seek and hold an elective office? Does not the Constitution speak in opposition to such an eventuality? In fact, I was even told that since other non-clergy candidates were now in that race, I should drop out and "stay in the pulpit, where you belong."[13] Since I was holding an elective office at the very time that question was being raised, I could only assume that the question became relevant only when a member of the clergy sought to run for a statewide or federal position.

NO CONSTITUTIONAL BASIS FOR EXCLUDING CLERGY

Fourth, I ran because I knew that the phrase "separation of church and state" appears nowhere in the U.S. Constitution. The phrase originates with Roger Williams, founder of the first Baptist church to be established in British North America in 1638. In a pamphlet he wrote in 1644, entitled "Mr. Cotton's Letter Examined and Answered," Williams wrote, "When they have opened a gap in the hedge or wall of Separation between the Garden of the Church and the Wilderness of the world, God hath ever broke down the wall it selfe, removed the Candlestick, and made his Garden a Wilderness, as at this day."[14]

Historian John Barry, writing in *Roger Williams and the Creation of the American Soul: Church, State, and the Birth of Liberty*, sheds light on this phrase by Roger Williams: "He was saying that mixing church and state corrupted the church. He was saying that when one mixes religion and politics one gets politics."[15]

That idea first appears within the American political context as a phrase, or a metaphor, employed by Thomas Jefferson in a letter that he wrote to a group of Baptists in Danbury, Connecticut, in 1802. In fact, Jefferson himself had no hand in drafting or signing the Constitution, since he was in Paris, France, during that period serving as ambassador to that country. In that letter Jefferson wrote,

> Believing that religion is a matter that lies solely between Man and his God that he owes account to none other for his faith or his worship, that the legislative powers of government reach actions only, and not opinions, I contemplate with sovereign reverence that act of the whole American people which declared that their Legislature should "make no law respecting an establishment of religion, or prohibiting the free exercise thereof," thus building a wall of separation between Church and State.[16]

What Jefferson was arguing for, and what the First Amendment stands to safeguard against, is the intrusion of the government into any aspect of religious activity, ranging from the use of taxpayer dollars to support any religion, to declaring any one religion to be the official or "established" religion of the country, to considering one's religious affiliation or the lack thereof as a basis upon which to determine a person's suitability for public service. In fact, the idea that a person's religious preferences should not be considered when running for or being appointed to public office is not merely implied in the First Amendment to the Constitution; it is stated plainly in Article 6 of the main body of that document: "No religious test shall ever be required as a qualification to any office or public trust under the United States."

Thus, there was never any attempt to insert into the Constitution the idea that clergy or any people of religious faith should be excluded from serving in political office on that basis. This was a point that my opponents in 1998, both of them attorneys, seemed either unaware of or unwilling to concede. It was, however, a point about which I was absolutely certain!

Notes

1. "10 Facts You Should Know About American Baptists" (Valley Forge, PA: American Baptist Churches USA, n.d.).

2. Marvin McMickle, *An Encyclopedia of African American Christian Heritage* (Valley Forge, PA: Judson Press, 2002), 160.

3. E. J. Dionne, "Jackson Share of Votes by Whites Triples in '88," *New York Times*, June 13, 1988, A1.

4. Mittie Olion Chandler, "Black Clergy Electoral Involvement in Cleveland," in *Black Churches and Local Politics: Clergy Influence, Organizational Partnerships, and Civic Empowerment*, ed. R. Drew Smith and Fredrick C. Harris (New York: Rowman & Littlefield, 2005), 137–50.

5. Ibid., 143.

6. Ibid., 144.

7. Ibid.

8. Marvin A. McMickle, ed., *The Audacity of Faith: Christian Leaders Reflect on the Election of Barack Obama* (Valley Forge, PA: Judson Press, 2009).

9. Marvin A. McMickle, "Adam Clayton Powell, Jr.," in *An Encyclopedia of African American Christian Heritage* (Valley Forge, PA: Judson Press, 2002), 129–30.

10. John A. Ragosta, *Religious Freedom: Jefferson's Legacy, America's Creed* (Charlottesville: University of Virginia Press, 2013), 20.

11. Ibid.

12. "An Act for establishing religious Freedom." www.virginiamemory.com/docs/ReligiousFree.pdf

13. Chandler, "Black Clergy Electoral Involvement," 144.

14. John M. Barry, *Roger Williams and the Creation of the American Soul: Church, State, and the Birth of Liberty* (New York: Viking, 2012), 307–8.

15. Ibid., 308.

16. Adrienne Koch and William Rede, eds., *The Life and Selected Writings of Thomas Jefferson* (New York: Modern Library, 1944), 333.

3

"POLITICS IS A DIRTY BUSINESS"

The idea that politics could be a means of grace is often overshadowed by the belief, perhaps the all–too–frequent reality, that politics can be a dirty business. Many people opposed my candidacy in 1998 because they believed that serving in that office would have a negative effect on my character. They were convinced that the ugly side of the political process would "rub off on me." They were never able to accept the idea that my use of politics as a means of grace could rub off on others in the political process. One of my clergy colleagues was quoted anonymously in the local paper as saying, "Congregations sometimes are wary about their ministers personally crossing the line from the religious realm to the political. They may want you to stay with the flock. They may be suspicious about you delving into the world of smoke-filled back rooms."[1]

One of my opponents in that campaign, a highly respected member of the state senate, made a similar suggestion when he stated also in the local paper,

> To be a good politician, I think he has to deal with the fundamental question of mixing religion and politics. ... Although intellectually he can deal with the difference, there are still practical conflicts on a day-to-day basis. In the long run, he's going to have to choose between religion and politics. I don't think it's a good balance in the long run.[2]

Here is the tension that must be resolved. Do members of the clergy listen to voices like that of Robert McAfee Brown, who challenges us to see political involvement as a means of grace, and who warns us that we shirk in our fundamental duty if we do not at least attempt to influence and even wield some of the power that affects the lives of many millions of our fellow citizens, including members of our own congregations? Or do we placidly accept the view that not only do religion and politics not mix, but also the very attempt to mix them is a violation of the principle of the separation of church and state?

Reflecting back on the career of Robert Edgar, the white United Methodist minister who served in Congress from 1975 to 1987, political scientists and commentators said about him, "He always had this moralistic sense about him, a strong moral compass and moral focus," and "Mr. Edgar ruffled his elders in almost every conceivable way" and had a "marvelous touch of naïveté" in the rough and tumble world of Washington politics.[3] Washington did not rub off on Edgar; he turned politics into a means of grace.

That is the role clergy can play in the political process: not banging people over the head with verses from the Bible, but living out their faith commitments to justice and mercy on a daily basis. I am informed by the apostle Paul, who observed, "A little yeast works through the whole batch of dough" (Galatians 5:9). This principle can work as well in politics as it does in baking; a little bit can go a long way.

JOHN F. KENNEDY AND THE ELECTION OF 1960

Much can be learned about the issue of the separation of church and state and the role of religion in politics by recalling the campaign that resulted in the election of John F. Kennedy as the first Roman Catholic to be President of the United States. As the first Roman Catholic since Al Smith in 1928 to win the presidential nomination of a major political party, Kennedy met with strong opposition to his nomination based upon the understanding that many people at the time had of the separation of church and state.

Charles Stewart, in a chapter on the separation of church and state in essays by several authors in *Preaching in American History*, notes that many sermons were preached in 1960 warning that the election of Kennedy would open the doors of the White House to the direct influence of the pope. The fear was that Kennedy would use his office to elevate the views and influence of one religious tradition above all others. "This could mean an end to religious liberty and the separation of church and state."[4]

He quotes from one anti-Kennedy and anti-Catholic sermon preached in 1960:

> We call upon all Americans, let us preserve our Christian heritage for our wonderful children and their children. We must not turn our families over to Catholicism by electing a Roman Catholic as President or Vice-President. NOW IS THE TIME TO STOP ROMES'S [sic] MARCH INTO THE WHITE HOUSE. SPEAK UP. SPREAD THE WORD. SAVE AMERICA. VOTE AGAINST A ROMAN CATHOLIC FOR PRESIDENT.[5]

In the face of such virulent anti-Catholicism, Kennedy offered a reasoned reply that goes a long way in making the case for the appropriate way in which to approach the principle of the separation of church and state. In a speech before the Ministerial Alliance in Houston on September 12, 1960, Kennedy literally entered the lions' den as far as his candidacy was concerned. He said,

> I believe in an America where the separation of church and state is absolute; where no Catholic prelate would tell the President—should he be Catholic—how to act, and no Protestant minister would tell his parishioners for whom to vote; where no church or church school is granted any public funds or political preference; and where no man is denied public office merely because his religion differs from the President who might appoint him or the people who might elect him.[6]

The most famous words in that speech came when Kennedy said,

> I am not the Catholic candidate for President. I am the Democratic Party's candidate for President who happens also to be a Roman Catholic. I do not speak for my church on public matters; and the church does not speak for me. Whatever issue may come before me as President ... on birth control, divorce, censorship, gambling or any other subject, I will make my decision in accordance with what my conscience tells me to be the national interest, and without regard to outside religious pressures or dictates.[7]

Several phrases in this speech by President Kennedy bear closer examination in regard to the issue of clergy involvement in the political process. The first is the notion that no one "is denied public office merely because his religion differs from the President who might appoint him or the people who might elect him." At this point, the issue involves the right of every individual to be considered for and/or to seek a political office regardless of that person's religious affiliation or lack thereof. This certainly would be consistent with Article 6 of the U.S. Constitution.

The second important phrase here is "I will make my decision in accordance with what my conscience tells me to be the national interest, and without regard to outside religious pressures or influence." This is the standard by which all persons of religious faith should engage in political affairs. They are not there to advance the interests or the agenda of their congregation or denomination. They are there to advance the broad interests of all of their constituents and of the country as a whole.

In the *New York Times* obituary for Father Robert Drinan, who was mentioned in the preceding chapter, there was a clear indication that he operated in precisely this way: "And though he never pledged to ignore church dictates while in office, he did ignore Catholic teaching in his support for federal financing of birth control and abortion."[8] Any person of religious faith who can operate within this paradigm should be eligible for elective office, no matter what his or her religious affiliation might be.

THE PRINCIPLE IS NOT THE PROBLEM

My point here is that it is not the principle of the separation of church and state that prevents clergy from serving in politics in general and in elective office in particular; rather, that principle is designed primarily to prevent the government from having any intrusive role in matters of religion. That intrusion can involve things such as requiring taxpayer support of any religion, requiring religious affiliation within a certain group or tradition, limiting voting rights or political offices only to members of a certain religious group, recognizing any one religion as the "official state religion" of the nation, or failing to protect the religious liberties of those whose religious practices differ from those of the majority of members of the nation.

In this country such intrusion would mean preferring Christianity over all other religions and failing to protect the religious liberties of Jews, Muslims, Hindus, Buddhists, or other well-established and well-known world religions. However, it would also include protecting the religious liberties and the rights of those who profess agnosticism or atheism. All of this will be discussed in greater detail later in this book.

Suffice it to say at this point, that what the separation of church and state does not intend to do is unilaterally determine that members of the clergy cannot and should not be involved in political life as advocates, candidates, or officeholders. As long as they remain within the boundaries so eloquently set forth by President Kennedy, and as long as they see their service as a means of grace by which the issues of justice and compassion can be advanced, there should be no objection to their involvement on the basis of the First Amendment. Those who wrongly assert that clergy involvement in politics is unconstitutional should reread the Constitution. If anything, denying clergy the right to be involved in political activity is to deny them what is, in fact, the first clause of the First Amendment—freedom of speech.

WHAT ABOUT THOSE "EVANGELICAL CHRISTIANS"?

This chapter must give some preliminary attention to one of the main reasons why so many people in this country may be opposed to the active involvement of clergy, especially Christian clergy in the political process. Over the last twenty-five to thirty years much attention has been given to what has come to be known as the "evangelical vote." That phrase is intended to describe the social values and voting habits of a sector of the electorate that appear to be linked by two things: a very conservative understanding of Scripture and theology, and the ways in which that theology informs them primarily on the issues of abortion, human sexuality, and marriage equality.

The movement began with clergy such as Jerry Falwell and the Moral Majority, and Pat Robertson and the *700 Club* television program. It went on to include laypersons such as James Dobson of Focus on the Family and Ralph Reed of the Christian Coalition. These four men, as much as anyone else in the country over the last three decades, have politicized a significant group of Christians into a voting bloc that has become closely associated with the right wing of the Republican Party. In essence, they have elevated what was little more than a regional subculture of religious and social values into a mandate for how the entire country should act and think.

THE FAITH & FREEDOM COALITION

Ralph Reed organized a new group in 2009, the Faith & Freedom Coalition. The group has often been referred to as "Teavangelicals" because it seeks to be a bridge between conservative evangelical Christians and the Tea Party movement. The stated mission of that group says, "The Faith & Freedom Coalition is a non-profit organization committed to educating, equipping, and mobilizing people of faith and like-minded individuals to be effective citizens." Based solely upon that mission statement, the Faith & Freedom Coalition could almost serve as an advertisement for this book and its central thesis about politics as a means of grace. However, as the old adage says, "The devil is in the details."

Ralph Reed's organization hosted a conference in June 2013 called "The Faith and Freedom Forum." The theme of the conference was "The Road to Majority," and speakers included political leaders such as Sarah Palin, Herman Cain, Rand Paul, Michelle Bachman, Alan West, Marco Rubio, Jeb Bush, Newt Gingrich, and Paul Ryan. Speakers also included conservative media figures such as Glenn Beck and Michael Medved. The point of the conference was to have conservative Republican politicians, most of whom are either seeking national office in 2016 or seeking to influence the outcome of that election, appeal for the support of the religious right in the 2014 and 2016 elections.

The website for the group is also revealing of the overtly conservative nature of its political agenda. There are a series of displays, all featuring President Obama in a most unfavorable way, and each scene carries a message: "Suspend state funding of Obamacare," "Stop Obama's assault on Israel," "Stop Obama's war on religious liberty." It ends with a scene that says, "Marriage is defined as the union of one man to one woman." However, it offers no source for that definition, including the Bible. While all of those scenes are rotating, what remains constant is an endorsement of the Faith

& Freedom Coalition by conservative radio talk show host Sean Hannity. His message says,

> Ralph Reed has built an incredible organization and I'm gonna tell you, it's going to grow into a force to be reckoned with. And that's the Faith & and Freedom Coalition. It's going to be the modern day Christian Coalition and it's gonna have a big impact.[9]

The website also features a petition called "Fight Obama's War on Religion." One might think at first that the issue is about the First Amendment and government interference in the free exercise of religion by some sector of the faith community. It even carries this declaration of concern: "Pro-family and pro-freedom Americans will not sit idly by as government attempts to compel us to violate our own conscience. For three years, the Faith & Freedom Coalition has pointed out this Administration's war on religion. This unconscionable edict is the final straw."[10]

What the website does not set forth is the content of "this unconscionable edict." Of course, this is a veiled reference to a portion of the Affordable Care Act ("Obamacare," as they call it) that requires most employers who provide medical insurance for their workers to include coverage for abortions and other human reproduction services. Given the Faith & Freedom Coalition's stated opposition to women having the right to choice concerning abortion, the group sees such a requirement in medical coverage as an infringement of the government on their religious liberty.

Through the lobbying efforts of "Teavangelicals", many states are refusing to accept any money from the federal government for their Medicaid programs, and ever more stringent antiabortion laws are being enacted in state after state across this country. It is a way to kill two birds with one stone: under *Roe v. Wade* abortion is legal in the United States, and provisions about abortion coverage are in the Affordable Care Act. Bear in mind that the provisions of the Affordable Care Act do not apply to churches, and they have nothing at all to do with the practice of religion in American life. It says only that private employers who offer medical coverage to their workers must include abortion services as part of that coverage.

The link between religion and politics within the Faith & Freedom Coalition is evident in statements such as the one featured on the website by Pat Robertson: "America will face divine punishment if it does not recriminalize abortion. ... Only anti-choice laws can avert the wrath of the Lord, but it will come upon the nation unless we do something."[11] There was also this quotation from Michael Medved: "We [Teavangelicals] lost because Barack Obama won crushing lopsided majorities among Americans who are single, poor, and irreligious. Who wants to live life as single, poor, and irreligious?"[12]

I OBJECT TO THE PHRASE "EVANGELICAL CHRISTIANS"

I cannot overstate how much I object to the way in which conservative Christians have hijacked the word "evangelical." They have taken a perfectly wonderful theological term with deep roots in American and European church history and transformed it into a metaphor for a handful of social agenda items. A true evangelical is defined by faith in the authority of Scripture, the divinity of Jesus, the fallen nature of humanity, the work of world missions and evangelization, and redemption from sin through faith in Jesus Christ. An evangelical is not someone whose primary agenda is anti-abortion or anti-homosexual, pro-school prayer or pro-religious displays in public buildings. An evangelical is not a person solely aligned with the most conservative wing of the Republican Party.

Former U.S. Senator John Danforth, mentioned in the preceding chapter, is an Episcopal priest and a member of the Republican Party. He wrote an op-ed in the *New York Times* about what has happened to that party in recent years in which he says, "By a series of recent initiatives, Republicans have transformed our party into the political arm of conservative Christians."[13]

People who hear the word "evangelical" do not think of its historic meaning dating back to the Protestant Reformation in Germany in the sixteenth century, or in the Great Awakening and the ministries of Gilbert Tennent, George Whitfield, and John and Charles Wesley, and so many others in colonial America in the eighteenth century. They do not think of "an unswerving belief in the need for conversion (the new birth) and the necessity of a life of active holiness (the power of godliness)."[14] Today the term "evangelical" is associated with a political agenda limited primarily to the issues of abortion and human sexuality, with a little anti-Obamaism tossed in for good measure. As James Sanders argues in his essay "The Betrayal of Evangelicalism," "The Constitution mandates the separation of church and state whereas evangelicals, professing belief in the Bible and the Constitution, have attempted a sort of amalgam of the two doing great harm to the public's understanding of both."[15]

Sanders continues,

> Southern evangelicals have recently launched a serious mission to convert the rest of the country to their political views, and the Republican Party has become a vehicle for doing so. More recently it has been manifest in the evangelical resistance to granting equal constitutional rights to gays and lesbians and to once again limiting the rights of women, in essence putting their view and interpretation of the Bible above the mandates of the Constitution.[16]

RALPH REED VERSUS RACHEL MADDOW

On June 28, 2013, NBC's *Meet the Press* assembled a political panel that included Ralph Reed, of the Faith & Freedom Coalition, and Rachel Maddow, host of a news program on MSNBC. The discussion involved the recent ruling by the U.S. Supreme Court concerning same-sex marriage, a ruling that Ralph Reed referred to as "a stunning and indefensible display of judicial activism." He spoke about his efforts to organize the evangelical vote in states across the country to outlaw same-sex marriage at the state level. He continued to refer to "the evangelical vote."

Rachel Maddow mentioned that efforts to turn out the evangelical vote in the 2008 and 2012 national elections to defeat President Obama had been unsuccessful. As a result, energy was now being directed at the state level. For instance, no sooner had the U.S. Supreme Court thrown out certain provisions of the 1965 Voting Rights Act than states such as Texas, Mississippi, and North Carolina began implementing voter suppression laws to lessen the impact of persons who had voted for President Obama in those two elections.

This focus on a social agenda involving abortion and human sexuality, and a political agenda designed to suppress the vote among African Americans and Hispanics, all done under the umbrella of the "evangelical vote," has led many people to believe that religious groups are using the political process to impose a strict moral agenda upon the entire country. There must be a standard or a litmus test for such involvement. This is where the words of Robert McAfee Brown, Carl F. H. Henry, and John Bennett need to be revisited. Brown said, "Politics can be a means of grace. It has become an arena where the most fastidious Christian must act responsibly and decisively if he is not to be derelict in his duties."[17] Henry said, "The church should urge members to engage in political affairs to their utmost competence and ability, to vote faithfully and intelligently, to engage in the public process at all levels, and to seek and hold public office."[18]

The litmus test of how to negotiate the issue of church and state is what John Bennett added to the discussion when he said, "No church, no matter how powerful, should bring pressure on the state to enact laws which are based upon principles that depend for their validity of its own doctrine or ethos. ... It is wrong to make the ethos of one part of the community the basis of law."[19]

WHY THIS FIXATION ON SEPARATING CHURCH AND STATE?

What are the reasons for walking this thin line of separation between church and state? What is the danger of turning the ethos of one part of the community into the basis of law that governs the whole of society? The answers to these questions are deeply rooted in American history, and even more deeply embedded in the principle of religious liberty that informed many of those who left the nations of Europe and settled in North America before the United States was founded. One cannot properly discuss what the separation of church and state means in the twenty-first century without understanding the roots of that idea in the seventeenth and eighteenth centuries in countries such as England, Holland, Germany, and France. We will turn our attention to that history in the next chapter.

However, in doing so, we also will be walking into one of the most morally and ethically hypocritical aspects of American history. At the very time when the founders of the United States were debating religious liberty for themselves, they were using religious language and metaphors to justify the practice of human slavery. In fact, the very religious freedoms that white Americans were demanding for themselves were being forcibly denied to black people in America out of concern that religious instruction might undermine the principles upon which human slavery had been established, and upon which it was being maintained.

The fight to end human slavery in this country would require the concerted efforts of the black church and black preachers working simultaneously in their roles as priestly, prophetic, national, and political leaders. What those black preacher/politicians did was not a violation of the separation of church and state. What they did was use political power to shape the society that for so long had held them captive. They used their religious sensibilities to shape governmental policies that would work to the benefit of the most disadvantaged persons in American society—the more than four million black people who were coming out of the unjust and inhumane condition of chattel slavery in a country that less than a hundred years earlier had fought a revolutionary war to free itself from the tyranny of oppression at the hands of the British.

PART I: QUESTIONS FOR DISCUSSION AND REFLECTION

1. Do you believe that the U.S. Constitution prohibits members of the clergy from running for and serving in public office? Why or why not?
2. Do you know, or are you aware of, any members of the clergy currently serving in public office at the local, county, state, or federal level? What do you know about their service, politically and ministerially?
3. In your judgment, when have clergy used their political office or political influence in order to advance a matter of religious doctrine or practice (e.g., school prayer, religious symbols on public property, religious holiday observances, mandatory attendance at or taxpayer support for a particular religious tradition)?
4. Would you vote for a member of the clergy who was seeking election to public office at any level of government? Why or why not?
5. Do you believe that the United States is a "Christian nation"? Why or why not? What does that phrase mean to you?
6. What does the First Amendment to the U.S. Constitution say about religion?
7. Who first used the phrase "separation of church and state," and what was intended by the phrase? What is the meaning

of the word "establishment" as far as the separation of church and state is concerned?
8. Should local churches host political events of any kind or provide an occasion for candidate forums and debates? Why or why not?
9. What does it mean to say that "politics can be a means of grace"?
10. What was the objection that some had to the candidacy of John F. Kennedy? What was the substance of his response to those concerns?
11. What is the Faith & Freedom Coalition, and what are its roots?
12. What is a "Teavangelical"?
13. What was Thomas Jefferson's initial view of clergy holding public office?
14. What was James Madison's response to that view by Jefferson?
15. What was Jefferson's final position in the 1789 Virginia Statute of Religious Liberty?
16. What is James Sanders's objection to the close connection between evangelical Christians and the Republican Party?
17. What is the meaning of the term *voter suppression*, and where is that effort underway?
18. What is historically problematic with the phrase "evangelical Christians"?

PART I: THINGS TO REMEMBER

1. In what year was John F. Kennedy elected to the presidency of the United States?
2. What was his religious affiliation?
3. Who was Father Robert Drinan?
4. Who was Rev. Robert Edgar?
5. Name four black clergy who served in the U.S. Congress in the twentieth century.
6. Who first coined the phrase "a wall of separation between church and state"?
7. To what group did Thomas Jefferson write a letter about religious liberty in 1802?

8. Who said that politics can be a means of grace?
9. What Presbyterian clergyman signed the Declaration of Independence?
10. Who hosts the MSNBC talk show *Politics Nation*?

Notes

1. Joe Hallett, "Candidates Seek Black Ministers' Support," *Cleveland Plain Dealer*, April 29, 1998, A1.
2. Jessie Tinsley, "Saving the Soul of the City," *Cleveland Plain Dealer Sunday Magazine*, August 30, 1998, 16.
3. Adam Bernstein, "Former U.S. Representative Robert Edgar Dies at 69," *Washington Post* (http://www.washingtonpost.com/local/obituaries/former-us-representative-robert-edgar-dies-at-69/2013/04/23/fea8d072-ac43-11e2-a8b9-2a63d75b5459_story.html).
4. Charles Stewart, "Separation of Church and State," in *Preaching in American History: Selected Issues in the American Pulpit, 1630–1967*, ed. DeWitte Holland (Nashville: Abingdon Press, 1969), 355.
5. Ibid.
6. John F. Kennedy, "Address to the Greater Houston Ministerial Association," Houston, Texas, September 12, 1960 (http://www.americanrhetoric.com/speeches/jfkhoustonministers.html).
7. Ibid.
8. Douglas Martin, "Robert Drinan Dies at 86; Pioneer as Lawmaker Priest," *New York Times*, January 30, 2007, C13.
9. The Faith and Freedom Coalition (http://ffcoalition.com).
10. Ibid.
11. Pat Robertson, "U.S. Abortion 'Holocaust' Worse Than Nazi Germany, Will Lead to 'Wrath of the Lord,'" June 25, 2013 (http://ffcoalition.com).
12. Elizabeth Flock, "Paul Ryan, Michelle Bachmann: 'Teavangelicals' Are Back: The Faith and Freedom Coalition Wants Faith-based Votes to Turn Out in Droves in Upcoming Elections," *U.S. News & World Report*, June 14, 2013 (http://www.usnews.com/news/blogs/washington-whispers/2013/06/14/paul-ryan-michele-bachmann-teavangelicals-are-back).
13. Quoted in Kevin Phillips, *American Theocracy: The Peril and Politics of Radical Religion, Oil, and Borrowed Money in the 21st Century* (New York: Viking, 2006), 218.
14. Mark A. Noll, *The Rise of Evangelicalism: The Age of Edwards, Whitefield, and the Wesleys* (Downers Grove, IL: InterVarsity Press, 2003), 15.
15. James A. Sanders, "The Betrayal of Evangelicalism," *Bulletin of Colgate Rochester Crozer Divinity School* (summer 2012): 13.
16. Ibid., 19.
17. Robert McAfee Brown, "Confessions of a Political Neophyte," *Christianity and Crisis*, December 24, 1953, 186.
18. Carl F. H. Henry, *Christian Countermoves in a Decadent Culture* (Portland, OR: Multnomah Press, 1986), 118.
19. John C. Bennett, *Christians and the State* (New York: Scribner, 1958), 207.

Part II

THE EVOLUTION OF RELIGIOUS LIBERTY AND THE SEPARATION OF CHURCH AND STATE

4

THE QUEST FOR RELIGIOUS LIBERTY

In the preceding chapters we saw that it is both historically and technically inaccurate to suggest that clergy running for or holding political office is a violation of the principle of the separation of church and state. Nothing in the U.S. Constitution, including the First Amendment to that document, in any way discourages, prohibits, or disallows clergy participation in electoral politics. There may be doctrinal or polity practices within various religious traditions that discourage clergy from being overtly politically active. However, that is a matter of theology and denominational policy, not a matter of constitutional law.

What is needed in order to make the point about clergy involvement in politics even clearer is an in-depth understanding of what the separation of church and state actually does intend to address and regulate. Stated succinctly, the intent is not how to keep religious leaders out of the affairs of the government; rather, the intent is, and always was, how to keep the government out of the affairs of the church. What the Constitution has sought to do is prevent from developing in this country some of the practices that were common in the nations of Europe in the years prior to the mass emigration of Europeans to what would become British North America.

Those practices would include such things as "established churches" that were supported by the government and by public funds, and then limiting the right to vote and to hold office only to those who belonged to the established church. Those practices also included a denial of religious liberty in the form of suppressing and persecuting all religious traditions other than the established church. In some instances, there were attempts at physically coercing people to convert to and confess faith in the established church. In other instances, the offices of the government were used to enforce such religious practices as church attendance, Bible reading, and the approved forms for observing baptism and Communion.

RELIGIOUS LIBERTY VERSUS RELIGIOUS TOLERANCE

The central principle to grasp in a discussion about the separation of church and state is the principle of religious liberty, or the freedom to worship God according to one's own conscience without fear of persecution or reprisal from the government or from those who observe other religious traditions. Care must be taken to talk specifically about religious liberty and not merely religious toleration. To speak of religious toleration is to suggest that there is some dominant and approved religious tradition in a society that is embraced by the majority of the population, but that allows other religious traditions to operate within their sphere. Religious toleration suggests that something is being "put up with" but not fully embraced as being of equal value to the dominant tradition. On the other hand, religious liberty suggests that a person is free to choose from any number of religious traditions active within a given society, and the government works to protect the rights of all of them to operate according to their own conscience.

Comedian Emo Phillips, in what has been declared to be the best God joke ever, reveals how quickly even the slightest differences in religious form and practice can result in conflict.

> Once I saw this guy on a bridge about to jump. I said, "Don't do it!" He said, "Nobody loves me." I said, "God loves you. Do you believe in God?"
>
> He said, "Yes." I said, "Are you a Christian or a Jew?" He said, "A Christian." I said, "Me, too! Are you a Protestant or a Catholic?" He said, "Protestant." I said, "Me, too! What franchise?" He said, "Baptist." I said, "Me, too! Northern Baptist or Southern Baptist?" He said, "Northern Baptist."

I said, "Me, too! Northern Conservative Baptist or Northern Liberal Baptist?" He said, "Northern Conservative Baptist." I said, "Me, too! Northern Conservative Baptist Great Lakes Region or Northern Conservative Baptist Eastern Region?" He said, "Northern Conservative Baptist Great Lakes Region."

I said, "Me, too! Northern Conservative Baptist Great Lakes Region Council of 1879 or Northern Conservative Baptist Great Lakes Region Council of 1912?" He said, "Northern Conservative Baptist Great Lakes Region Council of 1912."

I said, "Die heretic!" And I pushed him over.[1]

Without the principle of religious liberty and the insistence on a separation between church and state, these kinds of minor distinctions between religious traditions resulted not only in disputes, but often even in death. This piece of humor by an American comedian that ran in a British newspaper is more than a moment of comedy or levity. It is, as is the case with all good satire, a reflection on the nature of religious intolerance that has impacted and infected both the United States and the United Kingdom for hundreds of years.

Indeed, a very similar example of religious intolerance is found in Henry Fielding's 1749 novel *The History of Tom Jones: A Foundling*, in which the character Parson Thwackum says, "When I mention religion, I mean the Christian religion, and not only the Christian religion, but the Protestant religion; and not only the Protestant religion, but the Church of England."[2]

RELIGIOUS LIBERTY IN THE TWENTY-FIRST CENTURY

For those of us living in the United States of America in the twenty-first century, it is impossible to imagine a time when the definition of acceptable religious practice could be defined so narrowly. In fact, for most Americans born in this country, it is impossible to imagine a time when religious liberty and the separation of church and state were not the unquestioned norm. Consider the following indicators of twenty-first century American religious diversity. In this country, which was founded by an overwhelmingly Protestant majority, Roman Catholicism is the dominant religious affiliation of members of the U.S. Supreme Court, with two Jewish members as well. There are Muslims serving in the U.S. House of Representatives. Muslim mosques, Jewish synagogues, and Sikh temples exist in nearly every city in this country. There are legal protections for those who are Wiccans, along with those that practice certain Afro-Caribbean religions such as Vodun and Santería.

In the last half century or so, the Oval Office in the White House has been home to a Roman Catholic (John F. Kennedy), a Disciples of Christ (Lyndon Johnson), a Southern Baptist (Jimmy Carter), a Quaker (Richard Nixon), two United Methodists (George W. Bush and Bill Clinton), two Episcopalians (Gerald Ford and George H. W. Bush), a Presbyterian (Ronald Reagan), and a Congregationalist/United Church of Christ (Barack Obama). This shift not only in presidential leadership, but also in the religious affiliation of those who have served in that office, is something that most Americans today accept as the norm.

Not only does the United States make room for religious liberty among those who seek to worship and understand God in various ways; it is just as important to note that with every passing year the United States also makes room for people who express no religious faith whatsoever, and for atheists, who reject the very existence of God. Three years ago there was a billboard battle between Christians and atheists being waged at opposite ends of the Holland and Lincoln Tunnels connecting New York City to New Jersey and also in Times Square in midtown Manhattan. The billboard sponsored by the American Atheists Society showed a jovial Santa Claus and a crucifix with Christ on the cross. The text said, "Keep the Merry, Dump the Myth."

According to CNN Belief Blog, the same group has also sponsored billboards in largely Jewish and Muslims neighborhoods in and around New York City and northern New Jersey, written in English and Hebrew in one instance and in English and Arabic in the other. Those billboards say, "You know it's a myth, and you have a choice."[3] In addition to the billboards, the interest in, if not the affirmation of, atheism has been further reinforced by the presence of Christopher Hitchens's book *God Is Not Great* on the *New York Times* list of bestselling books for many months in 2007.[4]

On May 5, 2014, the U.S. Supreme Court ruled in the case *Town of Greece v. Galloway*, in which the issue of religious liberty and the constitutional rights of nonreligious persons was at stake. The case was brought by two citizens of Greece, one Jewish and the other an atheist, and it involved whether or not it was appropriate for prayers to be offered at the beginning of the meetings of the town council in Greece, New York, especially when 90 percent of those invited to offer those prayers were Christians who made explicit reference to Jesus Christ. The case was resolved in a split decision by the court that upheld the practice of opening prayers at town council meetings, ruling that such a practice was not a violation of the establishment clause of the First Amendment. The court took this action on the basis of the 1983 case *Marsh v. Chambers*, in which the court upheld the practice of the Nebraska legislature using public funds to hire a chaplain who offered daily prayers. "Chief Justice Warren Burger ruled that such prayers were part of the fabric of our society. The decision prohibited only those prayers that take sides by advancing or disparaging a particular religion."[5] The point here is that the rights of some citizens to exercise their religious beliefs are aggressively resisted through the federal courts by other citizens who do not want public gatherings of elected officials to become occasions when sectarian prayer is being used in the presence of believers and nonbelievers alike. The courts have ruled that while such prayers are allowed, they must be more ceremonial and theologically neutral in nature, rather than exalting one religious tradition above all others.

RELIGIOUS INTOLERANCE IN THE UNITED STATES

There have been isolated examples of religious intolerance in the United States. Let us look at three of them.

On August 5, 2012, in Oak Creek, Wisconsin, a self-described white supremacist walked into a Milwaukee-area Sikh temple and opened fire, killing six people and wounding five others. He then turned the gun on himself after he was wounded in the temple parking lot by a police sniper who had responded to a 911 call about an active shooting. However, the response from the interfaith community in and around Milwaukee was swift and immediate in support of the Sikh community and in defense of the principle of religious liberty and diversity.

On September 11, 2001, the radical Islamic group al-Qaeda conducted terrorist attacks in New York City, Washington DC, and in the skies over Shanksville, Pennsylvania. Those attacks resulted in thousands of deaths in the two towers of the World Trade Center, several hundred on the four hijacked planes, and dozens more inside the Pentagon. As a result, strong anti-Muslim sentiment arose all over the country, even in places not directly touched by the 9/11 attacks. In 2010 plans were announced to build a mosque very close to what has come to be known as Ground Zero, the site where the two World Trade Center towers once stood. A New York City firefighter, Timothy Brown, who lost friends and coworkers when the twin towers collapsed, filed a lawsuit to prevent a mosque from being built so close to the site of that terrorist attack.

The matter was finally resolved in April 2011, when New York State Supreme Court justice Paul Feinman dismissed the lawsuit. The court determined that Timothy Brown's right to grieve the death of his friends did not offset the right of Muslims to build a community center that had a mosque as part of its design. The court ruling was further supported by President Obama, who stated,

> As a citizen, and as President, I believe that Muslims have the same right to practice their religion as anyone else in this country. That includes the right to build a place of worship and a community center on private property in lower Manhattan in accordance with local laws and ordinances.[6]

Here is a case in which the government is not establishing or supporting one religion over another. Instead, the government is upholding the rights of a religious minority, perhaps a despised minority in some sectors of society, to enjoy the same constitutional protections that have long been enjoyed by citizens of other religious traditions. The fact that persons who happened to be Muslim carried out the 9/11 terrorist attacks should not, and did not, prevent Muslim Americans, more than eight hundred of whom were killed when the towers of the World Trade Center collapsed, from building a mosque near that site.

How is it possible that a state court and the president of the United States could take such positions? What are the legal and constitutional principles that allow even for this level of religious tolerance? How is it that a nation can focus on a city where the odor of the explosions was still in the air and protect the religious and citizenship rights of Muslims and the free and open practice of Islam?

More recently, two brothers who had been radicalized by a Chechen-based, extreme anti-American ideology set off two bombs at the Boston Marathon on April 15, 2013. That terrorist attack resulted in five deaths and 280 injuries. Once again, an anti-Muslim, anti-Islam sentiment popped up across the country in places far away from Boston. At an interfaith memorial service that featured speakers from the Muslim, Jewish, Greek Orthodox, Roman Catholic, and Protestant communities, each speaker invoked the principle that the whole Muslim community should not be blamed for the actions of two men who happened to observe a radical form of Islam.

Even when isolated acts of intolerance occur, they seem only to strengthen the nation's commitment to the right of people to worship God according to their own conscience and without fear of persecution from the government. It also offers the reassurance that their right to worship when faced with threats such as occurred in Wisconsin will be defended by the government.

RELIGIOUS INTOLERANCE IN EIGHTEENTH-CENTURY COLONIAL AMERICA

Wide-ranging religious liberty and religious pluralism were not always the norm in this country. In fact, in the years immediately before and after the founding of this nation religious liberty was anything but the norm. In eighteenth-century colonial America Jews and Catholics could not vote or serve in any government office, whether elected or appointed. By 1783, at the conclusion of the Revolutionary War, most states in the newly formed United States of America had lifted the ban on voting but continued to exclude non-Protestants from serving in any legislative position. New Jersey, Delaware, North Carolina, Georgia, South Carolina, and Vermont continued to bar Catholics and Jews. Pennsylvania and Maryland barred Jews but not Catholics.[7] Looking back on these realities from the vantage point of 230 years of history, contemporary Americans find it hard to believe that such religious discrimination not only existed, but also was actually codified by law and custom.

Consider the tone and content of this anti-Catholic rhetoric from the Massachusetts state constitution drafted in 1779 by John and Samuel Adams, both of whom signed the Declaration of Independence. The section on religious liberty or religious toleration begins with this statement:

> No subject shall be hurt, molested, or restrained for worshipping God in the manner and season most agreeable to the dictates of his own conscience provided he doth not disturb the public peace or obstruct others in their religious worship.[8]

The phrasing to that point sounds like the approach to religious liberty as observed in the United States in the twenty-first century. However, the Massachusetts state constitution then went on, in typical eighteenth-century fashion, to set forth exceptions to the policy of religious liberty and toleration in regard to holding elective office. Jews were entirely excluded because elected officials were required to take an oath of loyalty to Christianity that included the phrase "I believe the Christian religion, and have firm persuasion of its truth." Catholics who wished to serve in elected office were first required to renounce the authority of the pope and affirm that "no foreign ... prelate ... hath, or ought to have, any jurisdiction ... in any manner, civil, ecclesiastical, or spiritual, within this commonwealth."[9]

It goes without saying that during the colonial era and after the founding of this nation Native Americans and people of African ancestry, whether slave or free, were completely prohibited from any participation in the political process as voters or officeholders. This had absolutely nothing to do with their religious affiliation; instead, it sprang from the curious and clearly hypocritical reality that those who sought for themselves religious and political liberty from the tyranny of England were perfectly content to deny both forms of liberty to other people based upon color and ancestry.

That fact will play a crucial role in the next chapter of this book when I begin to discuss how and why it is that black clergy and black churches have historically felt less interested in and/or constrained by the issue of the separation of church and state. Black people themselves were separated from the whites-only church and the whites-only state. Their churches became the setting in which their quest for religious and political liberty was centered.

RELIGIOUS CONFLICTS AROUND THE WORLD

When speaking about the religious liberty that we take for granted in the United States today, we should not lose sight of the fact that religious intolerance and the resulting persecution that so often comes in its wake are quite common in the world today. One only needs to look at the headlines of newspapers or watch the television news reports to realize that our peaceful coexistence of various religious traditions is not the norm around the world. In places ranging from Egypt to Syria in the Middle East, from Bosnia to Chechnya in the Balkans and Russia, and from Pakistan to India with the region of Kashmir in between, civil wars are being waged, and religious differences are often at the heart of those conflicts.

In the nations of Chechnya and Georgia near Russia there have been intense interreligious struggles between Muslims and the Russian Orthodox Church. The archbishop of the Evangelical Baptist Church in Georgia writes,

> Chechnya is our neighboring country. Historically, Chechens and Georgians have been enemies. Our enmity was heightened by our religious differences as Muslims and Orthodox Christians, and also by the brutality committed by Chechens in recent wars in Georgia. The Berlin wall came down in 1991, but the wall of separation between Christians and Muslims is still very much there. This wall is not tangible, but it is solidly built with the mortar of fear, suspicion and hatred. For the last couple of decades, one fifth of the Chechen population has been eliminated by troops who had been blessed for this mission by Orthodox Christian clergy. Political Christianity came face-to-face with political Islam in Chechnya.[10]

Iraq and Iran share a common border, but they are divided by distinctions within a common religion. Iraq is comprised largely of Sunni Muslims, while Iran is comprised largely of Shiite Muslims. The differences between the two are not clear to most Americans, but they annually result in bloodshed and animosity between adherents of those two groups of Muslims. Sunni Muslims are those who believe that the father of the prophet Mohammed's wife was the designated leader after Mohammed's death. Shiite Muslims believe that leadership fell to Mohammed's cousin and son-in-law Ali, a blood relative of the prophet. Based upon that difference alone, great religious intolerance exists within the Muslim world.

As reported in *The Christian Century*, these intra-Muslim rivalries are also fueling hostilities in Syria and Lebanon.

> Whether the battle will be contained to Syria is in doubt now that Islam's two major strands have taken sides against one another, threatening to spark a wider war that is centuries in the making between Sunnis and Shiite Muslims. ... The royal families of Saudi Arabia and Qatar have been funneling arms and cash to rebels, and Sunni Muslims who dominate al-Qaeda have dispatched fighters to the front. Assad [Bashar-al-Assad, president of Syria] has appealed to the Shiites, who are helping him hang on to

his regime. The Shi'ite theocracy of Iran has deployed officers and fighters from its Revolutionary Guards. Hezbollah, designated a terrorist group by the United States, which has fought two wars with Israel from its base in Lebanon, is pouring militants into Assad's forces.[11]

The nation of Israel is a self-described Jewish state surrounded on three sides by large and often hostile Muslim populations in the so-called Arab world. Voting rights are tightly regulated so that there is no chance that a Muslim majority could come to power and take over the country. There is also a significant Christian population in Israel, but there is no possibility, numerically or philosophically, that any group other than the Jewish community will ever hold the majority of the power in every sector of Israeli society. This Jewish state, established in 1947 by United Nations Resolution 181, was undoubtedly a response to the Holocaust under the Nazis during World War II and the pogroms in Russia and other European nations prior to the Nazis. Nevertheless, it is difficult to imagine that a lasting peace will ever take root in Israel so long as largely Muslim areas of Palestine are occupied and controlled by the armed forces of that Jewish state.

India was once a single country inclusive of the nation now known as Pakistan. However, when India achieved independence from the British on August 15, 1947, the country had already split into two separate nations on August 14, 1947. One was Pakistan, a Muslim-dominated country, and the other was India, a Hindu-dominated country. The assassination of Mohandas Gandhi (Mahatma) in 1948 was the result of intense religious animosity. The same could be said for the assassination of Egyptian president Anwar el Sadat in 1981 and Jewish prime minister Yitzhak Rabin in 1992; both were killed by people who were fueled by the ongoing religious hatred between Jews and Muslims.

In Myanmar (Burma) the military-led government suppressed and persecuted Buddhist priests. In return, Buddhists have persecuted the Muslim minority in that country. A Buddhist monk, Wirathu, who has allegedly taken for himself the name of "the Burmese bin Laden," preaches unequivocal hatred of Muslims and declares, "We must keep Myanmar Buddhist." *Time* magazine reports,

> The trouble began last year in the far west, where machete-wielding Buddhist hordes attacked Rohingya villages; 70 Muslims

were slaughtered in a daylong massacre in one hamlet, according to Human Rights Watch. ... In the shadow of a burned-down mosque, I was able to meet the family of Abdul Razak Shahban, one of at least 20 students at a local Islamic school who were killed. "My son was killed because he was Muslim, nothing else," Razak's mother Rahamabi told me.[12]

In Nigeria there are intense hostilities between Christians and Muslims, often dividing members of the same family. When I served as a pastor in Cleveland, a student from Nigeria joined our church. He had been raised as a Muslim in his small village in Nigeria, but he converted to Christianity, and I baptized him into that faith. As a result, he was cut off from his family in Nigeria. He was even warned not to attend his father's funeral in their village in Nigeria because his life would be in danger. He actually left the United States and went into seclusion in Canada to reduce the likelihood of anyone knowing where he was. So intense is the Muslim suspicion of other religions and cultures that in April of 2014 several hundred school girls in the northern part of Nigeria were kidnapped by a group called Boko Haram who objected to those girls receiving a western education. "Boko Haram translates as 'Western education is a sin' in the Hausa language. The militant group says its aim is to impose a stricter enforcement of Sharia law across Nigeria, Africa's most populous nation."[13]

In 2011 something that has come to be known as the Arab Spring erupted in nations such as Tunisia, Libya, and Egypt. Overthrowing autocratic rulers was something that those nations could accomplish in a matter of weeks, but finding a suitable governing formula going forward has been far more challenging. This has been the case in large measure because of issues of religious diversity and religious liberty. As reported in the *New York Times*,

> Most of the uprisings have devolved into bitter struggles, as a mix of political powers battle over the rules of participation, the relationship between the military and the government, the role of religion in public life and what it means to be a citizen, not a subject.[14]

The report continues, "In many ways, the Arab Spring has revealed and exacerbated deep societal splits, between secularists and Islamists and between religious sects. 'This is political polarization on steroids,' said Jeffrey Martini, a Middle East specialist. ... 'You've got both sides trying to banish each other from politics.'"[15] As an example of this polarizing religious conflict, "In the Persian Gulf kingdom of Bahrain, overwhelming force by the ruling Sunni monarchy has failed to silence dissent by the country's Shiite majority."[16]

THE BARMEN DECLARATION

No discussion about recent struggles over religious liberty and the conflicts between rivaling religious groups would be complete without some reference to the Barmen Declaration of 1934 and the conflict between the German Evangelical Church, which had grown out of the Reformation of the sixteenth century, and the German Christian Church, which was a creation of the Nazi Party under Adolf Hitler. Led by such notable theologians as Karl Barth, Martin Niemoller, and Dietrich Bonhoeffer, the German Evangelical Church objected to changes in theology and polity that essentially resulted in making Hitler coequal with Christ in authority over church and society.

Here are three of the most important statements in the Barmen Declaration:

1. We repudiate the false teaching that there are areas of our life in which we belong not to Jesus Christ but another lord, areas in which we do not need justification and sanctification through him.
2. We repudiate the false teaching that the church can and may, apart from this ministry, set up special leaders (*Führer*) equipped with powers to rule.
3. We repudiate the false teaching that the state can and should expand beyond its special responsibility to become the single and total order of human life, and also thereby fulfill the commission of the church.[17]

ISSUES THAT TEST RELIGIOUS TOLERANCE IN THE UNITED STATES TODAY

Although Americans in the twenty-first century value and benefit from the principle of religious liberty, a number of social issues keep obscuring the lines between church and state. It is very likely that religious conflicts could easily break out in this country over contentious issues such as abortion, capital punishment, and doctrinal arguments about who is adhering to the "true religion," were there not some principle at work that keeps this country from such conflicts.

RELIGIOUS PLURALISM

When I was growing up in Chicago in the 1950s and 1960s, there was a significant presence of members of the Nation of Islam in my neighborhood. The national headquarters of that movement, led by Elijah Muhammad, was two blocks from the apartment where I lived with my family. The barbershop where I went to get my hair cut was owned and operated by the Nation of Islam. Malcolm X was a frequent presence in our community, and the anti-American, anti-Christian, and anti-white rhetoric of the Nation of Islam could be heard on street corners and on black-owned radio stations all over the city.

Not one trip to the barbershop went by without my Nation of Islam barber assuring me that Islam was my true religion, and that I should leave Christianity and "join the nation." One of my cousins accepted that invitation and remains a member of the Nation of Islam to this day. The Nation of Islam was outspoken in its criticism of America, especially during the 1960s, when there was so much white-on-black violence going on as part of civil rights demonstrations in Birmingham, Selma, and Anniston in Alabama, and in Jackson, Philadelphia, and Oxford in Mississippi. Nevertheless, the right of the Nation of Islam to assemble, to speak, to hold marches and protest rallies, and even to call for an all-black region within the country that would be legally separated from the United States was upheld. How was it possible that this religious and political diversity could have been allowed and not openly suppressed?

PEYOTE AND NATIVE AMERICANS

Certain Native American groups practice a prayer ritual that includes drinking a tea made from the peyote cactus. Though considered a sacred medicine by Native Americans, peyote was outlawed by the U.S. government in the 1940s because it produces a psychotropic substance, mescaline. After Native Americans protested for years that the use of peyote was an essential part of their religious life, the U.S. government voted to end the ban, and in 1978 the use of peyote was deemed legal under the Fourteenth Amendment to the U.S. Constitution. The use of peyote is now common in Texas, Utah, Colorado, Minnesota, Nevada, Kansas, New Mexico, and Oklahoma. What makes it possible for a country that has a legal ban on the nonmedical use of any and all substances that are narcotic or psychedelic in nature to allow its use in Native American religious ceremonies? Even more amazing, why are Christians in those states not in an uproar not only about the use of peyote, but also about the presence of a non-Judeo-Christian religion being practiced in their states?

THE BIBLE IN PUBLIC SCHOOLS

In an interesting development, an elected school board in Wilmington, Delaware, is considering a high school class that examines the Bible's role in society and history. The course that has been developed by the Bible Literacy Project is currently being taught in 580 schools in forty-three states. The Bible Literacy Project has been endorsed by the American Federation of Teachers, the National School Board Association, the Baptist Joint Committee on Public Affairs, and even the American Jewish Committee and the Council on Islamic Education.[18] Given that the U.S. Supreme Court has outlawed school-sponsored prayers in the classroom, is it not strange that the school district's curriculum committee would recommend a course that studies a religious text, even if the study focuses on literature and history and not on faith and belief?

Even the American Civil Liberties Union in Delaware has spoken in favor of this project. The local director of that group said, "It is perfectly constitutional for schools to teach about religious texts, as long as it is strictly an objective, academic context."[19] The school board president observed,

> I think once people understand what we're trying to do, a lot of the concerns you see go away. When people understand that you're teaching about the Bible but not teaching that people need to conform to any particular religion or religious thought, things become a lot less controversial.[20]

It is common in colleges and universities to encounter courses about the Bible as literature. In fact, there are some seminary and divinity school professors of Bible whose approach is far more literary and historical than it is faith-based and belief-centered. However, to have such a course taught in a public school, where almost certainly students of various faith traditions and students from no faith traditions are present in the classroom, might reasonably raise several issues in regard to the separation of church and state. Nevertheless, there is something about American society that allows for this class along with all the other diverse religious views and practices noted above.

CLERGY-LED PRAYER AT LEGISLATIVE MEETINGS

I live in Rochester, New York. As mentioned earlier, the Supreme Court heard the case *Town of Greece v. Galloway*. At issue was the practice of opening meetings of the town council with a prayer. In 2007 two citizens of Greece, New York, complained not only about the practice of offering a prayer before the meeting of a governmental body, but also about the fact that the vast majority of those invited to offer the prayer were Christian clergy. The Second U.S. Circuit Court of Appeals found the prayer practice to be an unconstitutional establishment of religion, not because of the prayer itself, but because between 1999 and 2010 only four invocations out of a possible 130 had been offered by someone other than a Christian clergyperson. Eighty-five members of the U.S. Congress signed an amicus brief in support of the town's position that its practice is not unconstitutional. The May 5, 2014 ruling by the court that such prayers are allowable and are not a violation of the establishment clause of the First Amendment impacts not only both houses of Congress where a prayer is offered before every daily session of the House and the Senate, but also state legislatures and city councils all across the country that begin their sessions with prayer.[21]

I have offered prayers before the Ohio legislature and the Cleveland city council. No one suggested in those instances I was violating the separation of church and state. A prayer is offered at the inauguration of a President of the United States, as well as at the beginning and end of Republican and Democratic national conventions. The issue is not whether those practices should be outlawed. In an earlier ruling, in the case of *Marsh v. Chambers* in 1983, the Supreme Court upheld legislative prayers as a practice that historical accounts revealed to be "deeply embedded in the history and tradition of the country."[22] The court found that such prayers were usually nonsectarian and "simply a tolerable acknowledgement of beliefs widely held among people of this country."[23]

While prayer at a local city council was being debated, the Supreme Court itself opened with a prayer that states, "God bless the United States of America and this honorable court." Every session of the U.S. Senate begins with a prayer offered by the official Senate chaplain, who at this time is Barry Black, a retired Navy admiral, former chief of Navy chaplains, and an ordained Seventh-day Adventist clergyman. He is the sixty-second person to serve as Senate chaplain, following such notable twentieth-century predecessors as Peter Marshall and Lloyd John Ogilvie. In fact, Chaplain Black gained a considerable amount of celebrity during the shutdown of the federal government in October of 2013 as he challenged members of the Senate with rebukes such as "Save us from the madness. ... Deliver us from the hypocrisy of attempting to sound reasonable while being unreasonable. ... Forgive them the blunders they have committed."[24] Not only does the President of the United States attend the National Prayer Breakfast sponsored every year by members of Congress, but also since 1937 prayers have been offered by Protestant, Catholic, and Jewish clergy at the inauguration of U.S. presidents.

The use of prayer at the beginning of a session of any governmental agency does not suggest an establishment of religion. However, since 1985 all those who have been invited to offer prayer at a presidential inaugural have been Protestants. The last rabbi to pray at an inauguration did so in 1985. Interestingly, a rabbi also prayed at the inauguration of John F. Kennedy, who was the first, and so far the only, Roman Catholic to serve in that office. Several Greek Orthodox clergy have prayed at these events. However, no Muslim, Buddhist, Hindu, or other non Judeo-Christian person has been invited to share in that role. That is part of what is at stake whenever prayer in political settings is debated.

VOTING ON THE "LORD'S DAY"

In 2013, in the state of North Carolina, a law was passed by the legislature to end all Sunday voting in political elections. The practice of Sunday voting has been a successful way of getting African American voters to the polls, especially in the 2008 and 2012 presidential elections. This legislative action, taken by a Republican-controlled legislature, is viewed as a form of voter suppression that was enacted as soon as the U.S. Supreme Court struck down certain provisions of the 1965 Voting Rights Act. When asked to justify this action, State Representative Bob Steinburg said, "There should be no voting on Sunday because Sunday is the Lord's Day."

Is it appropriate for an elected state official to take an action involving the right to vote by invoking the notion that Sunday should be set aside only for religious observances? First of all, there are undoubtedly people in North Carolina for whom Sunday is not the Lord's Day, including Jews, Muslims, Seventh-day Adventists, and others. Why should their right to vote on Sunday be abridged because it conflicts with what lawmakers consider to be the Lord's Day? Second, the right to vote is guaranteed to all citizens in the U.S. Constitution, but the observance of the Lord's Day is entirely a matter of conscience and personal conviction. Here is a clear case in which the meaning of the separation of church and state needs to be clarified.

ABORTION

Many Christians, both Roman Catholic and Protestant, are vehemently opposed to the practice of abortion. They are also opposed to any taxpayer money such as Medicaid being used to fund abortions. However, the U.S. Supreme Court ruling in *Roe v. Wade* has determined that an abortion is a legal right in this country. The government does not see it as its duty to support or defend the religious views of any portion of its citizenry, even if persons serving in the government may personally be sympathetic with those views.

Certain religious leaders and antiabortion activists vehemently oppose *Roe v. Wade* and exercise their First Amendment right to protest in front of abortion clinics and on the steps of the Supreme Court. However, the only way that legalized abortion will be changed at the federal level is either by a newly constituted Supreme Court that votes to overturn *Roe v. Wade* or by legislation passed by both houses of Congress and signed into law by the President of the United States. One of the reasons that every presidential appointment to the Supreme Court is so hotly debated is that there is currently a five-to-four majority on that court not to overturn *Roe v. Wade*. One vote in the Supreme Court cast by a justice who is opposed to the practice of abortion, or who is in favor of putting tighter restrictions on when an abortion can be performed, could reverse that 1973 court ruling. However, that remains a legal, democratic process and not a unilateral action by the government in favor of one religious group over all others.

There are attempts at the state level in more than thirty states, from Texas to Pennsylvania, to limit access to abortion by requiring that an abortions can be performed only within the first twenty weeks of pregnancy, only at a surgical center, and only by a doctor who has admitting privileges at a nearby hospital, and also that only a licensed physician can administer abortion-inducing drugs. It is anticipated that when taken together, these restrictions would result in most clinics that perform abortions being closed.

Of course, the end result of such requirements is that more than access to abortion will be affected. Many women also use clinics that perform abortions as the setting to receive other health care services, ranging from breast exams and pap smears to birth control information. The debate rages back and forth at both the state and federal levels. This issue puts the entire First Amendment to the test. The clause regarding freedom of speech is employed by persons on both sides of this issue. And there is the clause regarding the freedom of peaceable assembly to protest a particular issue, likewise regularly employed by both sides. And there is the clause regarding religious liberty and no establishment of religion, whereby the government does not take a side as religious communities debate the morality, but not the legality, of abortion.

Tragically, there have been horrific acts of violence taken by antiabortion activists who have bombed abortion clinics and killed doctors who provide abortions, such as Dr. George Tiller in Kansas in 2009. There have also been horrific abuses by doctors who provide abortions, such as Dr. Kermit Gosnell of Philadelphia, who confessed to cutting the spinal cord of three babies after they had been delivered alive, a crime for which he now serves a life sentence in prison. However, despite these extremes on both sides of the abortion debate, it has been, and continues to be, argued within the boundaries of a principle that puts legal restraints on both sides and carves out space for opposing biblical and theological views to be heard under the protection of the courts and the federal government.

HEALTH CARE LAWS AND SECULAR COMPANIES

A major issue has emerged around the question of whether devoutly religious owners of private companies can be exempted from that portion of the Affordable Care Act that requires them to provide health insurance coverage that includes birth control measures, including what is commonly called "the morning-after pill." People such as the owner of the arts and crafts company Hobby Lobby who personally oppose abortion or birth control won a lawsuit that was upheld by U.S. Supreme Court in June 2014. The federal government has already allowed for exemptions to this kind of medical coverage for churches and church-affiliated organizations, such as Roman Catholic hospitals and universities. The government acknowledged that it "can't compel [churches] to violate their faith."[25]

The question is whether national policy should be written in ways that conform to the religious views of persons doing business in the private, for-profit sector. In an earlier U.S. Supreme Court ruling involving Amish business owners who claimed that they should be exempt from paying Social Security taxes, the court ruled against such exemptions, deciding that for the government to grant such an exemption to a private company would be to impose the employer's religious faith on their employees, and that one secular business was being granted an exemption unavailable to other businesses. Religious liberty guarantees people in this country the right to practice their religion according to the dictates of their own conscience. The question in this case is whether a for-profit company can be exempted from health care coverage approved by Congress, signed into law by the president, and upheld as constitutional by the Supreme Court because portions of that law are in conflict with the religious convictions of the owner of that company.

The mere fact that such an issue can arise and be heard before the courts of the United States is an indication of the seriousness with which religious liberty is debated and decided in this country. People on both sides of this issue are earnest in their positions and determined to pursue a legal resolution to how the power of the federal government can and cannot intrude upon the personal religious convictions of companies whose owners are deeply religious, but which are not in any way affiliated with a religious institution.

YOGA CLASSES IN PUBLIC SCHOOLS

In the town of Encinitas, California, the school district received a grant to begin offering yoga classes as part of the physical education curriculum. A parent group filed suit to stop those classes on the grounds that yoga was rooted in the Hindu religion. The lawsuit suggested that by offering yoga classes the school district was promoting more than physical fitness; it was actively promoting religion. In July 2013 San Diego superior court judge John Meyer ruled against the parents and in favor of the school district, declaring that although yoga may have religious roots, its current use throughout American society serves a legitimate secular purpose. The court ruled that yoga neither advances nor inhibits religion.[26]

The judge employed a 1971 U.S. Supreme Court ruling in *Lemon v. Kurtzman* that established a three-part test to determine if any government agency was using taxpayer resources of money or space in ways that are neutral toward religion. Those three tests are: first, government institutions or legislation must have a secular purpose; second, the primary effect must be one that neither inhibits nor advances religion; third, there must not be an excessive government entanglement with religion.[27]

Even though the judge ruled in favor of the school district, the National Center for Law and Policy, representing the parents who brought the lawsuit, plans to appeal the judge's decision. The group's attorneys will claim that the judge has an anti-Christian bias.[28] One parent said, "We will have a society very soon where Christians will be the weirdest people. They will just be touted as crazy."[29] Here is another case in which the views and complaints of Christians about a threat to the preeminence of their faith tradition in the United States was heard and not upheld. Hinduism was not being advanced, and Christianity was not being inhibited simply by offering yoga classes in a public school.

THANK GOD FOR THE FIRST AMENDMENT

The principle that allows for the extensive religious diversity described above to peacefully exist in this country is called "religious liberty," which is guaranteed by the First Amendment to the U.S.

Constitution. That amendment says, in part, "Congress shall make no law respecting an establishment of religion, or prohibiting the free exercise thereof." Notice that the phrase "separation of church and state" does not appear in the First Amendment. What does appear are two critically important clauses: the "establishment" clause and the "free exercise" clause. What they mean, when taken together, is that the government will not use its force and power to favor the theology or policy views of one religious group over another. The government will not decide which religious traditions will and will not be allowed to function in the country, as long as no laws are being broken in the process.

Thanks to the First Amendment, taxpayer money will not be used to support any purely religious activity or organization. No persons will be coerced into any religious affiliation by the force of, or out of fear of retaliation from, the government. Employment in the public sector will not be limited to persons of a favored religious group, with adherents of other religious groups being excluded simply by virtue of their religious affiliation. No religious organization will be allowed to use its collective influence to shape public policies that conform to their particular theology, while ignoring and trampling on the views of other religious groups. Rather than religious coercion or the suppression of various religious views, the government will protect the rights of all religious groups, including small minority groups, to function without fear of reprisal.

Notes

1. Emo Phillips, "The Best God Joke Ever—And It's Mine!" *The Guardian*, September 28, 2005 (http://www.theguardian.com/stage/2005/sep/29/comedy.religion).
2. Quoted in Michael I. Meyerson, *Endowed by Our Creator: The Birth of Religious Freedom in America* (New Haven: Yale University Press, 2012), 14.
3. Dan Merica, "Atheist Group Targets Muslims, Jews with 'Myth' Billboards in Arabic and Hebrew," *CNN Belief Blog*, March 1, 2012 (http://religion.blogs.cnn.com/2012/03/01/atheist-group-targets-muslims-jews-with-myth-billboards-in-arabic-and-hebrew/).
4. Christopher Hitchens, *God Is Not Great: How Religion Poisons Everything* (New York: Twelve, 2007).
5. Richard Wolf, "Supreme Court upholds prayer at government meetings," USA Today, May 5, 2014, p. 1.
6. Reshma Kirpalan, "'Ground Zero Mosque' Clears Legal Hurdle to Build," *ABC News*, July 13, 2011 (http://abcnews.go.com/US/ground-mosque-wins-legal-battle-build/story?id=14062701).
7. Meyerson, *Endowed by Our Creator*, 82.

8. See Charles H. Lippy, "The 1780 Massachusetts State Constitution: Religious Establishment or Civil Religion?" *Journal of Church and State* 20 (1978): 533–49.

9. Meyerson, *Endowed by Our Creator*, 78.

10. Malkhaz Songulashvili, "My Threefold Grief: A Letter to My American Friends," *Baptist Peacemaker* 33, no. 3 (2013): 14.

11. Oren Dorell and Ahmed Kwider, "Sunni and Shi'ite Muslims Clash in Civil War," *The Christian Century*, June 26, 2013, 16.

12. Hannah Beech, "The Face of Buddhist Terror," *Time*, July 29, 2013, 42–45. Wirathu has since denied the allegations of taking such a name and asserted that he rejects all violence (see http://www.rfa.org/english/news/myanmar/monk-06212013182954.html).

13. Dana Ford, "Nigerian military official claims he knows whereabouts of kidnapped girls," CNN world.com, May 27, 2014.

14. Ben Hubbard and Rick Gladstone, "Arab Spring Countries Find Peace Is Harder Than Revolution," *New York Times*, August 15, 2013, A11.

15. Ibid.

16. Ibid.

17. John H. Leith, ed., "The Barmen Declaration 1934," in *Creeds of the Churches: A Reader in Christian Doctrine, from the Bible to the Present* (New York: Anchor Books, 1963), 520–21.

18. Matthew Albright, "Delaware School District Considers Class about Bible," *The News Journal*, July 24, 2013, 1.

19. Ibid.

20. Ibid.

21. Meaghan M. McDermott, "Members of Congress Add Voices to Greece Prayer Case," *Democrat & Chronicle*, August 6, 2013, B1.

22. *Magazine of The Baptist Joint Committee* 68, no. 6 (2013): 1.

23. Ibid.

24. Jeremy W. Peters, "Give Us This Day, Our Daily Senate Scolding," *New York Times*, October 6, 2013, A1.

25. "Don't Exempt Secular Business from Contraception Mandate," *USA Today*, August 12, 2013, A8.

26. Lilly Fowler, "Public School Yoga Classes Not Religious, Judge Says," *The Christian Century*, July 1, 2013, 17–18.

27. Stephen L. Carter, *The Culture of Disbelief: How American Law and Politics Trivialize Religious Devotion* (New York: Anchor Books, 1994), 110.

28. Fowler, "Public School Yoga Classes," 17.

29. Ibid.

5

THE UNITED STATES AS A SECULAR SOCIETY

Stephen Prothero, in his book *Religious Literacy*, puts this issue in context: "Thanks to the establishment clause, American government is secular by law. Thanks to the free exercise clause, American society is religious by choice."[1] I affirm two words in that last phrase: "religious" and "choice." The United States is not a Christian nation; it is a secular nation that protects the rights of all religious groups, as well as the rights of those who choose not to observe any religious tradition at all. In this country the observance of religion or the decision not to do so is a choice that every citizen can make without fear of being persecuted for one's faith or being denied any citizenship rights, such as voting or holding public office because of one's religious views. That is the essence of religious liberty and of the separation of church and state.

The United States is not the kind of theocratic society initially envisioned in the Old Testament, where the laws of God were the laws by which ancient Israelite society was governed. Interestingly, modern-day Israel itself does not presume to live under the authority of biblical law. Israel today is also a secular society governed by a democratically elected legislature and prime minister. I find it amusing to hear twenty-first century Christian clergy invoking the tenth-century BC Holiness Code (Leviticus 17–26) of ancient Israel, limited of course only to the issues of women in ministry and human sexuality and sexual orientation. They seem oblivious to the fact that the very people for whom those laws were intended have long since abandoned most of them as guidelines for their lives. Of course, there remains a small minority of Orthodox Jews in Israel and in the United States who still cling to the strictest possible interpretation of Jewish law.

The beauty of that religious diversity in both countries, the United States and Israel, is that their governments protect their right to practice religion as they choose without determining that the rest of society must follow their example. That is religious liberty. That is what it looks like to live in a country that insists upon the separation of church (or synagogue) and state.

Furthermore, there is no need to worry about the imposition of Sharia law, a strict interpretation of the Koran, upon the United States. Every now and then it is rumored that the very presence of Muslims in this country is a clear indication that an attempt to do so is underway. There are countries in the Muslim world, especially in places such as Afghanistan and Nigeria, and other largely Islamic nations where either the government or an influential group such as the Taliban, Boko Haram, or al-Qaeda is attempting to impose Sharia law upon the whole of society. But the likelihood of that happening in the United States is not just unlikely; it is impossible. First, there is no attempt or expressed interest among the Muslim population in this country to move in that direction. Second, if such a move were undertaken, it would immediately run into the impregnable roadblock of religious liberty and the separation of church and state. Anti-Muslim rabble rousers may use the idea of Sharia law as a way to galvanize attention for themselves and stir up further anti-Muslim sentiment in this country; however, their fears of the United States falling under the influence of Sharia law are, to borrow the words of Shakespeare, "much ado about nothing."

THE EARLY STRUGGLE FOR RELIGIOUS LIBERTY IN EUROPE

What must be understood is that religious liberty, or the right to worship God according to one's own conscience and convictions, is not just a matter of current religious and political significance. The appropriate interaction of church and state is a goal that has been debated, resisted, and fought over in the United States, Europe, and places around the world since the sixteenth century. Given that those who drafted the founding documents of this country came out of a European background, it would be especially useful to examine the struggle for religious liberty in that context.

In every nation of Europe there had been one so-called state-supported or established religion. That established religion usually was the religion practiced by the monarch and the ruling elite, imposed upon the entire country. There was a legal doctrine called *cuius regio, eius religio*, which meant that subjects would worship in whatever manner their ruler did.[2] As long as the Roman Catholic Church stood as the unchallenged religious tradition for all of Europe, with the exception of the Orthodox Church, the issue of religious liberty within the Christian portion of the population was not an issue. However, life for non-Christian groups in Europe during those years was another matter entirely.

THE SPANISH INQUISITION

There were, of course, two non-Christian religious traditions represented in some European countries: Islam and Judaism. Although these groups were basically forbidden from living in places such as England, Germany, and other northern European countries, there were fairly large Jewish and Islamic populations in Spain and Portugal. Nothing better epitomizes the fate of those two groups so far as religious liberty is concerned that the infamous Spanish Inquisition and the lesser known but equally intense Portuguese Inquisition of the fifteenth and sixteenth centuries.

The Spanish Inquisition was created in 1481 by King Ferdinand and Queen Isabella, the same people who would sanction the voyage of Christopher Columbus to the New World in 1492. The intent of the Inquisition was twofold. First, it was to impose orthodox Catholic teaching on any Christians who might have strayed from or spoken in opposition to anything being taught by the church. The second purpose was to force Jews and Muslims either to convert to Catholicism or to leave the country if they would not convert. The severest part of the Inquisition involved monitoring the activities of Jewish and Muslim converts to Christianity, known as *conversos*, in order to make sure they did not return to their earlier religious practices.

As often as not, those forced conversions came after episodes of torture, the threat of loss of property, and the public execution of those who claimed to have converted but were caught still observing aspects of their true religious faith. The ultimate penalty for failing to conform to orthodox Catholic teaching was to be burned alive. It was reported that between 1480 and 1504 more than two thousand persons had been burned at the stake. By the end of the Inquisition the number is estimated to have exceeded four thousand. That does not count the number of persons who were simply imprisoned, tortured, or intimidated by the threat of any of those punishments.[3]

The Spanish and Portuguese Inquisitions achieved their intended purpose: to rid their countries of what they believed to be heresies. Protestantism was suppressed, and non-Christian religions were banished. But what did they lose in the process of trying to prevent freedom of thought or room for dissent? The philosopher Will Durant, in *The Story of Civilization*, frames that answer:

> Spain lost an incalculable treasure by the exodus of Jewish and Muslim merchants, craftsmen, scholars, physicians, and scientists, and the nations that received them benefitted economically and intellectually. Knowing henceforth only one religion, the Spanish people submitted completely to their clergy, and surrendered all right to think except within the limits of the traditional faith.[4]

THE SPIRIT OF THE INQUISITION IN EUROPE

Harsh treatment of dissenters was not limited to the Spanish Inquisition. In England, a century earlier, John Wycliffe was charged with heresy, not only for his views that differed from the Roman Catholic Church, but also for translating the Bible into English, which was contrary to Catholic doctrine. He was ordered to appear before Pope Urban VI in Rome to answer to the charges brought against him, but he suffered a stroke while saying Mass and died, in 1384, before any sentence could be passed against him. However, in 1428 Pope Martin V ordered a posthumous execution, and Wycliffe's bones were exhumed and burned, and his ashes scattered.

In 1415 John Hus of Bohemia (modern-day Czech Republic), who had expressed support for the teachings of John Wycliffe, was burned at the stake after having been excommunicated and later imprisoned. In 1431 Joan of Arc, the renowned female warrior of France, was burned at the stake on the charge of heresy, declaring that the voice of God, which she said spoke directly to her, was of greater authority in her life than the authority of the church. In 1498 the Italian priest and noted preacher Girolamo Savonarola was burned for failure to conform to orthodox Catholic teaching. In 1536 William Tyndale was burned at the stake in England for translating the Bible into English without the permission of Henry VIII. In other words, although the Spanish Inquisition has received the most attention, in part because it continued for so long, the same practice of coercing religious conformity under penalty of death was in full force in every nation of Europe.

THE PROTESTANT REFORMATION

The total monopoly on religious practice that had long been enjoyed and assumed by the Roman Catholic Church throughout most of Europe began to change after the theological and political upheaval that was the Protestant Reformation in the sixteenth century. In Germany under Martin Luther, in England under Henry VIII, in Switzerland under John Calvin, and in Scotland under John Knox, there began the rise of various new Christian religious traditions, including the Lutherans, Calvinists, Anglicans, and eventually Baptists and Methodists. When viewed together, they were known as Protestants, those who protested some aspect of the forms and practices of the Roman Catholic Church.

MARTIN LUTHER IN GERMANY

For many people, the Reformation is most closely associated with the ministry of Martin Luther and his ninety-five theses, which he nailed to the door of the Roman Catholic Church in Wittenberg, Germany, on October 31, 1517. With that act, Luther was challenging various practices of the Roman Catholic Church, including the idea that the authority of the pope was at least coequal to the authority of Scripture, and that the papal-sanctioned practice of indulgences or the belief that money donated to the church could purchase the salvation of someone who had died. This resulted in two historic declarations forever associated with Martin Luther: *sola scriptura*, which means that final authority for Christian belief and action resides in the Bible alone, and *sola fide*, which means that salvation is achieved only by faith in the work of Christ and never by any works that we do ourselves.

When called upon to recant his views and resume full compliance with the teachings and practices of the Roman Catholic Church at the Diet of Worms in 1521 (a diet was an assembly of inquiry), Luther made this famous statement:

Unless I am convicted by the Scriptures and plain reason—I do not accept the authority of popes and councils, for they have contradicted each other—my conscience is captive to the Word of God. I cannot and I will not recant anything, for to go against conscience is neither right nor safe. God help me. Amen.[5]

After his failure to recant, Luther was excommunicated from the Roman Catholic Church by Pope Leo X. By the very next year, the ideas of Martin Luther sparked the birth of a new expression of Christianity that took the name of Lutheranism, or today's Lutheran Church. His appeal to religion based upon conscience and not conformity was the theological seed that resulted in the Reformation and that eventually gave birth to the idea of religious liberty.

ULRICH ZWINGLI IN SWITZERLAND

The next major phase of the Reformation era came in Switzerland in 1522 with the work of another former Roman Catholic priest, Ulrich Zwingli. Having been influenced by Martin Luther, Zwingli picked up and added even more emphasis to the idea that the sole authority for Christians is the Bible. Any practice required by the Roman Catholic Church but not explicitly demanded by Scripture was to be immediately abandoned. Zwingli set forth his views in sixty-seven articles,

> affirming that the Gospel derives no authority from the church, that salvation is by faith, and denying the sacrificial character of the mass, the salvatory character of good works, the value of saintly intercessors, the binding character of monastic vows, or the existence of purgatory. He also declared Christ to be the sole head of the church, and advocated clerical marriage.[6]

As a result of Zwingli's efforts, priests and nuns married, baptismal and burial fees were abolished, images and relics were removed, monasteries were confiscated by the state, and Mass was no longer celebrated after 1525. In short, almost everything that defined the structures and beliefs of the Roman Catholic Church was done away with in Switzerland.

HENRY VIII IN ENGLAND

Another breakaway from the Roman Catholic Church, in England in 1534, hinged on the issue of church and state. King Henry VIII was married to Catherine of Aragon for sixteen years, but she was unable to provide him with a male heir to his throne. He sought to have that marriage annulled by Pope Clement VII so that he could marry Anne Boleyn in the hopes that she could provide him with that male heir. When the pope refused to annul the marriage, Henry and the English Parliament began to pass a series of laws that placed England outside the authority of the pope and the Roman Catholic Church. Not only that, but they also established a new church, the English Church (*Ecclesia Anglicana*), with the king as the supreme head. All property and goods of the former Roman Catholic Churches throughout England were made property of the state. All monasteries were closed. The Bible was translated into English by Henry's authority more than seventy years before the appearance of the King James Bible in 1611. This so-called Great Bible was the first English-language Bible authorized for public use, unlike the earlier translations by John Wycliffe (1380) and William Tyndale (1525), actions that resulted in their martyrdom. More importantly for this study, the observance of religion as defined by the English Church (the Church of England, or the Anglican Church) was mandated by the state.

JOHN CALVIN IN SWITZERLAND

The next major breakaway from the Roman Catholic Church came with a former French Catholic priest, John Calvin. He fled from France to Basel, Switzerland, in 1534 to avoid the persecution that was being directed against Protestants in that country by the Roman Catholic monarch of France, King Francis I. By 1536, Calvin had written *Institutes of the Christian Religion*, which essentially upheld the teachings of the Protestant Reformation that was now underway in Germany, France, and England.

Like Luther's ninety-five theses, the ideas of John Calvin quickly took root in countries throughout Europe, giving birth to what came to be called the Reformed Church, which today would include the Presbyterian Church and the Dutch Reformed Church, among other Protestant groups. Central to Calvin's teachings was the total depravity of the human spirit, salvation by faith to those whom God has predestined or "elected" to be saved, the primacy of biblical authority, and church governance devoid of both the papacy and the episcopacy (bishops).

Calvin presents a significant challenge, however, to the notions of religious liberty and of the separation of church and state. He envisioned a blend of religion and politics that took shape in the city of Geneva. He wanted a city-state that was governed by certain Old Testament laws as well as by the practices of the New Testament Christian community. In his "holy city" every citizen took an oath to live to the glory of God by following a very strict code of moral conduct. Those who refused to adopt that code of conduct were eventually driven out of Geneva, and in some cases they experienced a Protestant form of excommunication.

Despite some initial resistance, all citizens of Geneva had either accepted the oath or left the city. The Oxford Dictionary of the Christian Church writes, "From 1555 to his death in 1563 Calvin was the unopposed dictator of Geneva, which through him had become a city of the strictest morality."[7] Remarkably, John Calvin ended up becoming the embodiment of the very principle against which both the Reformation tried to oppose: intolerance of freedom of thought and religious dissent.

THE CONTINUING EFFECTS OF THE REFORMATION

The Reformation under Martin Luther set in motion the concept of religious liberty and the right to worship God according to one's conscience. The English reformation under Henry VIII raised the specter of the idea of an established church continuing to exist even after that established church had ceased to be exclusively the Roman Catholic Church. The Reformation as influenced by John Calvin seemed to ignore both religious liberty and the separation of church and state. Instead, he actually established a city-state that was a theocracy in which the teachings of Scripture became the laws of the region. Those laws were in turn enforced by a governance structure that merged the authority of the church with the authority of the state.

From 1534 onward, the monopoly on how to worship God and relate to the practice of religion that was once solely held by the Roman Catholic Church for most Europeans was forever broken. However, that does not mean that the seeds of true religious liberty or the separation of church and state had been sowed. Instead, the practice of having state-sponsored or established churches in various European nations continued unabated. In most of the countries of Europe one still had to belong to the established church of one's country or suffer harsh consequences for expressing dissent or embracing a different faith tradition. In France and Spain one had to be a Roman Catholic. In other countries, such as England, Germany, and parts of Switzerland, one had to be an Anglican, a Lutheran, or a Calvinist.

INTERNAL EFFECT OF ESTABLISHED RELIGIONS

The continued practice of having established churches resulted in two problems, one internal and one external. The internal problem was that the established churches were financially supported by taxes. Churches were built, clergy were paid and otherwise supported, and program needs were underwritten by funds from the public coffers. In some countries there was something known as prescriptive support for the established church. That meant that all residents had to support the established religion financially, supporting its clergy and buildings. They were required to attend the worship services of the established church.

In sixteenth-century England, for instance, there was the Act of Uniformity, which required all subjects to attend weekly worship services at their parish church. Failure to attend worship or even refusal to participate in the full liturgy became a crime and a subversive act.[8] Only those belonging to the established church could vote in an election or hold public office. In other words, in order to be a full member of that society, one had to be an active member of the established church. To make matters worse, there was no toleration for the observance of any other religion. Those who sought to do so were often subject to arrest, fine, and even physical punishment.

In other countries there was a practice known as permissive support, which meant that other religions were allowed to exist alongside the established church, but those other religious groups received no financial support from the government. Members of those other religious groups were excluded from voting and from holding public office. Not to be a member of the established church was allowed, but that decision came with some severe consequences.

The most notable practice of permissive support occurred in England with the passage of the Act of Toleration in 1689. That act allowed freedom of worship to Protestant groups that dissented from belonging to the Church of England but took an oath of allegiance to the English monarch. It should be noted that the Act of Toleration excluded Roman Catholics and Unitarians. Needless to say, Jews continued to be persecuted and reviled in most of Europe during this period, as evidenced in the arts, for example, by the portrayal of Shylock in Shakespeare's *Merchant of Venice*.

EXTERNAL EFFECTS OF ESTABLISHED RELIGIONS

The external consequence of the rise of these various Protestant denominations was frequent conflicts between countries where one country's monarch was Roman Catholic and the other's belonged to a Protestant group. The famous naval battle between Spain and England in 1588 in which the great Spanish armada was defeated by a smaller British navy in the English Channel was as much a religious conflict between the Roman Catholic king Philip of Spain and the Protestant queen Elizabeth of England. Saying, "There cannot be two religions in one state,"[9] Elizabeth did everything in her power to suppress the Roman Catholic Church in England. Spain did everything in its power, including several assassination plots against Elizabeth, to return England to its earlier Roman Catholic roots.

The Thirty Years' War (1618–1648) was the longest war in European history, and it began as a struggle between Protestant and Roman Catholic monarchs and nations. As historian John Barry notes, "Christians killed other Christians because of how they worshiped Christ. ... They embraced with swords, muskets, and artillery."[10] It was these internal and external consequences of having an established religion supported by the power and might of the state, and the brutal suppression of any dissent from that established church, that gave birth to the idea of religious liberty and the separation of church and state. Initially, only members of the established church could serve in the government.

The goal of religious liberty was to level the playing field so that persons of any and all faith traditions and even persons of no faith tradition at all, could exercise their religious convictions according to their own conscience without fear of persecution from the state. In addition, religious liberty tried to guarantee that citizenship rights would not be denied to a person who chose not to belong to the established church. Initially, only members of the established church were protected in their person and property by the courts, and only they could serve in elective or appointed political office. The goal of religious liberty was to allow persons of any and all religious traditions to serve God according to the dictates of their own conscience, and to serve their country as full-fledged citizens.

ESTABLISHED CHURCHES IN COLONIAL AMERICA

The attainment of religious liberty throughout Europe came neither quickly nor easily. One way to trace this issue, as far as the antecedents for religion in the United States are concerned, is to view it through the lens of the group known as the Puritans. They were so named because they wanted to purify the Church of England of any and all practices and rituals that hinted of its Roman Catholic past. They rejected the use of all vestments, icons, and rituals that had been used in the medieval era. They opposed the use of the Prayer Book, and they rejected the continuation of the office of the bishop, preferring instead a congregational form of church government.

When many of their attempts at reforming the Church of England failed, and when they found their own ability to worship God according to their own conscience being impeded, thousands of Puritans sailed for the New World in search of religious liberty. This "errand into the wilderness" (to use Perry Miller's phrase from his book of that title) was intended to establish in the New World a model of Christian reformation that seemed to have become impossible in Europe.[11] The familiar story of the ship *Mayflower*, which arrived in what is now the state of Massachusetts in 1620, was part of this mass immigration of Puritans to America.

Among the actions that the Puritans in America took were to separate from the Church of England in terms of serving under bishops and diocesan control, choosing instead a form of control known as Presbyterian or Congregational. They also embraced the added emphasis on sanctification or the pursuit of the holiest life possible attained through adherence to a strict code of personal morality. The story of Hester Prynne in *The Scarlet Letter* by Nathaniel Hawthorne provides a good window through which to view seventeenth-century, New England Puritan morality.

Perhaps the most remarkable thing about the Puritans, the errand into the wilderness, and their search for freedom of conscience is how little time it took for the creation of an established church to take root in colonial America. Since the people who founded the earliest colonies of British North America came from a country that had an established church and a history of suppressing other religious traditions, perhaps it should not be surprising that early and constant conflict arose between those who wanted to make the

Church of England the established church in colonial America and those who preferred what came to be known as Congregationalism.

Either way, those who refused or resisted the idea of supporting a church of which they were not members were called "dissenters," and the treatment of dissenters was harsh and swift. Consider the following examples of what happened in colonial America when an established church was allowed to exist.

JAMESTOWN, VIRGINIA

The first charter for the colony of Virginia, written in 1606, said that all settlers were to be instructed in the one true religion. Historian Michael Meyerson notes, "Settlers were to employ their utmost care to advance all things pertaining to the Order and Administration of Divine Service according to the form and discipline of the Church of England."[12] The 1609 charter demanded "the Anglican Oath of Supremacy from everyone entering the colony. By 1619, the first colonial legislature formally established the Church of England for His Majesty's colony."[13] That charter of the Virginia colony also stated that the "true religion" excluded Roman Catholics. It said, "It would be loath that any person should be permitted to pass that we suspected to affect the superstitions of the Church of Rome."[14]

The language of the charter reveals how tightly the practice of religion was controlled by the authority of the state. Instructions found in Article 7 of the charter read as follows:

> Every man and woman duly twice a day upon the first tolling of the bell shall upon the working days repair unto the Church to divine service upon pain of losing his or her days allowance for the first omission, for the second to be whipped, and for the third to be condemned to the gallies for six months. ... No man shall speak any word or do any act which may tend to the derision of God's holy word upon pain of death. ... No man shall speak impiously or maliciously against the holy trinity or against the known articles of the Christian faith under penalty of death.[15]

This colony was committed to an established church and to the persecution of any persons who dissented from the prescribed and required observances. So it was that the first British colony to be established in what was to become the United States of America brought with it from England the practice of a state-supported established church. As a result, Jamestown is noted for having two significant firsts attached to its legacy: it was the first British colony in North America to begin the practice of importing Africans for the purpose of indentured servitude and then slavery, and also to have an established church that specifically targeted Roman Catholics and all other dissenters for persecution.

THE PLYMOUTH AND THE MASSACHUSETTS BAY COLONIES

The Plymouth and the Massachusetts Bay Colonies were founded by Puritans, so-called, as we noted above, because they wanted to purify the Church of England of all vestiges of its Catholic heritage. Eventually they abandoned the Church of England altogether in favor of a Congregationalist model that spread into Connecticut as well. However, as in Virginia, there was no tolerance for any expression of religion other than the Congregational church. Meyerson states, "Purity of religion required that those who differed in their views of the word of God be removed from the body politic."[16]

In 1635 Roger Williams was exiled from Massachusetts because he "hath broached and divulged diverse new and dangerous opinions against the authority of magistrates, and yet maintaineth the same without retraction."[17] In 1637 Anne Hutchinson was accused of heresy for criticizing local Congregationalist ministers and likewise was exiled from Massachusetts. Baptists and Quakers were especially despised in the Massachusetts colonies, and frequently they were whipped for refusing to abandon their professed faith and convert to the "true religion." Meyerson reports that on July 25, 1651, three men were arrested for attending a Baptist church service in a private home, and for that offense they were sentenced to a whipping. "Each prisoner received thirty strokes with a three-cord whip until his blood flowed in little streams down to the waist to soak into the clothing."[18]

Things did not improve as far as religious liberty was concerned over the next one hundred years in Virginia and Massachusetts. In Virginia in 1771 John Waller, a Baptist preacher, reported that at a service in which he was preaching people in the congregation were attacked by a mob. He stated, "Brother Wafford was severely scourged. Brother Henry Street received one lash from one of the prosecutors, who was prevented from proceeding to further violence by his companions." He further reported that other Baptist ministers were attacked with whips and clubs, hunted by dogs, pelted with apples and stones, and faced with guns. Many other ministers suffered similar beatings until mob violence became the usual practice.[19]

Such reports of harassment of dissenters continued:

> By the time of the Revolution, more than half of the Baptist ministers in Virginia had suffered jail time; scores of others—Baptists and Presbyterians—had been jailed, beaten, dunked, fined, or otherwise harassed. The condition of the records and the apparent common nature of the harassments and beatings suggest that the recorded instances of physical persecution and arrest probably significantly underreport the actual experience of Virginia's dissenters.[20]

All of this violence and suffering was spurred by the simple fact that there were people in colonial America who dared to hold religious views and engage in religious practices that varied from the established religion of the colony in which they lived. The quest for religious liberty, and eventually the principle of the separation of church and state, are rooted in this struggle between the power of the state to impose a particular religion upon all the residents under its jurisdiction and the impulse within a growing number of people to hold to religious views according to the dictates of their own conscience and not the mandates of the government.

RELIGIOUS LIBERTY THROUGH THE EYES OF ROGER WILLIAMS

For Baptists in the United States, the central figure in the quest for religious liberty both prior to and long after colonial America is Roger Williams. In Geneva, Switzerland, is the Reformation Wall, a monument built to commemorate the four hundredth anniversary of the birth of John Calvin. That monument features the statues of ten men deemed important enough to the Reformation to be included. Roger Williams is one of those ten men, and the only one with a direct connection to the spread of religious liberty in North America.

Williams was born into an Anglican family in England in 1603, but after graduating from Cambridge University, he dissented against the forced imposition of the Church of England. He migrated to Boston, Massachusetts, in 1631 in search of religious liberty. What he quickly discovered was that he had fled an established church in England (Anglican) only to find another established church in the Massachusetts Bay Colony (Congregational). As a result of his failure to conform to the policies of religion so rigidly enforced by the church and the state, Williams was officially banished from the colony in 1634 and had to flee to avoid arrest and a forced return to England to face trial for heresy.

After a torturous journey through the wilderness, the fugitive finally arrived in what would become Providence, Rhode Island. There he established a colony in 1635, and in reaction to the established church policy of Massachusetts from which he had been banished, he established the first Baptist church organized in North America, in Providence in 1638.

Williams wanted to adopt a style of worship and spiritual life that was as close as possible to the examples found in the Bible among the earliest Christians. This was especially true concerning the act of baptism. Williams had been baptized as an infant in England. However, as Barry observes, "Since no scriptural rule supported infant baptism, he came to reject it. When several men and women who believed in adult baptism appeared in Providence, he joined them, getting himself rebaptized and then cofounding the first Baptist church in America in Providence."[21] He continued with the Calvinist idea that only a select few had been predestined for salvation. This placed him among a group known as Particular Baptists.

Williams came to disavow the idea of apostolic succession, the authority of bishops, and the idea that anyone except Christ himself had the authority to organize a church. Thus, within a few months of helping to organize the First Baptist Church in Providence, Rhode Island, he withdrew from that fellowship and would never again be a member of any church. He simply became a seeker, pursuing both religious liberty and individual freedom of conscience.[22]

It was Roger Williams, not Thomas Jefferson, who first framed the concept of the separation of church and state, charging that the established Congregational Church in Massachusetts had "opened a gap in the hedge or wall of Separation between the Garden of the Church and the Wilderness of the world."

Williams was opposed to an established church for two reasons. First, it went against his core belief that there should be no coercion in the matter of how a person chooses to worship God. Second, he believed that when the power of the state is used to advance the work of the church, the results is more politics and less true religion. In other words, religion is strongest when it is able to exist and advance on the merits of its teachings and doctrines, and not when it requires the support of the state to maintain its buildings, clergy, doctrines, and disciplines.

Williams offered a definition of religious liberty that was more expansive than anything ever heard before. Writing while in England in 1644 in a treatise entitled *The Bloudy Tenent*, he said, "It is the will and command of God, that since the coming of his Sonne the Lord Jesus, a permission of the most Paganish, Jewish, Turkish, or Antichristian consciences and worships bee granted in all Nations and Countries."[23]

Williams also argued that the state had no business involving itself in any way in religion, and that those, including Calvin himself, who supported the doctrine of persecution for cause of conscience erred and erred grievously. "Parliament by using Civill force and violence to worshippers' consciences to compel a particular worship, hath committed a greater rape, than if they had forced or ravished the bodies of all the women in the world."[24]

It is worth noting here that another term that has become synonymous with religious liberty and freedom of conscience is "soul freedom" or "soul liberty." Baptist historian Walter Shurden defines soul freedom as "the historic affirmation of the inalienable right and responsibility of every person to deal with God without the imposition of creed, the interference of clergy, or the intervention of civil government."[25] Long before Roger Williams emerged as a major leader within the Baptist church in the American colonies, Thomas Helwys of Amsterdam, Holland, in 1609 gave expression to the idea of soul liberty or soul freedom:

> Let the king judge, it not most equal that men should choose their religion themselves, seeing they only must stand themselves before the judgment seat of God to answer for themselves, when it shall be no excuse for them to say, "We were commanded or compelled to be of this religion by the king or by them that had authority from him."[26]

Whether one uses the term "religious liberty" or "soul freedom," however, one is dealing with the same set of principles argued by Roger Williams more than 350 years ago.

Clearly, Roger Williams laid the foundations for the principles of religious liberty and the separation of church and state as they are observed in the United Sates to this day. The notion that persons should be free to relate to God based upon their own conscience without facing persecution or reprisal from the officers of the state or of the church was the legacy of Roger Williams to the U.S. Constitution.

Notes

1. Stephen Prothero, *Religious Literacy: What Every American Needs to Know—And Doesn't* (New York: Harper One, 2007), 22.
2. John M. Barry, *Roger Williams and the Creation of the American Soul: Church, State, and the Birth of Liberty* (New York: Viking, 2012), 46.
3. Will Durant, *The Story of Civilization*, vol. 6, *The Reformation* (New York: Simon & Schuster, 1957), 215–16.
4. Ibid., 220.
5. Quoted in Roland H. Bainton, *Christendom: A Short History of Christianity and Its Impact on Western Civiliation* (2 vols.; New York: Harper & Row, 1966), 2:21.
6. Williston Walker, *A History of the Christian Church* (New York: Scribner, 1918), 362.
7. F. L. Cross, ed., "John Calvin," in *The Oxford Dictionary of the Christian Church* (New York: Oxford University Press, 1957), 220.
8. Barry, *Roger Williams*, 11.
9. Ibid., 12.
10. Ibid., 46.
11. Perry Miller, *Errand into the Wilderness* (New York: Harper & Row, 1956).
12. Michael I. Meyerson, *Endowed by Our Creator: The Birth of Religious Freedom in America* (New Haven: Yale University Press, 2012), 14–15.
13. John A. Ragosta, *Religious Freedom: Jefferson's Legacy, America's Creed* (Charlottesville, VA: University of Virginia Press, 2013), 42.
14. Meyerson, *Endowed by Our Creator*, 15.
15. H. Shelton Smith, Robert T. Handy, and Lefferts A. Loetscher, *American Christianity: An Historical Interpretation with Representative Documents*, vol. 1, *1607–1820* (New York: Scribner, 1960), 42–43.
16. Meyerson, *Endowed by Our Creator*, 17.
17. Barry, *Roger Williams*, 205.
18. Meyerson, *Endowed by Our Creator*, 17.
19. Ragosta, *Religious Freedom*, 52.
20. Ibid., 72.
21. Barry, *Roger Williams*, 263.
22. Ibid., 262–63.
23. Ibid., 321.
24. Ibid.
25. Walter B. Shurden, *The Baptist Identity: Four Fragile Freedoms* (Macon, GA: Smyth & Helwys, 1993), 23.
26. Bill Leonard, *Baptist Ways: A History* (Valley Forge, PA: Judson Press, 2003), 26.

6

WHAT THE U.S. CONSTITUTION ACTUALLY SAYS

With the history sketched out in the preceding chapter in mind, we turn now to the actual language of the U.S. Constitution in regard to the issue of religious liberty. If the fear of an established religion was the problem confronting the founders of this country, then the separation of church and state and the guarantee of religious liberty was the solution that they adopted to protect these rights for all citizens. As has been stated repeatedly in this study, the actual words "separation of church and state" do not appear anywhere in the Constitution. The origin of that principle lies with Roger Williams in 1644, and the first known American usage of that term came with Thomas Jefferson in his 1802 letter to the Baptist Association in Danbury, Connecticut. The language that does appear in the Constitution that seeks to guarantee religious liberty is found first in Article 6 of the main body of that document, which was signed in 1787, and later the First Amendment to the Constitution, which was ratified in 1792 as part of the Bill of Rights.

ARTICLE 6, SECTION 3

Article 6, Section 3 says in part, "No religious test shall ever be required as a qualification to any office or public trust under the United States." Under this provision of the Constitution the religious affiliation of a person seeking public office should not even be a consideration, much less a basis for exclusion. One does not have to belong to any particular religious group to be qualified to serve in public office. In fact, one does not have to belong to *any* religious group in order to be qualified for public office. Remember that in colonial America and in the years after the Revolutionary War, Jews and Catholics were excluded from holding public office. Article 6, Section 3 of the Constitution removes that and all other prohibitions based upon religious affiliation.

I can remember sitting as a member of the audience at a candidates' forum in a church in suburban Cleveland in 2010 where all the candidates were asked in the presence of more than one hundred persons whether or not they were a member of a church. They were asked whether or not they believe that Jesus Christ is Lord. They were asked other questions that had to do with their religious views, and not with matters that pertained to the office they were seeking. Several of the candidates involved were attorneys, and they knew that such questions were inappropriate and unconstitutional so far as legally determining a person's qualifications for holding public office was concerned. There should be "no religious test." However, those candidates were afraid to offend the persons asking those questions, so they attempted to answer them while offering as little specifics as they could without violating their own conscience.

I was not a candidate for any office that year, but I was invited to offer closing comments and reflections on the discussion that had just transpired. I used that occasion to say that what happened that night was wrong and should not be repeated. Most of the people in that audience had no idea about Article 6, Section 3 of the Constitution and the prohibition against any religious test for those seeking public office. Paradoxically, there were some in that audience who had been sure that my running for public office a decade earlier was a violation of the principle of the separation of church and state. They did not perceive a contradiction in wanting to forbid a faith leader from holding public office, but wanting other candidates for office to share their faith.

It seems to be the case that many people are altogether unclear about the historic importance of the principle of religious liberty, and they are also unclear or totally misinformed about the meaning and purpose of the separation of church and state. It was as inappropriate to question those candidates about their religious views and beliefs as a precondition for election as it was to assume that my vocation in some form of clergy status should automatically disqualify me from running for or holding elective office. "No religious test shall ever be required as a qualification to any office of public trust under the United States."

THE FIRST AMENDMENT

The second part of the U.S. Constitution that pertains to the issue of religious liberty is the First Amendment, which says, "Congress shall make no law respecting an establishment of religion, or prohibiting the free exercise thereof; or abridging the freedom of speech, or of the press; or the right of the people peaceably to assemble, and to petition the Government for a redress of grievances." The relevant portion of the First Amendment for this study involves two clauses working together to create the desired outcome.

The first clause revolves around the word "establishment," which, as I have pointed out in chapters 1 and 2, indicates that the government is not to be in the business of preferring and supporting one religious group over all others. Persons do not have to belong to a particular religious group in order to vote or to qualify for service in an elective office. Membership in any particular religious group will also not serve to disqualify a person from any of the rights of citizenship, including voting and holding public office. Persons who belong to some religious minority will be protected by the government in their pursuit of religious liberty according to their conscience. No taxpayer money or other public funding will be provided for the support of any strictly religious institution. No particular religious doctrines will be a required part of the curriculum in any publicly supported schools. None of the laws or teachings of any religious text will be considered as the laws by which American society will be governed.

The second clause revolves around the words "free exercise," which means that in the United States people are free to choose whether or not they want to be involved in religious activity, and if they do, what form that might take. No coercion by the government will be employed to require any person to worship God in ways that conflict with his or her own conscience. This means that the rights of those who choose not to believe in or worship God are as protected by the "free exercise" clause as the rights of those who do believe and express their belief in worship.

It should be noted that Thomas Jefferson's use of the phrase "separation of church and state" is best understood as a reinforcement of the language of the First Amendment. Jefferson wrote:

> Believing that religion is a matter that lies solely between Man and his God, that he owes account to none other for his faith or his worship, that the legislative powers of government reach actions only, and not opinions, I contemplate with sovereign reverence that act of the whole American people which declared that their Legislature should "make no law respecting an establishment of religion, or prohibiting the free exercise thereof," thus building a wall of separation between church and state.[1]

WE HAVE COME A LONG WAY SINCE THE REFORMATION

It is a historical fact that the majority of the persons who founded and helped to establish this country were Christians of one stripe or another. However, having learned some lessons from European history, those who drafted the U.S. Constitution and the Bill of Rights made sure that the rights of all persons were protected in regard to religious liberty. This was a far cry from the religious principles that prevailed during the years of colonial America before the Declaration of Independence, and especially before the ratification of the Constitution and the First Amendment to that document. The founding documents of the colonies in Jamestown, Virginia, and Plymouth, Massachusetts, would have made impossible the kind of protections for religious liberty that we enjoy today.

U.S. SUPREME COURT RULINGS ON RELIGIOUS LIBERTY

It should be noted that the principle of separation of church and state has been upheld by several U.S. Supreme Court rulings. In the 1947 case *Everson v. Board of Education* the issue was a New Jersey law that required public school districts to transport to parochial schools any students living in that district whose parents opted for those parochial schools. The court ruled that the issue was one of student safety and not a matter of providing any direct financial support to parochial schools. Writing for the majority, Justice Hugo Black said,

> The establishment of religion clause of the First Amendment means at least this: Neither a state nor the Federal Government can set up a church. Neither can pass laws which aid one religion, aid all religions, or prefer one religion over another. No person can be punished for entertaining or professing religious beliefs or disbeliefs.[2]

The second major Supreme Court ruling dealing with separation of church and state was the 1963 case *Engel v. Vitale*, which resulted in the elimination of required prayer and Bible reading in public schools. This was the case that involved, to a limited degree, the atheist Madalyn Murray O'Hair. In 1951 the New York State Board of Regents recommended that all public schools begin their day with this prayer: "Almighty God, we acknowledge our dependence upon Thee, and we beg Thy blessings upon us, our parents, our teachers and our country." Justice William O. Douglas wrote for the majority and said,

> The price of religious freedom is double. It is that the church and religion shall live both within and upon that freedom. There cannot be freedom of religion, safeguarded by the state, and intervention by the church or its agencies in the state's domain or dependency on its largess. The great condition of religious liberty is that it be maintained free from sustenance as also from interferences by the state. For when it comes to rest upon that secular foundation it vanishes with the resting.[3]

Over the years, the position of the Supreme Court has been that government must remain neutral as far as the role of religion in society is concerned, favoring none and prohibiting none as long as no other laws are being violated in the process. The 1971 case *Lemon v. Kurtzman* set forth this policy of neutrality with the use of a three-part test. The court ruled, "First, government institutions or legislation must have a secular purpose; second, the primary effect must be one that neither inhibits nor advances religion. Third, there must not be an excessive government entanglement with religion."[4]

One of the most important proofs of the enforcement of the "free exercise" clause in the First Amendment came with a Supreme Court ruling in 1993 involving the city of Hialeah, Florida, and the Afro-Cuban religion Santería. Santería involves animal sacrifice as part of its liturgy. The city was concerned about the disposal of the carcasses of animals that had been ritually sacrificed, and in 1987 it voted to ban the act of animal sacrifice anywhere within city limits that was not directly related to food consumption.

The Santería community filed a lawsuit that reached the U.S. Supreme Court, whose nine judges ruled unanimously that animal sacrifice was a central part of the religious life of an identifiable segment of the community in question. Whatever the public health concern was about the disposal of animal carcasses, that concern did not overrule in importance the "free exercise" clause in the First Amendment. Justice Anthony Kennedy, writing on behalf of the court, said,

> The record in this case compels the conclusion that suppression of the central element of the Santeria worship service was the object of the ordinances. ... Careful drafting ensured that although Santeria animal sacrifice is prohibited, killings that are no more necessary or humane in almost all other circumstances are unpunished.[5]

Here was a case in which religious liberty and the separation of church and state were front and center in defense of a religious practice observed only by a tiny minority of the population of the United States. People are protected in their right to worship God in any way they choose, and the government does not have the right to prohibit them from doing so. In fact, it is the duty of the government to protect and uphold the religious liberty of all citizens, even a tiny minority group like the followers of Santería, when their rights are being threatened or abridged.

WHAT ABOUT CLERGY INVOLVEMENT IN POLITICS?

Returning to the central issue of this book, we should now see clearly that nothing in the U.S. Constitution in any way speaks to, much less seeks to prohibit, the active involvement of members of the clergy in the electoral political process. Neither clergypersons nor adherents of any religious tradition should seek to use elected office in order to advance the doctrinal views of their own tradition or seek to repress or punish those who hold differing views in regard to religious belief and practice. That would clearly violate the three-part test of the *Lemon v. Kurtzman* case of excessive government entanglement with religion.

Religious liberty implies the right of each individual to relate to God and to claims about faith according to his or her own conscience. Religious liberty also seeks to protect each individual from being denied any right of citizenship based upon that person's religious views and practices. It would be as wrong to deny a clergyperson the right to serve in elective office based solely upon his or her vocation as it would be for that same clergyperson to use an elected office to force or compel others to adopt his or her religious views and practices. The First Amendment and Article 6, Section 3 protect society from both of those infringements on religious liberty.

ANOTHER PARADOX IN THE AGE OF RELIGIOUS LIBERTY

There is a dark side to the search for religious liberty both in Europe and the United States from the sixteenth through the eighteenth centuries. At the very time when the Enlightenment, the Renaissance, and the Reformation were celebrating individual liberty and freedom from oppressive and dominating institutions, the entire Western world was caught up in the cruelty and brutality of the transatlantic slave trade. The nations of Holland and England, which led the way during the quest for religious liberty for white people, were also providing the ships and sails that powered the forced enslavement of millions of Africans who were brought to Brazil, Cuba, Jamaica, and Haiti, as well as to Savannah, Jamestown, Baltimore, and other port cities in North America populated by Christians who were debating their religious liberty. As noted by historian Edwin Redkey, from the fifteenth to the nineteenth centuries European nations were busy "stealing Africans from Africa," and for most of the twentieth century they were busy "stealing Africa from the Africans."[6]

In almost every respect, the liberty and freedom that whites wanted for themselves, both religious and political, they totally and completely denied to people of African roots based solely on their color and ancestry. That conflict has set up a separate discussion about the separation of church and state as far as the sons and daughters of Africa are concerned. Since the same government that protected the rights of white people was the chief instrument used to deny those rights to black people, many black people began to realize that one of the surest ways to alter and improve their condition was to aspire for influence within the political system that sat approvingly over their oppression and subjugation.

Beginning in the Reconstruction era (1865–1877) and continuing to this very day, beyond their roles in the church, many black preachers and clergy have also served as their community's political leaders. From Hiram Revels of Mississippi, who served in the U.S. Senate, to Emanuel Cleaver, who currently serves in the U.S. House of Representatives, the unfinished work of freedom and liberty has been advanced by the work of these politically active preachers. In the next chapter we take a longer and deeper look at this important intersection between church and state.

PART II: QUESTIONS FOR DISCUSSION AND REFLECTION

1. Why is Martin Luther considered an important figure concerning religious liberty?
2. What is the meaning of the term "established church"? How does that term inform a discussion of religious liberty?
3. What is the meaning of the phrase "wall of separation between church and state"? Name two persons associated with that term.
4. Who wanted to turn the city of Geneva, Switzerland, into the "city of God"? What was his understanding of the meaning of that term?
5. Who were the Puritans, and why did they come to British North America?
6. What is the meaning of the term "prescriptive" in regard to religious liberty?
7. What other term associated with Roger Williams can be used to describe religious liberty?
8. What was the moral contradiction between religious liberty and chattel slavery? What contemporary issues present comparable moral contradictions?
9. What other faith group besides Christians existed in Europe? What was their experience of religious liberty?
10. What groups were denied voting rights in colonial and in early American history?
11. What does the First Amendment say regarding religious liberty?

12. What is the importance of Article 6, Section 3 of the U.S. Constitution in regard to religious liberty?
13. Name three instances of religious intolerance currently at work around the world today.
14. In what year and in what context did Thomas Jefferson use the phrase "wall of separation between church and state"?
15. What is the meaning of the term *sola scriptura*, and what two Reformation leaders saw that term as central to their views?
16. What is the meaning of the term *sola fide,* and what Roman Catholic doctrine did it oppose?
17. What is the difference between religious "tolerance" and religious "liberty," and how do you see these principles or dynamics at work in the United States or in global society today?

PART II: THINGS TO REMEMBER

1. What was the Protestant Reformation, and in what century did it begin?
2. Who started the Church of England, and for what reason was that church started?
3. In what year was the Spanish Armada defeated by the British navy? What was the reason for that naval battle?
4. In what year did Roger Williams establish the first Baptist church in America?
5. In what city was that church established, and how did Williams come to reside there?
6. What was the established church for the Massachusetts Bay Colony? What was the established church for the Jamestown and Virginia colonies?
7. In what year was William Tyndale burned at the stake, and why?
8. In what way was John Wycliffe an important voice for religious liberty?
9. What is Santería, and how does it relate to the issue of religious liberty?
10. What was the Thirty Years' War in Europe, and what was at the heart of that conflict?

Notes

1. Adrienne Koch and William Rede, eds., *The Life and Selected Writings of Thomas Jefferson* (New York: Modern Library, 1944), 333.
2. Robert L. Maddox, *Separation of Church and State: Guarantor of Religious Freedom* (New York: Crossroad, 1987), 116.
3. Ibid., 120.
4. Stephen L. Carter, *The Culture of Disbelief: How American Law and Politics Trivialize Religious Devotion* (New York: Anchor Books, 1994), 110.
5. Linda Greenhouse, "Animal Sacrifice: Court Citing Religious Freedom, Voids a Ban on Animal Sacrifices," *New York Times*, June 12, 1993, A1.
6. Edwin S. Redkey, *Black Exodus: Black Nationalist and Back-to-Africa Movements, 1890–1920* (New Haven: Yale University Press, 1969), 36.

Part III

THE RISE AND THE ROLE OF THE BLACK PREACHER/POLITICIAN

7

MORAL CONFLICT IN THE NEW UNITED STATES OF AMERICA

Part I challenged the incorrect claim that the involvement of clergy in partisan, electoral politics is unconstitutional and in violation of the principle of the separation of church and state. It was demonstrated that any such claim is wholly unsubstantiated, citing (among others) James Madison, one of the principal drafters of the U.S. Constitution, who stated that excluding clergy from any aspect of the political process (including holding public office) would deny clergy the very religious liberty and freedom of speech that the First Amendment of the Constitution was drafted to protect.[1] Not only are clergy at liberty to be involved in the political process of this country, but also their involvement, when done with no attempt to use politics as a means to advance a doctrinal or sectarian agenda, can "be a means of grace that advances the justice agenda of the gospel"[2] (see Matthew 25:31-46).

From Presbyterian clergyman John Witherspoon of New Jersey, who was one of the signers of the Declaration of Independence, to Congregational minister Abraham Baldwin of Georgia, who was among those who signed the U.S. Constitution, clergy have been involved in the political process from the founding of this country. Consider such notable persons as Rev. Hiram Revels (African Methodist Episcopal), who represented Mississippi in the

U.S. Senate from 1870 to 1871, and Father Robert Drinan (Roman Catholic) who served in the U.S. House of Representatives from 1973 to 1981. Consider also Rev. Emanuel Cleaver (United Methodist), who was mayor of Kansas City, Missouri, from 1991 to 1999 before being elected to the House in 2005, and Rev. Al Sharpton (Church of God in Christ), who not only ran for political office but also now hosts a political talk show on the national cable television network MSNBC.

As previously noted, many other clergy were active in politics even if they were not seeking or holding a political office themselves. In fact, it is impossible to discuss American politics over the last sixty years without reflecting on the role played by clergy. From Martin Luther King Jr. (Progressive National Baptist) and the Civil Rights movement of 1955 to 1968, to Abraham Joshua Heschel and Arthur Lelyveld (Jewish), who were deeply involved in the quest for voter rights for African Americans in the 1960s and in the group Clergy and Laity Concerned About Viet Nam; and from Daniel and Philip Berrigan (Roman Catholic), who were leaders in the anti–Vietnam War movement in the 1970s, to Jerry Falwell (Southern Baptist), who led the Moral Majority of the 1980s, the question has never been whether or not clergy should be involved in the political process. The real question has been about how such involvement should occur.

Part II discussed the history and evolution of the concepts of religious liberty and of the separation of church and state, examining the reformation movements that began in sixteenth-century Europe, the quest for religious liberty that caused thousands of Puritans and others to migrate to English colonies in Virginia and Massachusetts in the seventeenth century, and the actual language of the U.S. Constitution, both in Article 6, Section 3 and in the First Amendment. Part II also looked at multiple instances in twenty-first century America in which the issues of the free exercise of religion (religious liberty), on the one hand, and no establishment of religion (religious pluralism), on the other, are very much at the center of our society. It is doubtful that any member of the clergy of any denomination or faith tradition currently active in the United States can faithfully exercise his or her office without being politically informed at the very least, and, ideally, without being politically engaged to one degree or another.

Part III focuses on the moral conflict that arose when whites in America who were speaking about and even fighting a Revolutionary

War for their religious and political liberty were simultaneously engaged in the trans-Atlantic slave trade, which brought millions of Africans to the colonial Americas and later into the United States. The religious liberty and freedom from tyranny that this nation's founders wanted for themselves was summarily denied to the millions of human beings who were subjected to the brutality and inhumanity of lifelong chattel slavery.

ANOTHER PRINCIPLE FOUND IN THE U.S. CONSTITUTION

It is important to point out that in the U.S. Constitution the very humanity upon which any discussion of rights would be based was specifically discounted in regard to persons held in slavery. They were regarded as fractional human beings, only three-fifths of them counting for the purpose of determining apportionment of representatives and taxes in Article 1, Section 2, Clause 3, which says,

> Representatives and direct taxes shall be apportioned among the several States which may be included in this Union, according to their respective numbers, which shall be determined by adding to the whole number of free persons, including those bound to service for a term of years, and excluding Indians not taxed, three fifths of all other persons.

In deciding how to determine how many congressional seats any state would have, and given the disproportionate number of slaves in the Southern states, whose numbers could give a political advantage to slaveholding states, it was agreed to in the so-called Three-Fifths Compromise that all whites, free and indentured, would be counted (i.e., taxed) as full citizens. Native Americans (American Indians) would not be counted at all. All others (slaves) would be counted as three-fifths of a person. (The U.S. Constitution made no provision for the designation or recognition of free black people in this clause. The issue at hand was about congressional representation allotted to the various states based upon population. The question was how to count the large number of slaves then living primarily in the Southern states, who, if counted as whole persons, would give certain Southern states a far larger congressional delegation than most northern states.)

Professor Mark Lewis Taylor, of Princeton Theological Seminary, sheds light upon the hidden message of the clause. He notes that the desire of the founders to enjoy freedom for themselves did not in any way extend to an equal desire to grant freedom to the slave population that was resident in the country when the Revolutionary War had been fought and won. He states, "That slavery, declaring slaves to be but three-fifths human in spite of fervent cries for abolition at that time, was enshrined in the U.S. Constitution, is exemplary of the founders' way of limiting the drives toward revolutionary emancipation."[3]

The long and torturous history of race relations in the United States can be traced to this 1787 compromise that removed Native Americans from having any role in the country that had been their ancestral homeland and reduced enslaved individuals of African ancestry to the status of being 60 percent of a whole person. The near decimation of the Native American tribes and nations over the next hundred years was set in motion by this language in the U.S. Constitution. The continuing economic exploitation and political exclusion of black people in the United States for another 175 years was rooted in this decision. A European-based culture whose people had spent hundreds of years advancing the cause of religious liberty for themselves took as one of its first actions the complete and total dehumanization of Native American and African people.

To realize the full depth of the subjugation of African people in post–Revolutionary War America, one must look not only at the Three-Fifths Compromise. One must also examine the language contained in the U.S. Constitution about runaway slaves and the lawful continuation of the slave trade. Consider first Article 1, Section 9, which allows the importation of slaves into the United States to continue until 1808, with no restrictions whatsoever on the internal, domestic slave trade. Consider next Article 4, Section 2, which requires that any slaves who manage to escape from bondage into a state that does not allow slavery must be returned to their owners and not aided in their escape if they are captured or identified.

Little wonder, then, that in the March 16, 1849, edition of *The North Star* Frederick Douglass referred to the U.S. Constitution as a pro-slavery document.[4] Little wonder that on July 5, 1852, that same Frederick Douglass asked, "What to the slave is the Fourth of July?" He said in part,

> The rich inheritance of justice, liberty, prosperity and independence, bequeathed by your fathers, is shared by you, not by me.

The sunlight that brought life and healing to you has brought stripes and death to me. This Fourth [of] July is *yours*, not *mine*. *You* may rejoice, *I* must mourn.[5]

Douglass was fully cognizant of the shameful hypocrisy of people who were willing to fight a war to win freedoms for themselves, freedoms that included the freedom to worship God as they chose on the basis of individual conscience, all the while consciously and intentionally denying not only freedom, but even simple humanity, to others solely on the basis of color and ethnicity.

BLACK PREACHER/POLITICIANS AND THE MARCH TO FREEDOM

One of the ways by which that long history of slavery, oppression, and injustice was halted and a march toward equality and opportunity was begun was through the courageous actions of a small number of black preacher/politicians from the years following the Civil War until the present day. In fact, the very circumstances of oppression brought on by the slave regime unwittingly gave birth to a form of leadership unmatched both within and beyond the black community from the slave era until the present time—the black preacher in general, and the black preacher/politician in particular.

The purpose of this part of the book is to trace the emergence and evolution of the black preacher/politician, not simply as a vocation or profession but as a counterforce to the prevailing political winds of their time, winds that were intended to keep black people powerless and voiceless in a country that was otherwise founded on the principles of liberty and freedom. When all other voices from within the black communities across this country were muted, murdered, or manipulated by the white power structures of those areas, there always seemed to be at least one preacher/politician who was willing and able to push back against the forces amassed against his or her people. Recalling the language of Robert McAfee Brown, which we noted first in chapter 1, there have always been black preacher/politicians who were able to use the political process as "a means of grace."[6]

It must be noted that not all black preachers have engaged in politics to the same degree as others, although as Eric Foner has noted in *A Short History of Reconstruction*, "Every AME preacher in Georgia was said to be active in Republican Party organizing, and political materials were read aloud at churches."⁷ He then quotes Rev. Charles H. Pearce of Florida, who said, "A man in this State cannot do his whole duty as a minister except he looks out for the political interests of his people."⁸ Foner goes on to suggest one of the main reasons why black clergy often found themselves engaged in politics:

> Even those preachers who lacked ambition for political position sometimes found it thrust upon them. Often among the few literate blacks in a community, they were called upon to serve as election registrars and candidates for office. Over 100 black ministers would be elected to legislative seats during Reconstruction.⁹

One hundred black preachers hardly constitute the majority of black preachers in the post–Civil War years, also known as the Reconstruction era. History does not instruct, nor does this book suggest, that all black preachers were, are, or should be actively, personally involved in electoral politics. However, history does instruct, and this book most certainly does seek to suggest that the black communities of this country need some black preachers who will continue to serve in this role as political as well as spiritual leaders. No baseless, historically uninformed claims about this being a violation of the principle of the separation of church and state should be allowed to prevent this model of leadership from taking shape.

Eric Foner's observation that political leadership was as much thrust upon the black preacher as it was pursued by them points to some of the major reasons for the disproportionate influence of the preacher in black communities over the last 150 years. First was the central role of the church in the black community as the largest institution wholly owned and operated by black people. Second was that until very recently a rigidly segregated society prohibited talented and ambitious blacks from pursuing careers in almost any profession except as teachers and ministers. People with few other career opportunities turned to the ministry and became leaders in the most important institution in the black community. Therefore, as the only major professional group within the black community of the nineteenth century, preachers often were drafted or recruited to serve in political roles.

This point is reinforced by Benjamin Quarles, in *Black Abolitionists*, when he observes that black preachers had great influence because "colored men of other professions were in short supply."[10] Quarles refers to correspondence between Martin Delany and Frederick Douglass, two significant non-clergy leaders of that era, in which Delany writes, "As among our people generally in 1849, the church is the alpha and omega of all things."[11] This point must be kept clearly in mind in order for the political leadership role of the black preacher to be understood. Historical circumstances and necessity both allowed and required the black preacher to be more than a spiritual leader.

W. E. B. DU BOIS AND OTHERS ON THE BLACK PREACHER

The preacher represents the oldest continuing model of political leadership in the history of the black communities of America. From the Reconstruction era (1865–1877) to the present day, no other group of persons in the black communities of this country has been as consistently involved in providing political leadership as preachers have. There is no major scholar of this era in black history who has not made note of the unique leadership role of the preacher in the black community, usually with a direct reference to their role as political as well as spiritual leaders.

Writing in *The Souls of Black Folk* (1903), W. E. B. Du Bois said,

> The preacher is the most unique personality developed by the Negro on American soil. A leader, a politician, an orator, a boss, an intriguer, an idealist ... all these he is, and ever too, the centre of a group of men, now twenty, now one thousand in number. The combination of certain adroitness with deep-seated earnestness, of tact with consummate ability, gave him his preeminence, and helps him maintain it.[12]

Writing in *Out of the House of Bondage* (1910), Kelly Miller said this about the leadership and influence of the black preacher:

> Within the Church the opportunity for the talented tenth is almost unlimited. The Negro preacher has a larger influence and function than his white confrère, he is not only the spiritual adviser of his flock, but also their guide, philosopher and friend. Almost every feature of leadership and authority comes within his prerogative.[13]

Miller continues by offering a rationale for why the black preacher emerged as such an important leader within that community:

> The Negro preacher will be the spokesman of the people because his support comes directly from them. The teacher, on the other hand, whose stipend is controlled by the officers of the state, dares indulge in only such utterances as will not displease those upon whose good graces his tenure of place depends.[14]

That point about economic independence serving as a central reason for the freedom of the black preacher to be the leader and spokesman for the black community is reinforced by St. Clair Drake and Horace Cayton in their book *Black Metropolis*, a study of black life in the city of Chicago in the 1940s. They state,

> Negro preachers have the greatest freedom of any race leaders. Politicians must fit themselves into machine politics. Most civic leaders are dependent upon white philanthropy. Most of Bronzeville's [Clayton and Drake's term for the black communities of Chicago] preachers are answerable to no one except their congregation. They can say what they please about current affairs and race relations. There are no church superiors to discipline them and no white people to take economic reprisal.[15]

Howard Brotz, writing in *Negro Social and Political Thought, 1850–1920*, comments, "The preacher was, even before the Civil War, the group leader of the Negro."[16] Writing in 1927, James Weldon Johnson, then serving as the national executive director of the NAACP, observed that "the Negro today is the most priest-governed group in the country."[17] Leon Litwack, in *North of Slavery: The Negro in the Free States, 1790–1860*, makes a similar point: "Indeed the minister was unquestionably the most important and influential figure in the antebellum community. While exercising a powerful political, social, and moral influence, he also contributed some of the most militant leadership to the Negro's struggle for human rights."[18]

In *The History of the Negro Church*, Carter Woodson devotes an entire chapter to this topic, "The Call of Politics." There he notes,

> There were during the Reconstruction period, moreover, so many other necessities with which the Negroes had to be supplied that the Negro preacher, often the only one in their community

sufficiently well developed to lead the people, had to devote his time not only to church work but to every matter of concern to the race.[19]

Charles Hamilton, in *The Black Preacher in America*, notes that, from the perspective of the 1970s, one hundred years after Reconstruction, the central leadership role of the black preacher continues, for reasons that include, but also reach beyond, the preacher's economic independence from white society.

All of these scholars point out that only the black preacher enjoys an institutional base that can be tapped and mobilized without seeking permission from, or paying a user's fee to, some segment of white society. That base is the network of black churches. Hamilton further observes,

> The black lawyer, the black labor leader, the black politician—all these people are growing in number in the black community. But until they develop pervasive, indigenous black organizational structures, they will have to rely heavily on the black preachers for help in reaching and mobilizing the masses.[20]

In the twenty-first century other groups of professionals have emerged to provide significant leadership within the black community. They include black scholars, media groups, various nonprofit groups such as the National Urban League and the NAACP, political organizations such as the Congressional Black Caucus, and scores of other such groups in cities across the country. However, each of them lacks two ingredients long enjoyed by the black preacher and without which any sustained attempt at offering leadership is difficult to establish and exert.

The first ingredient for the exercise of leadership in the black community is regular access to masses of people who gather on a weekly basis (without having to be summoned to do so) to hear what a respected speaker has to say, or to hear from whomever the leader decides to bring before them on any given week. This privilege is the preacher's alone. The second ingredient for leadership is a building and facility where meetings can be held without added cost, where information can be produced and distributed, and where issues of various concern can be freely discussed and debated.

Until black leaders in other professions can meet these two criteria, the importance of the black preacher as a leader in the community will not soon be eclipsed. To this day, non-clergy black political leaders turn to churches and local pastors to host the rallies and events that they would like to sponsor, counting on the faith community to provide both the place and the access to most of the people.

In the 1998 political campaign for Congress in which I was a candidate this practice certainly was true. One of my opponents in that race, himself a well-respected attorney and a sitting member of the state senate in Ohio, was quoted in the local paper as saying, "You seek as many ministers' blessings as possible. You literally seek each minister."[21] The reporter who covered the Congressional primary campaign for the 11th District of Ohio in 1998 also acknowledged that the black church was the primary arena in which that campaign was conducted. He wrote, "In a district that is 60% black, the campaign largely played out in black churches, where the level of political discourse in a series of debates was higher than I had ever heard."[22]

WHITE AMERICA HAS NEVER HAD TO RELY ON PREACHER/POLITICIANS

The issues outlined above explain the essential difference between black preachers and their white counterparts in regard to leadership in the political realm. The white community has never had to rely upon their clergy to play a leading political role because leaders were able to arise within that community from every available sector of society: law, business, finance, publishing, the military, philanthropy, and higher education.

There were no Jim Crow laws that kept white people from advancing in all sectors of society. There were no Ku Klux Klan rallies designed to discourage white people from aspiring to achieve within any profession available in American society. There were no voter-suppression tactics such as the so-called grandfather clause, which limited the right to vote only to those whose grandfathers had already exercised that right two generations earlier (something that clearly prevented almost all black people from voting in most parts of this country). It was not just theology or polity that limited the political role of most white clergy in the United States; it was an absence of necessity. White clergy simply were not needed in the role of political leaders.

Even those white clergy who did play major roles in the political sphere of this country often made their mark on history in roles other than those specific to the parish or pastoral ministry. For instance, John Witherspoon, a signer of the Declaration of Independence, was a Presbyterian minister, but his greater contribution to the country was much more in relationship to his role as president of the College of New Jersey, which later became Princeton University. Abraham Baldwin, who signed the U.S. Constitution, was a clergyperson who served as chaplain during the Revolutionary War, but his major contribution to the country was as the founder and first president of the University of Georgia. Robert Drinan, a Jesuit priest who served in the U.S. Congress from 1973 to 1981, came to that position not as parish priest, but after fourteen years as the dean of the Boston College Law School. John Danforth, an Episcopal priest who was the attorney general of Missouri, later served in the U.S. Senate from Missouri from 1976 to 1995.

For most of this nation's history, such opportunities were unavailable to African Americans. As a result of limited access to other vocations and professions, the first wave of black political leadership included a significant number of persons who came directly from serving within the life of the black church. Not surprisingly, the black preacher continues to play a leading political role by virtue of the continuing influence of the black church within that community. Whether as an officeholder, an advocate on political issues, an endorser of political candidates, or a host for political forums and debates, black preacher/politicians have played a role totally unlike that of their white counterparts in ministry.

BLACK PREACHER/POLITICIANS OF THE RECONSTRUCTION ERA

As Eric Foner has pointed out, more than one hundred black preachers served in legislative positions during the period in American history known as the Reconstruction (1865–1877).[23] Carter Woodson reports on the surprising number of black preacher/politicians who emerged both before and during Reconstruction. James Poindexter was elected to the city council of Columbus, Ohio, in 1883. In 1885 Benjamin W. Arnett was elected to represent an 85 percent white district from Green County in Ohio in the Ohio general assembly. J. T. White served in the Arkansas legislature beginning in 1868. G.

W. Gayles served in both houses of the Mississippi legislature in the 1870s and 1880s.

Serving in that same body one decade earlier was Jesse Freeman Boulden, who was instrumental in having Hiram Revels appointed by the Mississippi legislature to serve in the U.S. Senate from that state. P. H. A. Braxton and D. F. Rivers, both Baptist pastors, also served in the Tennessee legislature in the 1870s. As late as 1896, Christopher Payne, a Baptist pastor and president of the West Virginia Baptist State Convention, was the first black person ever elected to the West Virginia legislature. James W. Hood, an African Methodist Episcopal Zion bishop from North Carolina, was a delegate to the 1876 Republican National Convention and was for a time the chair of the Republican State Convention in North Carolina.[24]

James Poindexter of Ohio gave voice to all of the black preacher/politicians of the Reconstruction era when told that they should not be involved in religion and politics:

> Nor can a preacher more than any other citizen plead his religious work or the sacredness of that work as an exemption from duty. Going to the Bible to learn the relation of the pulpit to politics, and accepting the prophets, Christ, and apostles, and the pulpit of their times, and their precepts and examples as the guide of the pulpit today, I think that their conclusion will be that wherever there is a sin to be rebuked, no matter by whom committed, and ill to be averted or good to be achieved by our country or mankind, there is a place for the pulpit to make itself felt and heard.[25]

The following is a brief look at three of the most widely known black preacher/politicians to serve during that period.

HIRAM REVELS

The African Methodist Episcopal preacher Hiram Revels began his career as a recruiter for two of the all-black regiments in the Union Army during the Civil War from Missouri and Mississippi. In 1870, following one term in the Mississippi state legislature, Revels was appointed by that legislature to a seat in the U.S. Senate from Mississippi. He was the first black person to serve in that chamber. John Hope Franklin in his landmark historical study of black history *From Slavery to Freedom* points out that Revels ironically filled the seat that had been vacated when Jefferson Davis resigned from the

U.S. Senate after Mississippi seceded from the Union, and Davis went on to become president of the Confederate States of America.[26] After his brief term ended in 1871, Revels went on to become president of what is now Alcorn State University in Mississippi.

RICHARD CAIN

Richard Cain was another African Methodist Episcopal preacher who became active in politics after having served in local churches. He was born free in Illinois and served churches in Brooklyn, New York, prior to the Civil War. After the war he migrated to South Carolina, where he got involved in Republican Party politics. He was a delegate to the state constitutional convention in 1868 and then served in the South Carolina state senate from 1868 to 1872. He went on to serve two non-consecutive terms in the U.S. House of Representatives from South Carolina, from 1872 to 1874 and from 1876 to 1878. During his tenure in office he was a leading advocate for the 1875 Civil Rights Bill, which sought to broaden and guarantee the rights of former slaves (freedmen) throughout the country. He was elected a bishop of the African Methodist Episcopal Church in 1880, serving the district that covered Texas and Louisiana. He also served as one of the founders and the first president of Paul Quinn College in Dallas, Texas.

HENRY McNEAL TURNER

The most influential of all the preacher/politicians of the Reconstruction era was undoubtedly Henry McNeal Turner of Georgia. He was another African Methodist Episcopal preacher of the nineteenth century who also had an earlier Civil War connection, being the first black man ever named to be an Army chaplain. He was appointed by Abraham Lincoln in 1864 as chaplain to various all-black regiments in the Union Army.[27] After the Civil War he became active in Republican Party politics in Georgia and was elected to the Georgia state legislature in 1868.

In regard to Turner's political influence, John Dittmer writes, "At thirty-three, Turner was the most influential religious and political leader in Georgia, the state with the largest black population."[28] Turner was an outspoken and proactive member of the Georgia legislature. He called for the formation of an armed black militia to allow for protection against Ku Klux Klan violence. He opposed the sharecropping system that he saw as a path to the re-enslavement of hundreds of thousands of black people throughout the South. To correct that abuse, he called for an eight-hour workday and an end to the convict lease system.[29] This is a clear example of "politics as a means of grace."

Turner and the other thirty-one African American members of the Georgia state legislature became so aggressive in defense of the rights of black people that the white majority in that legislature voted in 1869 to expel all black members from that body. This resulted in Turner's renowned "Speech on the Eligibility of Colored Members to Seats in the Georgia Legislature."[30] In that speech he declared, "I am here to demand my rights, and to hurl thunderbolts at the men who would dare to cross the threshold of my manhood."[31] Those black members were reinstated to the Georgia legislature in 1870, but only under the protection of the fixed bayonets of the Union Army, still stationed in Georgia.

In subsequent weeks and months those black members, including Henry McNeal Turner, were met with increased resistance to anything they sought to do on behalf of their black constituents. The Reconstruction era in Georgia gradually gave way to the reemergence of former Confederates to political power. That soon resulted in the rise of voter-suppression tactics that minimized and eventually eliminated the black vote throughout the South. As a result, black politicians, including preacher/politicians, were removed from office at every level of government. The era known as the Post-Reconstruction was dawning, and the political power and political leadership that black people in the South temporarily enjoyed was wiped out for many generations to come. (It should be noted that no black person would be elected to Congress from any Southern state until Rev. Andrew Young was elected to the U.S. House from Georgia in 1972, more than one hundred years after Henry McNeal Turner and other black politicians had been driven from office.)

Having been deprived of his once-formidable political base, and realizing the indifference of whites at both the state and federal levels both to violence directed against black people and the voter fraud that was denying their political power, Turner returned full-time to his church activities. Turner would go on to become a bishop in the African Methodist Episcopal Church in 1880. When he served in the Georgia legislature, he had introduced a bill to give women the right to vote, an act that was decades ahead of its time. As bishop, he championed the cause of women in ministry, going so far as to ordain a woman to be a deacon in the African Methodist Episcopal Church in 1888, an act that was rescinded by vote of the Council of Bishops on the grounds that it was not authorized by Scripture.

More importantly, he became an outspoken advocate of black emigration to Africa, believing that black people would never gain full equality or enjoy full citizenship in a nation that had so recently and brutally held black people in slavery. It was in that context of black nationalism and black emigration to Africa that Turner introduced the phrase "God is a Negro."[32] With that phrase, he became an early influence in what would come to be known as black theology. In fact, according to Edwin Redkey, Turner's use of the phrase "God is a Negro" was not only a theological observation about the *imago Dei*, but also it served to bolster the self-esteem of those black people who had been beaten down by white racism and made to believe that blackness was something of which they should be ashamed. "Even the heathen in Africa believed that they were created in God's image."[33]

The rest of what Turner had to say about "God is a Negro" is rarely mentioned, and it deserves equal attention. He believed that every race of people had portrayed God in their own image, and he lashed out at those whites and "fool Negroes" who "believe that God is a white-skinned, blue-eyed, projecting-nosed, compressed-lipped and finely robed *white* gentleman, sitting upon a throne in heaven."[34]

BLACK PREACHERS AND THE POLITICS OF THE POST-RECONSTRUCTION ERA

It is impossible to know how many more black preacher/politicians would have emerged in the years between the Reconstruction and today had it not been for the Post-Reconstruction era, which began in 1877, immediately after the election of Rutherford B. Hayes as president of the United States. In his campaign against Samuel Tilden, Hayes promised the Southern states that if elected president, he would immediately withdraw the Union Army troops from those states, effectively returning political power into the hands of the same people who had seceded from the Union and formed the Confederacy. As indicated in the story of Henry McNeal Turner of

Georgia, black political power in terms of black people holding any elective or appointive office came to a complete halt throughout the South, where the vast majority of black people still resided.

The loss of access to elective office did not necessarily mean the end of the black preacher/politician. As James Washington points out in his book *Frustrated Fellowship*, black preachers began to offer political leadership in new and different ways. Washington quotes Rev. Walter Brooks: "Our political leaders are few, and even those we have cannot reach the people. Therefore, it becomes our duty to speak out upon all questions that affect our people socially, economically, as well as spiritually."[35] However, most of that political leadership was shifted into congregational and denominational activity, where the organizational skills of black preachers could be organized, even if the impact of those organizations was nowhere near as far-reaching as it could have been had they been allowed to remain active in electoral politics at the federal, state, county, and local levels.

With the end of Reconstruction came an extended period of time referred to by historian Rayford Logan as the "nadir" of race relations in America, which stretched from 1877 through 1925. In *The Betrayal of the Negro: From Rutherford B. Hayes to Woodrow Wilson*, Logan makes two observations. First, he asserts, "The last decade of the nineteenth century and the opening decade of the twentieth century marked the nadir of the Negro's status in American society."[36] He sheds further light on that concept when he says, "At the beginning of the twentieth century, what is now called second-class citizenship for Negroes was accepted by Presidents, the Supreme Court, Congress, organized labor ... indeed by the vast majority of Americans, North and South. ... One is tempted to refer to this quarter of a century as the Dark Ages of recent American history."[37] It was during that time when several forces came together, like the proverbial "perfect storm," that removed black Americans from the nation's political equation, a storm that even the black preacher/politician could not resist.

THE TRIPARTITE SYSTEM OF OPPRESSION

Nothing better defines the forces that were amassed and maintained by whites to deny freedom and opportunity to blacks during that period in American history than what Aldon Morris calls "the tripartite system of oppression" in his book *The Origins of the Civil Rights Movement*.[38] Morris talks about the first aspect of that tripartite system, which was an economic system designed to keep the vast majority of black people locked into grinding poverty that was so suffocating that they had little energy left to protest their condition.

The second part of that tripartite system of oppression, crucial for the argument being made in this book, was to keep as many black people as possible in a state of political powerlessness. This involved all of the preconditions designed to render blacks ineligible to vote, devices ranging from the grandfather clause to literacy tests, from poll taxes to giving the precise number of bubbles in a bar of soap.

At a time when, in 2014, various voter suppression tactics are once again being employed to drive down the percentage of blacks and other minorities who can register and vote, one is reminded of how absolute the suppression of the black vote was within just ten years of the adoption of the Fifteenth Amendment to the U.S. Constitution in 1870, an amendment that theoretically guaranteed black males the right to vote.

For example, the grandfather clause stated that a person was qualified to register and vote in any county in a Southern state in which that person's grandfather had earlier been a registered voter. Given the 250-year legacy of slavery in the Southern states, that requirement guaranteed that virtually no black people were eligible to register, much less to actually vote. These obstacles to voting were not removed until the 1965 Voting Rights Act. Shockingly, in June 2013 the U.S. Supreme Court overturned portions of the Voting Rights Act, and within days of that action the states of Texas, North Carolina, South Carolina, Louisiana, and Virginia began to set up new obstacles to the right to vote that will have a disproportionate impact upon black and other minority voters.

The literacy test required black people to read aloud certain portions of a state constitution and then explain its meaning to the satisfaction of a white registrar of voters, a registrar who himself might be illiterate. Given that for the preceding two hundred years it was against the law for anyone to teach a black person to read or write, this was another way that blacks, who might well be the majority of the population in the counties of some Southern states, were rendered virtually absent from the voting booths. Similarly, Akhil Reed Amar, writing in *America's Constitution*, described something known as the poll tax, which he described as "one of several race-based suffrage rules"[39] that required black people to pay a sum of money as a prerequisite for being able to vote. Given the aforementioned poverty experienced by most black people, there simply was no money available to pay such a tax. Thus, as Amar points out, there was a third layer of voter suppression "that excluded blacks from the ballot."[40] John Hope Franklin, in *From Slavery to Freedom*, points out that the poll tax and the literacy test did impact white voters as well, but to a much lesser degree. He notes that by the year of 1890 in Mississippi alone that "the poll tax and education requirements would disenfranchise 123,000 Negroes and only 11,000 whites."[41]

The third part of the tripartite system involved intimidation and violence against those who challenged the political and social status quo. Black people had cause to fear violent attacks, which ranged from cross burnings and bombings of churches and homes to beatings, lynchings, and other torturous forms of death. Between 1895 and 1935 alone there were more than three thousand known instances of the lynching of a black person in this country.

It is impossible to tell the story of the Civil Rights movement without noticing how frequently some great achievement was countered by some gruesome act of terror. The 1954 U.S. Supreme Court ruling that desegregated public schools in America was answered by the murder of Emmett Till in 1955. The heroic Montgomery Bus Boycott was met with repeated bombings, including the bombing of the home of Martin Luther King Jr. The Freedom Riders of 1961 experienced brutal beatings and the firebombing of several buses at stops in Alabama. The 1963 March on Washington, where Dr. King gave his "I Have a Dream" speech, was answered just one month later by the bombing of the Sixteenth Street Baptist Church in Birmingham, in which four young girls were killed.

The Freedom Summer of 1964 was the time when people from across the country came to Mississippi to encourage and assist blacks in registering to vote. Within one week of their arrival, three of those volunteers were kidnapped and killed: Andrew Goodman, Michael Schwerner, and James Chaney. The march from Selma to Montgomery in 1965 was marred by the use of tear gas, electric cattle prods, and baton-wielding, mounted state troopers who attacked marchers on a day that came to be known as Bloody Sunday. Just a few weeks later, after participating in subsequent Selma marches, white activist Viola Liuzzo was run off the road and shot to death by four Ku Klux Klan members as she and Leroy Moton, a nineteen-year-old black man, were driving several black marchers back to their colleges. Obviously, the assassinations of Medgar Evers in 1963 and Martin Luther King Jr. in 1968 were further displays of the violence used to maintain black political powerlessness across parts of this country.

Again, the point here is not just to recount the gore and the glory of those historic events. The point, first of all, is to draw the stark contrast between the aspirations for freedom that whites had for themselves when they came to this country in the seventeenth and eighteenth centuries and the total absence of concern that was exhibited by this country in denying those very same things to Africans, African Americans, and Native Americans. The second point, and the one to which we now turn our full attention, involves the emergence of black preacher/politicians who were able to use their status within the black community to emerge as leaders in the effort first to encounter and later to begin to overcome that tripartite system of oppression.

Notes

1. John Ragosta, *Religious Freedom: Jefferson's Legacy, America's Creed* (Charlottesville, VA: University of Virginia Press, 2013), 20.
2. Robert McAfee Brown, "Confessions of a Political Neophyte," *Christianity and Crisis*, December 24, 1953, 186.
3. Mark Lewis Taylor, *Religion, Politics, and the Christian Right: Post-9/11 Powers and American Empire* (Minneapolis: Fortress Press, 2005), 12.
4. Frederick Douglass, "The Constitution and Slavery," *The North Star*, March 16, 1849 (http://teachingamericanhistory.org/library/document/the-constitution-and-slavery/).
5. Philip S. Foner, ed., *Frederick Douglass: Selected Speeches and Writings* (Chicago: Lawrence Hill Books, 1999), 194.
6. Brown, "Confessions of a Political Neophyte," 186.
7. Eric Foner, *A Short History of Reconstruction, 1863–1877* (New York: Harper & Row, 1990), 41.
8. Ibid.
9. Ibid.
10. Benjamin Quarles, *Black Abolitionists* (New York: Da Capo Press, 1969), 69.
11. Ibid.
12. W. E. B. Du Bois, *The Souls of Black Folk* (Greenwich, CT: Fawcett, 1969), 141.

13. Kelly Miller, *Out of the House of Bondage* (New York: Schocken Books, 1971), 203–4.
14. Ibid., 213.
15. St. Clair Drake and Horace R. Cayton, *Black Metropolis: A Study of Negro Life in a Northern City* (Chicago: University of Chicago Press, 1945), 427.
16. Howard Brotz, ed., *Negro Social and Political Thought, 1850–1920: Representative Texts* (New York: Basic Books, 1966), 256.
17. James Weldon Johnson, *God's Trombones: Seven Negro Sermons in Verse* (New York: Viking Press, 1969), 3.
18. Leon F. Litwack, *North of Slavery: The Negro in the Free States, 1790–1860* (Chicago: University of Chicago Press, 1961), 187.
19. Carter G. Woodson, *The History of the Negro Church* (Washington, DC: Associated Publishers, 1921), 220–21.
20. Charles V. Hamilton, *The Black Preacher in America* (New York: Morrow, 1972), 221–22.
21. Joe Hallett, "Candidates Seek Black Ministers," *Cleveland Plain Dealer*, April 29, 1998, A1.
22. Joe Hallett, "11th District Race Was Too Clean to See," *Cleveland Plain Dealer*, May 8, 1998, B11.
23. Foner, *Short History of Reconstruction*, 41.
24. Woodson, *History of the Negro Church*, 198–215.
25. Ibid., 202.
26. John Hope Franklin, *From Slavery to Freedom: A History of Negro Americans* (New York, Alfred Knopf: 1967), 319.
27. John Dittmer, "The Education of Henry McNeal Turner," in *Black Leaders of the Nineteenth Century*, ed. Leon Litwack and August Meier (Urbana: University of Illinois Press, 1991), 255.
28. Ibid., 257.
29. Marvin A. McMickle, *An Encyclopedia of African American Christian Heritage* (Valley Forge, PA: Judson Press, 2002), 184.
30. Dittmer, "Education of Henry McNeal Turner," 258.
31. Ibid., 258–59.
32. Ibid., 260.
33. Edwin S. Redkey, *Black Exodus: Black Nationalist and Back-to-Africa Movements, 1890–1910* (New Haven: Yale University Press, 1969), 40.
34. Dittmer, "Education of Henry McNeal Turner," 260.
35. James M. Washington, *Frustrated Fellowship: The Baptist Quest for Social Power* (Macon, GA: Mercer University Press, 1986), 158.
36. Rayford W. Logan, *The Betrayal of the Negro: From Rutherford B. Hayes to Woodrow Wilson* (New York: Collier Books, 1965), 62.
37. Ibid., 9.
38. Aldon D. Morris, *The Origins of the Civil Rights Movement: Black Communities Organizing for Change* (New York: Free Press, 1984), 1–4.
39. Akhil Reed Amar, *America's Constitution: A Biographical Study* (New York: Random House, 2005), 392.
40. Ibid., 394.
41. John Hope Franklin, 339.

8

FOUR MODELS OF BLACK CLERGY LEADERSHIP FOR THE TWENTY-FIRST CENTURY

Peter Paris is especially helpful at this point in reminding us of the various ways in which black preachers in the nineteenth and twentieth centuries went about their work, and in doing so, he establishes a set of models that can serve as guidelines for black preachers in the twenty-first century. Writing in *Black Religious Leaders: Conflict in Unity*, Paris points out four distinct models of clergy leadership, each of which he associates with a specific figure from black religious history in the United States. Those four models are priestly, prophetic, nationalistic, and political.

THE PRIESTLY MODEL

The priestly model, typified for Paris by Joseph H. Jackson of the National Baptist Convention USA, is used to describe those preachers who seek to focus their ministry efforts almost entirely on matters within their own local congregations. Paris writes, "Priests helped the people to endure things they could not readily change, and to make constructive use of every opportunity for self-development under the conditions of bondage."[1] Paris is quite clear about the fact that those operating out of the priestly model are not likely to engage in any form of social or political agitation against any of the conditions that confront them, since "the priestly function has tended to accommodate itself to the conditions of racism without affirming these conditions."[2]

Black preachers operating out of the priestly model tend to limit themselves to matters such as weddings, funerals, Bible study, hospital visitation, church administration, planning and leading various worship services, and generally tending to the work of individual spiritual formation. These are important areas of ministry that neither Peter Paris nor I seek to demean or downplay. It is simply a fact that once the door of opportunity closed in that nadir period in black history, many black preachers saw it as their primary duty to bring to life the words of the black spiritual that says, "There is a balm in Gilead to make the wounded whole."

It could be said that from the mid-to-late nineteenth century until this very day most black preachers continue to operate within this framework. I have already written books that have urged and instructed leadership within this realm.[3] While I acknowledge with Paris the value of the priestly model of ministry, it is clear to me that there is no need for a book designed to encourage preachers to adopt that model. Hence, I acknowledge but will not dwell on the black preacher in the role of a priestly leader.

THE PROPHETIC MODEL

The second model of clergy leadership mentioned by Peter Paris is the prophetic model, typified by Martin Luther King Jr. This style, says Paris, is characterized by the principle of social critique. "Prophets are reformers. They never accommodate to the status quo."[4] Central to this model of leadership is the target of one's activism and agitation. Black preacher/prophets in the nineteenth and twentieth centuries focused their attention on the sins of, and the need for transformation in, the broader American society. They may have been ordained preachers, and they may continue to serve as local pastors, but they have the capacity to focus their attention and the attention of others on what is happening well beyond the walls of the local church.

In an essay entitled "Missions of Patriotism: Joseph H. Jackson and Martin Luther King," Sam Hitchmough adds another level of contrast between the priestly and prophetic models of leadership. He argues that both men were deeply patriotic, but how they expressed their patriotism was what divided them.

Hitchmough writes, "For Jackson, correction of faults—the elimination of inequality—had to come through commitment to, and confidence in, the existing system, a belief that the structure was inherently capable of resolving problems."[5] On the other hand, he wrote this about the approach of Martin Luther King Jr., "King's later, more radical, philosophy affirmed his progressive patriotism, a belief that society's values had to be fundamentally altered, and the moral centre had to be re-orientated."[6]

In other words, Jackson believed that progress in the area of race relations in the United States would come through gradual steps involving white leaders of good will who would eventually do the right thing without having to be prodded by protests or acts of civil disobedience by the aggrieved black community. For instance, Jackson believed that King's presence in Chicago in 1966 was not necessary to dramatize the issue of neighborhood segregation in that northern city. Jackson thought that Chicago mayor Richard J. Daley would lead the way in bringing about the desired improvements because Daley was, in Jackson's words, "a friend of civil rights and a supporter of the NAACP."[7]

King, on the other hand, believed, "You cannot depend upon American institutions to function without pressure."[8] That is why King and the Southern Christian Leadership Conference went to Birmingham, Alabama, in 1963 to create the pressure that would result in the end of segregation in that city. It was while sitting in jail in that city that King wrote these words: "Human progress never rolls in on the wings of inevitability; it comes through the tireless efforts of men willing to be co-workers with God, and without this hard work, time itself becomes an ally of forces of social stagnation."[9]

James and Christine Ward, writing in *Preaching from the Prophets*, help differentiate between the priestly and the political mode of leadership:

> The natural inclination of the Christian community, like all religious communities, is to adapt its witness of faith to its most immediate human needs. In doing this the community always runs the risk of obscuring the wider dimensions of the gospel, particularly the wider implications of God's demand for righteousness and justice. What is needed, therefore, is preaching that recovers these wider dimensions and illuminates the ways in which the community obscures them.[10]

In my book *Where Have All the Prophets Gone?* I try to further distinguish between the priestly and the prophetic modes of leadership. I argue there that within congregational life there is a tendency for the preacher to become preoccupied with matters such as new-member orientation, confirmation classes, the maintenance or renovation of the church building, and whether or not the annual budget is being met. What may be lost in the face of those priestly concerns is the congregation's responsibility to respond to an escalating problem of homelessness in their community, the problem of black mass incarceration, the use and abuse of drugs and alcohol among young people, and the problems brought on by gun violence. It is the preacher's job in the prophetic mode of leadership to remain watchful and sound the alarm about the injuries being inflicted upon people by unjust policies and practices (see Ezekiel 3; 33).

Prophetic preaching shifts the focus of a congregation from what is happening to them as a local church to what is happening to them as part of society. Prophetic preaching then asks, "What is the role or the appropriate response of our congregation, our association, and our denomination to the events occurring within our society and throughout the world?" Prophetic preaching also never allows the community of faith to believe that participation in the rituals of religious life can ever be an adequate substitute for that form of ministry that is designed to uplift the "least of these" in our world.[11]

In the twentieth century, no black preacher better embodied the prophetic mode of leadership than Martin Luther King Jr. and the band of clergy who gathered around him between 1955 and 1968. That band included Wyatt Tee Walker, Andrew Young, Hosea Williams, Ralph Abernathy, James Lawson, Jesse Jackson, C. T. Vivian, and James Bevel, among others. It was while serving as pastor of Dexter Avenue Baptist Church in Montgomery, Alabama, in the years 1955–1956 that King also served as president of the Montgomery Improvement Association. From that position he led the 381-day boycott of the segregated system of seating on that city's buses.

When King moved on to become president of the Southern Christian Leadership Conference in 1957, that group took as its motto and its challenge "To save the soul of America."[12] In constantly shifting and broadening his focus from segregation in Montgomery and Birmingham to segregation and poverty in northern cities such as Chicago and Cleveland, in his opposition to the Vietnam conflict, and in his advocacy for the sanitation workers in Memphis this twentieth-century prophet was trying to save the soul of a nation rather than, in the manner of the priestly model, focusing on saving individual souls.

Cornel West points out that there is a specific task for anyone who wants to undertake the work of operating out of a prophetic model of leadership: "Prophetic beings have as their special aim to shatter deliberate ignorance and willful blindness to the sufferings of others, and to expose the clever forms of evasion and escape we devise in order to hide and conceal injustice." He continues by saying that the work of a prophetic being is "to stir up in us the courage to care and empower us to change our lives and our historical circumstances."[13] It is that last phrase about having the courage to care and being empowered to change historical circumstances that is the challenge of the prophet: not only to care about things personally, but also to persuade others to care and to act.

THE NATIONALISTIC MODEL

The third model mentioned by Peter Paris is the nationalistic model, typified primarily by Malcolm X and the Nation of Islam. However, that model clearly stretches back to the nineteenth-century black emigration or expatriation movement that included black preachers such as Alexander Crummell and Henry McNeal Turner. It is also important to remember that, although not a member of the clergy, no less a figure than W. E. B. Du Bois finally abandoned all hope of the redemption of the soul of America and relocated to the African nation of Ghana, where he became an official citizen on February 17, 1963. News of his death in Ghana on August 27, 1963, was announced at the March on Washington the next day, where Martin Luther King Jr. would speak passionately about his dream of a transformed American society.[14]

Paris describes a nationalistic leader as follows:

> This type is convinced that the society lacks the capacity for repentance, since it is viewed as morally decadent to the core. Evil is thought to be endemic; pervading every dimension of the society's life. This type of leader calls on its followers to disassociate themselves completely from the society and to set themselves to constructing a new society that bears no trace of the old.[15]

One can hear echoes of Dr. King's "I Have a Dream" speech from 1963 in the lament of Lott Carey, a black Baptist preacher from Richmond, Virginia. In 1815 Carey spoke about his reasons for wanting to abandon his life in the United States and to work to establish a colony for freed slaves in the country of Liberia. Carey said,

> I am an African, and in this country, however meritorious my conduct, and respectable my character, I cannot receive the credit for either. I wish to go to a country where I shall be esteemed by my merits, not by my complexion; and I feel bound to labor for my suffering race.[16]

As far back as 1795, a Baptist minister, David George, led a group of freed slaves from Georgia to Nova Scotia in Canada and then to Sierra Leone in Africa in search of freedom and to escape white oppression that was heaped upon both free and enslaved blacks in the United States.[17] George was a black preacher operating as a nationalistic leader.

In 1820 Daniel Coker, who had been the initial choice to be the first bishop of the African Methodist Episcopal Church until he deferred to Richard Allen, migrated from Baltimore to Sierra Leone as well. According to scholar Gayraud Wilmore, Coker saw two distinct reasons for the colonization movement: "Daniel Coker saw Negro colonization not only as a bid for independence and freedom for America's blacks, but as part of God's plan to bring the Christian faith to the land of his fathers through the ministry of the black church."[18]

Another major proponent of what would come to be known as the colonization and Christianization movement among black preachers of the nineteenth century was Henry Highland Garnet. In 1840 he was one of the founders of the American and Foreign Anti-Slavery Society. According to historian Benjamin Quarles, all of the eight founding members of that group were black preachers.[19] Garnet first burst onto the national stage with a speech he delivered before an annual session of the National Colored Convention meeting in Buffalo in 1843. In an address entitled "An Address to the Slaves of the United States," Garnet called upon slaves across the South to rise up against their owners, much as Nat Turner had done in 1831, and gain their freedom through force of arms. The most famous lines of that speech say,

> Let your motto be resistance! Resistance! Resistance! No oppressed people have ever secured their liberty without resistance.... Rather die freemen than live to be slaves. ... If hereditary bondsmen would be free they themselves must strike the blow.[20]

In 1858 Garnet founded the African Christianization Society to aid free blacks who wanted to emigrate to Liberia or Sierra Leone. That move was to have two purposes, the first of which was to introduce the Christian faith to those African nations. The second purpose was to create an agricultural economy that could produce and sell cotton to European nations at a substantially lower price than the cotton being grown by slave labor in the United States. If Europeans began buying cotton produced by paid labor from Africa, it would deal a death blow to the Southern slave economy. Unfortunately, the outbreak of the Civil War and the disruption of the emigration movement prevented Garnet's plan from taking effect.[21]

The first major nationalistic leader of the twentieth century was Marcus Garvey, who proposed a back-to-Africa movement as early as 1916. Through the Universal Negro Improvement Association, he made the case that wherever black people lived under the control of white authority they faced second-class status. He encouraged black people from the United States, the West Indies, Canada, and throughout Europe to establish their own country in Africa. Garvey was famous for these words:

> Where is the black man's government? Where is his king and his kingdom? Where is his president, his country, and his ambassador, his army, his navy, his men of big affairs? I could not find them. I will help to raise them up.[22]

Garvey's inquiry about an independent black African nation was a continuation of a similar vision and passion held by African Methodist Episcopal bishop Henry McNeal Turner, another strong advocate for a nationalistic ideology with a back-to-Africa methodology. Turner even raised the same concern about the absence of an independent black nation that could earn the respect of other nations. He said, "I do not believe any race will ever be respected, or ought to be respected, who do not show themselves capable of founding and manning a government of their own creation."[23]

By 1919, Garvey had raised over $630,000 for a venture that he called the Black Star Line, which included three steamships that would transport black people to Liberia. The plan fell apart for two reasons. First, Garvey never reached a final agreement with the government of Liberia to receive those who would be arriving on his ships. Second, he never received permission to sell stock in his company or to use the postal system in the United States to advertise his company. That resulted in his arrest and imprisonment for mail and securities fraud. His movement never recovered after he returned to his native Jamaica as a condition for his release from prison in 1927.[24]

However, no group more embodied the nationalistic model than the Nation of Islam under Elijah Muhammad. Rather than talking about emigrating from the United States to some other location in the world, they called upon the United States to pay restitution for slavery by designating several states in the Deep South as a separate region where black people could migrate and live as a nation unto themselves. He also demanded that the United States government support that emigration movement for a period of twenty-five years until the new black nation could become self-sufficient.

The suggested states were Mississippi, Alabama, Arkansas, Tennessee, and Louisiana. These were the states made rich by slave labor in the cotton and sugarcane fields. Muhammad's desire was to see that land offered to the descendants of those who once toiled there in slavery.[25] Needless to say, the most virulent form of racism was at work in those very states, and there was absolutely no likelihood that whites would abandon them under any circumstances as restitution for slavery.

There have been other movements within the borders of the United States that might more closely resemble separatist efforts than outright nationalistic efforts. For instance, Black Christian Nationalism as imagined by Albert Cleage Jr. in the 1960s was an attempt to establish a separate church body that he called The Shrine of the Black Madonna. This church, located in Detroit, was intended to be the first of a series of such churches that would place a separatist black religious movement at the heart of the resurrection of the black community in the United States. Cleage stated,

The present crisis, involving as it does the black man's struggle for survival in America, demands the resurrection of a Black Church with its own Black Messiah. Only this kind of a Black Christian Church can serve as the unifying center for the totality of the black man's life and struggle. Only this kind of a Black Christian Church can force each individual black man to decide where he will stand—united with his own people and laboring and sacrificing in the spirit of the Black messiah, or individualistically seeking his own advancement and maintaining his slave identification with the white oppressor.[26]

THE POLITICAL MODEL

The fourth model for Peter Paris is the political model as typified by Adam Clayton Powell, Jr. According to Paris, "This type of leadership is goal oriented and unafraid of compromise. It prefers to obtain a portion of its goal rather than none, and is the most pragmatic of all ideal types."[27] As was stated earlier, the problem for this model of leadership was the impact of the Post-Reconstruction period and the suppression of the black vote for nearly ninety years. Paris says,

> This type of Black religious leadership was born during the Reconstruction period in America and is, therefore, the most recent of all leadership types. Both the brevity of the period and the subsequent disfranchisement of Blacks seriously limited its development. The civil rights bills of the 1960s provided the necessary conditions for its rapid growth during the past two decades.[28]

ADAM CLAYTON POWELL JR.

The black preacher/politician model that was being forged by Henry McNeal Turner, Hiram Revels, Richard Cain, and dozens more during Reconstruction was reinstated and is epitomized by Rev. Adam Clayton Powell Jr. of New York. While continuing to serve as senior pastor of Abyssinian Baptist Church in New York City, Powell was elected to the city council of New York in 1941, and subsequently he was elected to the first of eleven terms in the U.S. House of Representatives between 1944 and 1968.

In a sense, Powell brought the passion of the prophet and the compassionate concern of the priest to his work as a political leader. As a prophet, he worked with the NAACP in the creation of something that they called the "Powell Amendment." This amendment would be attached to every piece of legislation that came through the House Education and Labor Committee, and it would deny any federal funding to any group that operated under segregated conditions. Beginning in 1946, when segregation was quite intense in this country, Powell's amendment began with this language: "No funds under this Act shall be made available to or paid to any school or state that maintains segregated facilities."[29] While the Powell Amendment was never actually attached to any bill, especially given the dominance of Southern politicians in Congress at that time, his continued use of the amendment served as a way to keep before Congress and the nation the evil of racial segregation.

From 1961 to 1967 Powell showed the compassionate spirit of the priest while serving as chairperson of the House Education and Labor Committee. During those years that corresponded with the presidencies of John F. Kennedy and Lyndon B. Johnson, Powell either introduced or saw through to passage by Congress and signing by the president more than sixty pieces of legislation that improved the lives of millions of Americans. Powell's leadership resulted in an increased minimum wage, free school lunches for poor children, rules for workplace safety, the War on Poverty, student loans for college, and services for the deaf, the elderly, and migrant workers.

Powell's time as chair of that committee was recognized in a letter from President Johnson that said in part,

Dear Adam:
The fifth anniversary of your Chairmanship of the House Education and Labor Committee reflects a brilliant record of accomplishment. It represents the successful reporting to the Congress of 49 pieces of bedrock legislation. And the passage of every one of these bills attests to your ability to get things done. ... Only with progressive leadership could so much have been accomplished by one committee in so short a time. I speak for millions of Americans who benefit from these laws when I say that I am truly grateful.[30]

Adam Clayton Powell Jr. picked up precisely where Henry McNeal Turner had been laboring one hundred years earlier before the end of Reconstruction, by using the power of the political process to create wholesale advances for people who had long been ignored, marginalized, or oppressed. The difference was that the laws that Powell helped to enact benefited not just black Americans, but all Americans. Once again, we have a clear example of a black preacher/politician who used politics as "a means of grace." The goal was not to amass political power for personal, selfish reasons; rather, it was to employ political power in order to have a positive, direct impact upon the quality of life of millions of people.

It would be quite wrong to think about the Civil Rights Movement of the 1950s and 1960s as being limited only to the street protests conducted by Martin Luther King Jr. and the Southern Christian Leadership Conference or to John Lewis and the Student Non-Violent Coordinating Committee. One has to think about the work of Thurgood Marshall and the NAACP as they worked within the courts to bring about the landmark 1954 Supreme Court ruling, *Brown v. Board of Education*, which declared segregation in public schools to be unconstitutional. One would also have to think about Adam Clayton Powell Jr. and his leadership of the House Education and Labor Committee that turned the energy of the street protests and the pronouncements of Supreme Court rulings into actual legislative action that transformed the United States for the better. He was the personification of the black preacher/politician of the twentieth century.

OTHER TWENTIETH-CENTURY PREACHERS IN THE POLITICAL MODEL

Adam Clayton Powell Jr. was the first black preacher/politician to emerge after the end of Reconstruction, but he was by no means the last one to seize upon that model of black political leadership that was rooted in the black religious experience of the nineteenth century. Many other black pastors and clergy would follow Powell into the halls of Congress. They would include Andrew Young from Georgia, who had been a top aide to Martin Luther King Jr. His election in 1972 made him the first black person elected to Congress from a Southern state since the end of the Reconstruction era almost one hundred years earlier. He was reelected in 1974 and 1976. In 1977 he was appointed by President Jimmy Carter as ambassador to the United Nations, and in 1981 he was elected to the first of two terms as Mayor of Atlanta.

Andrew Young was joined in Congress by other black preacher/politicians. There was William Gray III from Philadelphia. While continuing to serve as pastor of the Bright Hope Baptist Church of that city, he served in the U.S. House of Representatives from 1979 to 1991 and became chairman of the House Budget Committee. Floyd Flake served in the House on the Banking Committee from 1987 to 1997 while continuing as pastor of Allen Temple African Methodist Episcopal Church in Queens, New York. Walter Fauntroy, another close aide to Dr. King, served as the nonvoting delegate from the nation's capital to Congress from 1971 to 1990 while he continued to serve as pastor of the New Bethel Baptist Church. He was a founding member of the Congressional Black Caucus, and he was an outspoken critic of the apartheid regime in South Africa.

While all of the preacher/politicians listed above subsequently left their positions in Congress, that role of a black preacher/politician continues with the presence of Emanuel Cleaver. After serving twelve years on the city council of Kansas City, Missouri, he went on to serve two terms as mayor of that city beginning in 1991. He has served as a member of Congress since 2005. In 2010 he served as chair of the Congressional Black Caucus. He also served as pastor of St. James United Methodist Church in Kansas City from 1972 to 2009.

From Henry McNeal Turner, to Adam Clayton Powell Jr., to Emanuel Cleaver, the fourth model of black religious leadership has operated at the level of the federal government. Each of them has worked against the racism and discrimination imposed upon black people by a government that was founded on the principle of liberty and justice for all, things that were denied to people of color for most of this country's history. No one has charged these preacher/politicians with violating the principle of the separation of church and state. Quite the contrary, their status in the black church is what launched them and sustained them in their political positions. Their commitment to the principles taught in the black church concerning the equality of every person and their right to freedom and opportunity has been the underlying agenda of each of their political careers.

It may surprise many people to realize how many black preachers moved back into the role of preacher/politician once access to the voting booth was reestablished for black people in this country.

In addition to those listed above, all of whom have served at the federal level as members of the U.S. House of Representatives, many other black preacher/politicians have served at the state and local levels of government as well. Among them are some of the most illustrious names in black church history.

In 1936 black history was being made by others besides Jesse Owens in the Berlin Olympics, where he won four gold medals, and Joe Louis, when he was working his way toward the boxing heavyweight championship. In that same year Rev. J. C. Austin, pastor of Pilgrim Baptist Church in Chicago, was elected to be a voting delegate to the Republican National Convention.[31]

Gardner C. Taylor was pastor of Concord Baptist Church in Brooklyn, New York, from 1948 to 1990. He served as president of the Progressive National Baptist Convention in the mid-1960s, but in 1958 he became the first African American elected as a member of the New York City public school board.[32]

Sandy F. Ray was pastor of Cornerstone Baptist Church in Brooklyn, New York, from 1944 to 1979. He was a regional vice-president of the National Baptist Convention. However, in 1942, while serving Shiloh Baptist Church in Columbus, Ohio, he was elected to serve in the Ohio legislature.

Rev. Marshall L. Shepard Sr. served on the city council of Philadelphia from 1956 to 1967 after having served three terms in the Pennsylvania legislature from 1935 to 1942. In 1936 he served as chaplain to the Democratic National Convention.[33] All the while, he also served as pastor of Mount Olivet Tabernacle Baptist Church.

In 1947 Archibald Carey Jr. was elected to the Chicago city council. Later he was appointed as a deputy United Nations ambassador by President Eisenhower, and he ended his political career as a circuit court judge in Illinois. During all of that time Carey was pastor of Quinn Chapel African Methodist Episcopal Church in Chicago. Writing about Carey's tenure on the Chicago city council, historian Dennis Dickerson observes,

> Carey believed that his election to the Chicago City Council did more than satisfy personal ambition. Rather, it enabled him to advance Social Gospel objectives by improving the conditions of African Americans in the Third Ward. ... Carey's most important legislative effort focused on the elimination of racial discrimination in Chicago housing.[34]

In 1952 Carey addressed the Republican National Convention, and in that speech, which invoked language and images that would later be incorporated into Martin Luther King Jr.'s "I Have a Dream" speech, Carey said,

> Let freedom ring—from every mountainside let freedom ring. Not only from the Green Mountains and the White Mountains of Vermont and New Hampshire; not only from the Catskills of New York; but from the Ozarks in Arkansas, from the Stone Mountain in Georgia, from the Great Smokies of Tennessee and from the Blue Ridge Mountains of Virginia. ... From every mountainside, LET FREEDOM RING![35]

The list of black preacher/politicians in the twentieth century goes on to include Benjamin L. Hooks, who was elected in 1965 to be a judge for the Shelby County court in Memphis while serving two churches, one in Memphis and one in Detroit. Hooks was appointed by President Richard Nixon to be a member of the Federal Communications Commission in 1972. He left elective and appointed office to become executive director of the national office of the NAACP in 1977.

In 1976 Rev. Robert Harris became the first African American elected to the Utah state legislature. Bishop J. O. Patterson Jr. of the Church of God in Christ was a member of the city council in Memphis, the first African American member of the Tennessee state legislature, and for twenty days in 1982 he was the first African American mayor of Memphis.[36] After serving as president of Morehouse College for twenty-seven years, Dr. Benjamin Mays served as president of the board of education for the city of Atlanta. While serving as pastor of High Street Baptist Church in Roanoke, Virginia, Noel C. Taylor became mayor of that city from 1975 to 1992.

In 1962 S. Howard Woodson was elected to the city council of Trenton, and in 1963 he was elected to the first of his thirteen terms as a member of the New Jersey state legislature. He was elected speaker of the state assembly in 1974, the first African American to hold that position in any state since Reconstruction. He did all this while pastoring Shiloh Baptist Church in Trenton, where he served for fifty-three years. Leonidas B. Young served on the city council of Richmond, Virginia, from 1992 to 1999, and he was mayor of Richmond from 1994 to 1996. During that time he was pastor of Fourth Baptist Church of Richmond. And, while serving as senior pastor of First Baptist Church Lincoln Gardens in Somerset, New

Jersey, DeForest "Buster" Soaries Jr. was elected in a statewide election to be secretary of state of New Jersey. He served in that position from 1999 to 2002.

The list goes on. Darius Pridgen serves as pastor of True Bethel Baptist Church in Buffalo, New York, and has been a member of the Buffalo city council since 2011. Matthew Carter was associate pastor of Union Baptist Church in Montclair, New Jersey, while serving as mayor of that city from 1968 to 1972. L. Maynard Catchings, an ordained Congregationalist minister, served first as president of the board of education in Montclair from 1972 to 1976, and then he served on the city council from 1976 to 1980. E. T. Caviness was a member of city council in Cleveland in the 1970s while serving as pastor of Greater Abyssinian Baptist Church in that city. Today, Dwight Jones serves as mayor of Richmond, Virginia, and previously, from 1994 to 2008, he was a member of the Virginia state legislature. During all of that time he also served as pastor of First Baptist Church South in Richmond. While he was successful in getting elected, it should also be noted that in 2014 Delman Coates, pastor of Mt. Ennon Baptist Church in Clinton, Maryland, and a Ph.D. graduate of Columbia University in New Testament, was a candidate for the office of lieutenant governor for the state of Maryland.

This list is meant to be suggestive, not exhaustive. It is likely that in towns and cities all across the United States black preacher/politicians are serving as mayors, elected judicial officers, members of city councils, state legislatures, and boards of education, and holding administrative positions in county governments. These persons are a continuation of a model of clergy leadership that dates back almost 150 years to the era of Reconstruction. They serve the Lord by serving in the church, and they serve the Lord's people in many other ways by serving in political positions that grant them access to the levers of power in American society. As Anthony Pinn suggested, they bring their "religious sensibilities" to the task of political leadership."[37]

RUN JESSE, RUN! PRESIDENTIAL CAMPAIGNS OF JESSE JACKSON

No study of the role of the black preacher/politician would be complete without a closer look at the 1984 and 1988 campaigns by Rev. Jesse L. Jackson for the Democratic Party nomination for President of the United States. Although Jackson was unsuccessful in gaining the nomination in either of his attempts, he was more than successful in bringing his religious sensibilities and moral convictions into the American political mainstream. Issues of poverty, racism, gender equality, the high cost of American militarism, universal health care, and concerns dealing with sexual orientation were front and center in all of his campaign speeches as well as in the candidate debates and forums in which he participated.

Jesse Jackson was not the first black person to campaign for the presidency. The first serious contender was U.S. Representative Shirley Chisholm of Brooklyn, New York, who ran for the Democratic Party nomination in 1972. What made Jackson's candidacy unique was that he had been a national figure in the civil rights community for more than twenty years, first as a leader of the sit-in movement at North Carolina Agricultural and Technical State University in Greensboro, and then as a close aide to Dr. Martin Luther King Jr.

King named Jackson to head the Southern Christian Leadership Conference program called Operation Breadbasket, which negotiated with various corporate groups for fairness in hiring, promotion, and wages. Following the death of Dr. King, Jackson went on to organize Operation PUSH (People United to Save Humanity). He was instrumental in the voter registration efforts that resulted in the election of Harold Washington as the first black mayor of Chicago in 1983.

Through a combination of weekly radio and television programs, his presence at civil rights hot spots across the country, and personal appearances before various black church groups and conventions, Jesse Jackson was the most visible and perhaps the most influential black person in the United States by the time he had reached the age of thirty-five. By the age of twenty-seven he had already appeared on the cover of *Time* magazine. Thus, when he began his first campaign for the presidency, he had an enormous political base from which to run. In both 1984 and again in 1988 many of the major black church annual conventions were virtually campaign appearances for Jackson. Given the six million members of the National Baptist Convention USA and the six million members of the Church of God in Christ, not to mention the black churchgoers from other historically black and predominantly white denominations, Jackson had at the national level the kind of church support that other black preacher/politicians in Congress such Adam Clayton Powell Jr. enjoyed at the local level. That explains a remark that Jackson made about his Democratic and Republican rivals in a 1988 appearance on the ABC program *Nightline*. He said, "Mondale has big labor. Reagan has big business. I have big church."[38]

1984 CAMPAIGN

The Jackson candidacy in 1984 resulted in many significant outcomes. First, more black people registered to vote in 1984 than for any previous election in American history. Second, Jackson was able to appeal to Louis Farrakhan and the Nation of Islam for their support, resulting in 1984 being the first time members of the Nation of Islam had been encouraged by their leader to register and vote. Third, and most important for this study, were the electoral results for Jackson's candidacy for president. He garnered 3,282,431 votes in the Democratic primary, equaling 18 percent of the total votes cast. He also won five primaries and/or caucuses, in Louisiana, Mississippi, Virginia, his native South Carolina, and the District of Columbia.

THE 1988 CAMPAIGN

The results for Jackson's campaign were even more impressive when he ran again 1988. He won 21 percent of the votes cast that primary season for a total of 6.9 million votes. He won seven primaries, in Alabama, the District of Columbia, Georgia, Louisiana, Mississippi, Puerto Rico, and Virginia. He also won four caucuses, in Delaware, Michigan, South Carolina, and Vermont. Beyond that, his speech delivered at the Democratic National Convention in 1988 was, in my opinion, one of the greatest political speeches of the twentieth century.

THE "SHADOW" SENATOR

In 1990 Jesse Jackson won his first political position when he was elected to the U.S. Senate as a non-voting member to represent the people of the District of Columbia and advocate for their right to statehood. Since that time, Jackson has remained in public life, but not as a candidate for any office. However, it is difficult to calculate the number of other African Americans who ran for and now hold public office as a result of his example, not to mention the far-reaching impact that he has had on the American political landscape. Many people rightly think about the election of President Barack Obama as a partial fulfillment of the dream of Martin Luther King Jr., but it is equally accurate to observe that President Obama greatly benefited from the trailblazing efforts of Jesse Jackson in 1984 and 1988. For most African Americans of my generation, Barack Obama was the second or even third black person for whom they voted to be President of the United States.

"REV. AL"

It must not be forgotten that there was another black candidate for President of the United States between Jesse Jackson and Barack Obama, Rev. Al Sharpton. After a highly visible career as a civil rights advocate in New York City and across the country, Sharpton made his first venture into the world of electoral politics with two unsuccessful bids for the Democratic Party nomination for the U.S. Senate from New York in 1992 and 1994. In his second bid for that office he won 18 percent of the vote statewide, 21 percent of the vote in New York City, and more than 70 percent of the African American vote.[39] In 1997 he garnered 37 percent of the vote in a bid for the Democratic Party nomination for mayor of New York City.

In 2004 Al Sharpton made a bid for the Democratic Party nomination for president of the United States. He did not match the number of votes or the level of excitement generated by the presidential campaign of Jesse Jackson, garnering only 384,766 votes, or 2 percent of the total votes cast in that primary election process. Nevertheless, Sharpton did manage to inject into that election contest a sharp focus on an urban agenda for the United States, and also he was a charismatic and compelling orator during all of the debates in which he participated. In addition, he was another link in the thirty-six-year-old chain of black candidates running for president of the United States (1972–2008) that paved the way for the election of Barack Obama just four years later.

Sharpton has not pursued another elective office, but he remains very much engaged in politics. Since 2011 he has been the host of the MSNBC talk show *Politics Nation*, in which he both interviews leading politicians and policymakers and gives his own insights into the urgent social and political issues of the day. He is also a frequent commentator on other programs that appear on MSNBC during the day. In addition, he hosts a syndicated radio talk show that can be heard on stations across the country. He also maintains a high-profile presence away from the radio and television studios, coming to local communities across the country to call attention to civil and human rights violations in those places. He was instrumental in having Florida's attorney general pursue criminal charges against George Zimmerman after the police had released him from custody following the shooting death of Trayvon Martin.

In 2013 Sharpton led a march of more than two hundred thousand people who gathered in the nation's capital to mark the fiftieth anniversary of the 1963 March on Washington and the "I Have a Dream" speech of Martin Luther King Jr. During his own speech at that event Sharpton pledged himself to work against any and all attempts to suppress voting rights in this country, something that began to occur as soon as the U.S. Supreme Court declared portions of the 1965 Voting Rights Act to be unconstitutional.

THE VALUE OF RELIGIOUS SENSIBILITIES

In speaking about the effect of black preacher/politicians, scholar Anthony Pinn observes, "These political leaders ... used their religious sensibilities as a way of shaping government policies for the welfare of the underprivileged."[40] That is what so many black preacher/politicians have brought to their political assignments: religious sensibilities. I take Pinn's term to mean that black preacher/politicians have brought a passion for justice, a commitment to the equal worth of every person, the pursuit of a fairer and more inclusive society, and the belief that some of the work that God expects from every believer in every faith tradition can be accomplished or at least advanced through the political process.

For Christians, the mandate of Matthew 25:31-44 is always before the church as we seek ways to feed the hungry, clothe the naked, care for the sick, meet the needs of the stranger, and minister to those who are imprisoned. While there are things that individual Christians and individual congregations can do to address these areas of human need, it cannot be doubted that concentrating the combined resources of the various levels and branches of government is one way to make a powerful impact in all of these areas.

That was the work of Henry McNeal Turner in the nineteenth century and Adam Clayton Powell Jr. in the twentieth century.

Looking further into the twenty-first century, we can see that this is precisely what black preacher/politicians with their "religious sensibilities" can bring to the community. There will always be a need for the priest. God will, as God always does, send forth prophets in God's own time. In the meantime, there is an urgent need for the black preacher/politician to carry on the work that stretches back to the Reconstruction era.

Notes

1. Peter J. Paris, *Black Religious Leaders: Conflict in Unity* (2nd ed.; Louisville: Westminster/John Knox Press, 1991), 19.

2. Ibid.

3. Marvin A. McMickle, *A Time to Speak: How Black Pastors Can Respond to the HIV/AIDS Pandemic* (Cleveland: Pilgrim Press, 2008); *Battling Prostate Cancer: Getting from "Why Me" to "What Next"* (Valley Forge, PA: Judson Press, 2004); *Before We Say I Do: Seven Steps to a Healthy Marriage* (Valley Forge, PA: Judson Press, 2003); *Caring Pastors, Caring People: Equipping Your Church for Pastoral Care* (Valley Forge, PA: Judson Press, 2011); *Deacons in Today's Black Baptist Church* (Valley Forge, PA: Judson Press, 2009); *Living Water for Thirsty Souls: Unleashing the Power of Exegetical Preaching* (Valley Forge, PA: Judson Press, 2001); *Preaching to the Black Middle Class: Words of Challenge, Words of Hope* (Valley Forge, PA: Judson Press, 2000); *Shaping the Claim: Moving from Text to Sermon* (Minneapolis: Fortress Press, 2008); *The Star Book on Preaching* (Valley Forge, PA: Judson Press, 2006).

4. Paris, *Black Religious Leaders*, 20.

5. Sam Hitchmough, "Missions of Patriotism: Joseph H. Jackson and Martin Luther King," *European Journal of American Studies* 6, no. 1 (2011): 6.

6. Ibid., 9.

7. Ibid., 5.

8. Lotte Hoskins, ed., *I Have a Dream: The Quotations of Martin Luther King, Jr.* (New York: Grossett, 1968), 111.

9. Martin Luther King Jr., "Letter from Birmingham Jail," in *Why We Can't Wait* (New York: Signet Books, 1964), 86.

10. James Ward and Christine Ward, *Preaching from the Prophets* (Nashville: Abingdon Press, 1995), 11.

11. Marvin A. McMickle, *Where Have All the Prophets Gone? Reclaiming Prophetic Preaching in America* (Cleveland: Pilgrim Press, 2006), 2–3.

12. Hak Joon Lee, "To Save the Soul of America: Martin Luther King, Jr. and the Renewal of America Today," *Perspectives* 23, no. 3 (2008): 5–9 (www.rca.org/page.aspx?pid=3804). There is also a sound clip of Dr. King making this same point, available at http://www.hark.com/clips/lrkqrmtvhs-to-save-the-soul-of-america. The concept is further explored by Adam Fairclough, *To Redeem the Soul of America: The Southern Christian Leadership Conference and Martin Luther King, Jr.* (Athens: University of Georgia Press, 1987).

13. Cornel West, *Democracy Matters: Winning the Fight against Imperialism* (New York: Penguin Books, 2004), 114–15.

14. Manning Marable, *W.E.B. Du Bois: Black Radical Democrat* (Boston: Twane, 1986), 212–13.

15. Paris, *Black Religious Leaders*, 23.
16. Leon Fitts, *Lott Carey: First Black Missionary to Africa* (Valley Forge, PA: Judson Press, 1978), 27.
17. Carter G. Woodson, *The History of the Negro Church* (Washington, DC: Associated Publishers, 1921), 116.
18. Gayraud S. Wilmore, *Black Religion and Black Radicalism: An Interpretation of the Religious History of African Americans* (Garden City, NY: Doubleday, 1972), 143.
19. Benjamin Quarles, *Black Abolitionists* (New York: Da Capo Press, 1969), 68.
20. Earl Ofari, *Let Your Motto Be Resistance: The Life and Thought of Henry Highland Garnet* (Boston: Beacon Press, 1972), 153.
21. Marvin McMickle, *An Encyclopedia of African American Christian Heritage* (Valley Forge, PA: Judson Press, 2002), 142–43.
22. Lawrence W. Levine, "Marcus Garvey and the Politics of Revitalization," in *Black Leaders of the Twentieth Century*, ed. John Hope Franklin and August Meier (Urbana: University of Illinois Press, 1982), 109.
23. Edwin S. Redkey, *Black Exodus: Black Nationalist and Back-to-Africa Movements, 1890–1910* (New Haven: Yale University Press), 34.
24. McMickle, *Encyclopedia of African American Christian Heritage*, 180–81.
25. Ibid., 182, 246.
26. Albert B. Cleage Jr., *The Black Messiah* (New York: Sheed & Ward, 1968), 9.
27. Paris, *Black Religious Leaders*, 22.
28. Ibid.
29. James S. Haskins, *Adam Clayton Powell: Portrait of a Marching Black* (Trenton, NJ: Africa World Press, 1993), 56.
30. Adam Clayton Powell, Jr., *Adam by Adam: The Autobiography of Adam Clayton Powell, Jr.* (New York: Dial Press, 1971), 204.
31. Dennis C. Dickerson, *African American Preachers and Politics: The Careys of Chicago* (Jackson: University Press of Mississippi, 2010), 72.
32. "Honoring a Preaching Icon," *Baptist World Magazine* 50, no. 4 (2012): 8.
33. Dickerson, *African American Preachers and Politics*, 72.
34. Ibid., 98–99.
35. Ibid., 119.
36. Anthony B. Pinn, *The Black Church in the Post–Civil Rights Era* (Maryknoll, NY: Orbis Books, 2002), 76.
37. Ibid.
38. Michael Corbett and Julia Mitchell Corbett, *Politics and Religion in the United States* (New York: Garland, 1999), 307.
39. McMickle, *Encyclopedia of African American Christian Heritage*, 160.
40. Pinn, *Black Church in the Post–Civil Rights Era*, 76.

9

BLACK PREACHER/POLITICIANS AS PUBLIC THEOLOGIANS

In recent years the term "public intellectual" has worked its way into the vocabulary of American society. The term refers to scholars and university professors who are called upon by various news media outlets to comment on significant events occurring across the country and around the world. A number of African Americans have been called upon to function in this role: Melissa Harris Perry of Tulane, Cornel West of Union Theological Seminary, Michael Eric Dyson of Georgetown, and James Peterson of Lehigh regularly appear on TV stations and at public events. These persons are not journalists whose job it is to report on the news. They are thoughtful and insightful observers of the contemporary social and political scene who seek to help the public understand what is happening in the world with greater clarity and context. The work of public intellectuals is to bring a lifetime of research and writing to bear as they share their wisdom with the world. It is an important and a noble undertaking reserved for those who are capable of having one foot in the academic world and the other foot in the world of public policy.

When I think about the work of the black preacher/politician, I am led to introduce yet another term into the vocabulary of American society: "public theologian." According to historian Dennis C. Dickerson, that was the role that Archibald Carey played at the 1952 Republican National Convention when he spoke those words that were a precursor of Dr. Martin Luther King Jr.'s 1963 "I Have a Dream" speech. Dickerson said that "Carey was the embodiment of a public theologian who connected the pulpit and the public square to facilitate black advancement."[1] That was the role played by all of the black preacher/politicians mentioned in the preceding chapter, from Henry McNeal Turner to Adam Clayton Powell Jr. to Emanuel Cleaver. These are persons who consciously and intentionally bridge the worlds of religion and politics for the express purpose of facilitating black advancement and the advancement of all people who find themselves burdened by injustice.

We should note that the term "public theology" has been used by Peter Paris, in his contribution to the essays collected by Dwight Hopkins in *Black Faith and Public Talk*, to describe the writings and public witness of James H. Cone and Martin Luther King Jr.[2] That same volume has a chapter by James H. Cone himself that employs the term "public theology."[3] In both instances the terms suggest the ways in which Cone and King brought serious theological reflection to bear on the issues that impacted the lives of black and poor people in America, most notably issues of racism and poverty. Rather than being an academic discipline that is confined to the classroom or the pulpit, public theology is presented by Paris as what happens when people of faith take the next step and address contemporary social issues from a biblical and theological perspective.

What is being argued here, in this book, is that public theology can take yet another step and enter into the mix of religion and politics. What happens when people of deep religious faith, especially those with at least a basic training in theology and biblical interpretation, bring those skills to bear on whether public tax dollars should be allocated to ever-increasing and immensely expensive military expenditures or instead directed toward affordable and accessible medical care for all citizens? What happens when political leaders who happen to have a shepherd's heart think about the effects that the so-called War on Drugs has had in the black community, specifically in terms of staggering rates of incarceration and the lingering effects of a felony conviction? This is not theology that debates the nature of God or the divinity of Christ. This is theology that puts legs on Isaiah 61 (and Jesus' claim to it in Luke 4:16-21) and stands up on behalf of the neediest and most marginalized members of our society.

I am reminded of how many times people mention the fact that Henry McNeal Turner used the phrase "God is a Negro" as a precursor for black theology.[4] While that is true, and while it was a groundbreaking declaration when he uttered those words in the 1880s, what is invariably left unsaid in reference to Turner is the political activism in which he was engaged a full decade before his observation about God. Both of these aspects of Turner's life are indicators of a public theologian: denouncing the racist images of God offered by most white Christians, on the one hand, and pushing back against the racist practices of American society, on the other hand.

"I WAS HUNGRY. ..."

The call for black preachers to enter into the political arena should not be driven by the partisan and contentious agendas of party politics. The call should not be driven by the desire to denigrate one political point of view as opposed to another. The call certainly has nothing to do with the political stalemate that seems to dominate the political process in the United States at the present time. Rather, it should be a direct call to action to black preachers and pastors to put legs and feet and to give voice and expression to the very issues that Jesus lifted up in Matthew 25:31-44.

Many preachers speak the words about caring for the hungry, the thirsty, the naked, the stranger, the sick, and the imprisoned, but when limited solely to the influence of their local church or even that of their denomination, there is only so much that those preachers can do to significantly impact or alter those conditions. On the other hand, like so many of the black preacher/politicians mentioned in this study, casting a vote in a legislative assembly that has the potential to raise the minimum wage, to issue contracts for public sector jobs to minority contractors and vendors, or to establish fair workplace hiring practices in the private sector—such political action may do more to end hunger and poverty than one or one hundred food pantries or clothing drives.

The call that is being sounded here is consistent with the insight derived from Jim Wallis in his book *God's Politics: Why the Right Gets It Wrong and the Left Doesn't Get It*. He argues that most conservative Christians have already entered the political arena, but they do so with a fairly limited agenda that focuses on abortion and human sexuality. At the same time, people of a more progressive attitude seem reluctant to raise their voices in matters of faith and religion. Wallis observes, "Republicans are more comfortable talking about their religious values and issues, and they are quick to promise that their faith will affect their policies."[5] Meanwhile, he notes, "Democrats stumble over themselves to assure voters that while they may be people of faith, they won't allow their religious beliefs to affect their political views."[6]

That would make sense if the debate were about some partisan, doctrinal issue such as baptism, or the nature of Communion, or the rules that govern the practice of ordination to ministry. Those are matters in which government should never involve itself. That is where the separation of church and state makes sense. However, as public theologians, black preacher/politicians need to see that there are a great many cutting-edge issues for which religious sensibilities can bring great clarity.

As Wallis declares, "Failure to support working families is a religious issue. Neglect of the environment is a religious issue. Fighting preemptive and unilateral wars based on false claims is a religious issue."[7] To that list, public theologians might add that access to affordable health care is a religious issue. Controlling access to guns with large-capacity magazines (America's weapon of mass destruction) is a moral and religious issue. Reversing the practice of the mass incarceration of black and Hispanic people in this country is a moral and a religious issue.

When speaking, or advocating, or shaping policy from the position of a public office, black preacher/politicians can become public theologians. They can bring to bear their theological training, their biblical insights, their pastoral instincts, and their prophetic impulses as they give their attention to the issues of justice and equal opportunity that will come across their desks every day. Rather than being the mere puppets of some entrenched ideological group whose only interest is in maintaining its power, these public theologians can raise the debate about law and policy to a higher level.

For instance, at the funeral of Samuel Proctor, under whom I served at Abyssinian Baptist Church, Jesse Jackson was one of the speakers. He was president of the student body at North Carolina

Agricultural and Technical State University in 1961 when Dr. Proctor was serving as president of that school. When Jackson decided to run for president of the United States in 1984, he went to Proctor for advice and blessing. Jackson reported in his comments at that funeral service that what Dr. Proctor challenged him to do was to "raise the moral level of the conversation." That, of course, is exactly what Jesse Jackson did in 1984 and again 1988. That is what black preacher/politicians can and should do when they serve in public office: raise the moral level of the conversation.

"WHO WILL GO FOR US?"

I am not concerned that most black preachers will not answer this call, preferring instead to walk the safer and less challenging path of purely pastoral ministry, where the focus is entirely internal and limited to the issues within a single congregation. Pastoral ministry is a high calling, one that I followed as a senior pastor from 1976 to 2011. Indeed, the call to politics is not for every preacher or pastor, whether by temperament, ability, or opportunity. However, we do need some pastors to reach beyond the walls of their local church and beyond the specific concerns of their congregation. We need them to inject their religious sensibilities into discussions of public policy that can have a positive impact upon the broader American society.

This is what biblical scholars James and Christine Ward had in mind when they wrote in *Preaching from the Prophets* about preachers who need to move beyond the immediate concerns of their local church and to help people both inside those churches and beyond to consider "the wider implications of the gospel, particularly the wider implications of God's demand for justice and righteousness."[8] In the language of Isaiah 6, God may be asking, "Who will go for us?" Who will take on this responsibility of political leadership? Who will see politics not simply as a potentially corrupting influence, but as a means of grace? Not every black preacher needs to answer this call, but the hope is that some of them will see their ministry through this lens and cry out, "Here I am, send me."

We could use more black preacher/politicians who bring their religious sensibilities to local school boards, which make decisions about curriculum, testing, diversity training, and local versus state control of schools. These decisions impact the lives of millions of children and their families. We could use more black preacher/politicians on city councils, which make decisions about the allocation of tax revenue, access to city services, supervision and oversight of law enforcement personnel, fair treatment in the hiring of city workers, and policies that determine what companies can receive contracts to work on public projects. We could use more black preacher/politicians in state legislatures, which make decisions that determine access to health care, the adjudication of illegal drug offenses, and the drawing of congressional district lines that can allow one party to enjoy a "safe seat" and thus be immune from challenges by a primary or general election opponent.

It will no doubt be said that preachers do not have the time to invest in these matters; all of their time is tied up tending to their flock. The fact of the matter is that most clergy today are not full-time pastors. They are bivocational, serving as a pastor and also in some other capacity in order to make ends meet financially.[9] This concept of being bivocational is as old as Jesus, a carpenter from Nazareth, and Paul, a tentmaker from Tarsus. Is it unthinkable that instead of driving a bus, teaching in a school, laboring in a factory, or working in some other industry or profession that black preachers could devote themselves to the aforementioned forms of public service that, except for a local school board, could provide the additional income that they currently receive from their current bi-vocational secular employment?

Even those clergy who work full-time in their pastoral settings could serve at the local level. Pastors could serve in the state legislature if their church is not too far away from the state capital. Many state legislatures do not meet throughout the entire year; schedules could be arranged to allow for this kind of service. Serving in Congress is clearly more challenging in terms of time and distance, but the facts set forth in this chapter about black preacher/politicians speak for themselves. There have always been pastors and churches that saw the benefit of such involvement and so created the staff support and scheduling flexibility to make such service possible.

I remember my years at Abyssinian Baptist Church in New York City from 1972 to 1976, where the traditional midweek prayer service, so commonly held on Wednesday among black Baptist churches, was held on Friday to accommodate the schedule of Adam Clayton Powell Jr. when he served as senior pastor. He was in the nation's capital on most Wednesday evenings, so the church made that adjustment for their preacher/politician. The service that he delivered to his congressional district and to the country was well worth that small concession.

POLITICS IS MORE THAN HOLDING PUBLIC OFFICE

This part has intentionally focused on the issue of black preachers who have served in elective office since the days of Reconstruction. This was done to refute the notion that black preachers should not be involved in politics on the grounds that such service is a violation of the principle of the separation of church and state. To the contrary, when people of faith (including ordained clergy) use political office to advance issues of justice and human rights, and not to advance partisan theological or denominational concerns, such service can be of great benefit to the state and to the nation. The United States is a better place because of Henry McNeal Turner, Adam Clayton Powell Jr., Archibald Carey Jr., Floyd Flake, William Gray III, DeForest Soaries, Howard Woodson, J. C. Austin, Marshall Shepard, and countless other black preacher/politicians who served at the local, state, and federal levels of government.

However, running for and holding an elective or even an appointed political office is not the only way that black preachers and black churches can engage the political process for the benefit of the black community in particular and all of American society in general. There are many other ways in which they can and should serve as public theologians that bring together the power of the political process and the needs and grievances of the people who look to them for pastoral leadership. There are candidate forums to be hosted. There are voter registration drives to be held. There are voter-suppression tactics to be resisted. There are issues that need an advocate.

It may be that some reading this book may say that they just do not see themselves going through all that is required to win and maintain a seat as part of an elected body. Perhaps so, but there are myriad other ways in which black preachers can engage the political process. That will be the subject of the next part as we continue to examine how the black church should navigate the worlds of church and state.

PART III: QUESTIONS FOR DISCUSSION AND REFLECTION

1. What reasons can you offer for why black preachers became political leaders within their communities?
2. What were the reasons given by Charles Hamilton in *The Black Preacher in America*?
3. What are the four models of clergy leadership according to Peter Paris?
4. What persons did Paris use to typify or define those four models?
5. Which of the four models is most compelling to you? Why?
6. What reasons can you offer for why white clergy have not been as prominent in electoral politics as their black counterparts?
7. What characteristic does Anthony Pinn say that black preachers bring to the job of being a political leader?
8. What does it mean to say that black preacher/politicians are also public theologians?
9. Which black clergy do you know who might fit this definition, and how do they fulfill it?
10. What other black preacher/politicians can you name who are not mentioned in this book?
11. Who are the black preacher/politicians in the city or state where you reside?
12. What is the connection between black preacher/politicians and Matthew 25:31-44?
13. What is the connection between black preacher/politicians and Isaiah 61?
14. What was the tripartite system of oppression as defined by Aldon Morris and how did it affect the voting rights of black people in this country?
15. What is the famous description of the black preacher offered by W. E. B. Du Bois?
16. Why did Frederick Douglass say that the U.S. Constitution was a "pro-slavery document"?

PART III: THINGS TO REMEMBER

1. At what levels of government and of the African Methodist Episcopal Church did Henry McNeal Turner serve?
2. Who was the first black person elected to Congress from a Southern state since Reconstruction, and in what state and in what year did that election occur?
3. In which years did Jesse Jackson campaign to become president of the United States?
4. What black preacher was the nonvoting delegate in Congress from the District of Columbia?
5. What nineteenth-century black Baptist preacher from Richmond, Virginia, said that he wanted to go to a country where he would be judged by his merits and not his complexion?
6. To what country in Africa did he eventually emigrate?
7. What twentieth-century African Methodist Episcopal preacher from Chicago used the phrase "Let freedom ring from the Blue Ridge Mountains of Virginia"?
8. Who was Adam Clayton Powell Jr., and what was his contribution during the Civil Rights movement?
9. On what congressional committee did Adam Clayton Powell Jr. serve, and what things were accomplished by that committee during his tenure as chair? What American president commended Powell for his leadership of that committee?
10. What other black preachers ran for election as president of the United States in the twentieth century?
11. What black preacher served as secretary of state for New Jersey?
12. What black preacher/politician from Kansas City, Missouri, serves in Congress, and what other political offices did he hold?
13. What black preacher filled a vacant U.S. Senate seat from Mississippi soon after the Civil War, and what other contributions did he make during his career?
14. What political offices were held by Andrew Young of Georgia?
15. For which political offices did Al Sharpton campaign and in what years? What role does Al Sharpton play today?

16. How many black preachers served in political office during the Reconstruction era?

Notes

1. Dennis C. Dickerson, *African American Preachers and Politics: The Careys of Chicago* (Jackson: University Press of Mississippi, 2010), 119.
2. Peter Paris, "Comparing the Public Theologies of James H. Cone and Martin Luther King, Jr.," in *Black Faith and Public Talk: Critical Essays on James H. Cone's Black Theology and Black Power*, ed. Dwight N. Hopkins (Maryknoll, NY: Orbis Books, 1999), 218-31.
3. James H. Cone, "Looking Back, Going Forward: Black Theology as Public Theology," in Hopkins, *Black Faith and Public Talk*, 246–57.
4. See Dwight N. Hopkins, introduction to Hopkins, *Black Faith and Public Talk*, 5; also John Dittmer, "The Education of Henry McNeal Turner," in *Black Leaders of the Nineteenth Century*, ed. Leon Litwack and August Meier (Urbana: University of Illinois Press, 1991), 260.
5. Jim Wallis, *God's Politics: Why the Right Gets It Wrong and the Left Doesn't Get It* (San Francisco: HarperSanFrancisco, 2005), 57.
6. Ibid.
7. Ibid., 58.
8. James Ward and Christine Ward, *Preaching from the Prophets* (Nashville: Abingdon Press, 1995), 11.
9. Jeffrey MacDonald, "Churches turn to part-time clergy," www.*ChristianCentury.org*, September 18, 2013.

PART IV

THE BLACK CHURCH AND POLITICAL ACTIVISM

10

THE DOs AND DON'Ts THAT EVERY CHURCH SHOULD KNOW

To this point, it has been argued that nothing in the U.S. Constitution or any other state or federal regulation in any way prohibits or even seeks to discourage members of the clergy from seeking and serving in elective office in any level of government. Any notion that preachers involved in politics is a violation of the principle of separation of church and state, such as I faced in 1998, is completely without merit. The right of members of the clergy to participate with voice and vote in the political life of this country was resolved by James Madison and later by Thomas Jefferson in the 1780s.[1]

BLACK CLERGY AND THE POLITICAL PROCESS

It has also been demonstrated here that black preachers have emerged not only as spiritual leaders within their communities, but also as political leaders. A combination of the importance of the church within black communities across the country and the relative independence of the black preacher from being directly accountable to white society resulted in a scenario where the black preacher/politician emerged as a natural leader in this country at the end of the Civil War. The passage of the Fifteenth Amendment to the U.S. Constitution gave black males the right to vote, and with that vote they quickly elected over one hundred black preacher/politicians and over two thousand black people in general to serve in various political offices during the Reconstruction era, 1865–1877.[2]

With the end of Reconstruction and the return to power in the South of those same whites who formerly had been slaveholders or supporters of the slave system, black people throughout that region saw their voting rights denied by various voter-suppression tactics, including physical intimidation. As a result of that, all of the political progress that blacks had enjoyed, including the emergence of those preacher/politicians, was reversed. It would not be until the 1940s that any significant number of black people would be elected to political positions in the United States. Once that door to political office reopened, the role of the black preacher/politician quickly returned with the election of such notable black preacher/politicians as Adam Clayton Powell Jr., Marshall Shepard, Archibald Carey Jr., J. C. Austin, Sandy Ray, Gardner Taylor, and many others who continue to serve in that role to this day at every level of government—local, state, and federal.

Two concepts have been shared that have offered both logic and rationale for the involvement of black preachers in politics. One comes from Robert McAfee Brown, who speaks about politics as being "a means of grace."[3] Rather than focusing on the corrupting influences that have often been associated with political life, it is possible to focus instead on the ways by which politics can help to realize the mandate of Matthew 25:31-44 to care for the hungry, the naked, the stranger, the sick, and the imprisoned. The other concept offered to justify the involvement of black preachers in politics comes from Anthony Pinn, who observed that when black preachers got involved in politics beginning with the Reconstruction era, they "used their religious sensibilities as a way of shaping governmental policies for the welfare of the underprivileged."[4]

Thus, from Hiram Revels, who entered the United States Senate in 1870, to Emanuel Cleaver, who entered the U.S. House of Representatives in 2005, there has been a long and distinguished legacy of black preacher/politicians that has left an indelible mark on American history in general and on African American history in particular. From Adam Clayton Powell Jr., who was elected to the New York city council in 1941, to Jesse Jackson, who ran for president of the United States in 1984 and 1988, and on to Al Sharpton, who ran for that same office in 2004, the black preacher/politician has become something of a fixture on the American political landscape. In fact, there is likely not a single urban community in this country that has not encountered at least one black preacher—win, lose, or draw—seeking election to a political office.

BLACK CHURCHES AND THE POLITICAL PROCESS

This chapter focuses not on the political activism of the black preacher/politician in particular, but rather on the political activism of black churches in general. It is important to note the ways in which black clergy have been involved in the political process, but that involvement raises several questions. For instance, do the congregations or denominations with which those activist clergy are engaged support and encourage the political involvement of their pastor or staff ministers? Does the activism of the pastor have the result of generating new or added activism among the members of congregations and denominations? In other words, does political activism reside only among those standing at the pulpit, or does it extend to the people seated in the pews?

Here are some more questions that need to be asked. Do local congregations embrace the practice of having political candidates come before them for campaign purposes, whether in a candidates' forum or when addressing the congregation on a Sunday morning? Do local churches welcome the idea of their church being a distribution center for campaign materials such as yard signs, handbills, voter-registration forms, and sign-up sheets for people who would be willing to make themselves and their cars available to drive voters to the polls on election day? And then we must answer why or why not.

I raise these questions about the involvement of church members and church facilities in political events because I have noticed over the years that too many people in most churches are perfectly content to allow their pastor or some other black preacher in the community to be actively involved in many worthy causes outside the church, including political involvement. However, when those members are invited to get more directly involved in those things themselves, their level of enthusiasm falls off considerable. I have also noticed that there are some people in every church who do not want to see their pastor or any other preacher involved in the political process, believing that politics is a dirty and corrupting business and thus an unfit place for members of the clergy.

Dennis Dickerson, in *African American Preachers and Politics*, tells of one observer who expressed this view regarding the political involvement of Archibald Carey Jr. of Chicago.

> "Who will bury the dead ... ?, who will visit the sick ... ?, who will baptize our children ... ?, who will say the prayers and give comfort when we need them most ... ?" Therefore, Carey needed to decide whether "to be a minister of the Gospel or a Politician." If Carey continued to "dabble in politics," he would become contaminated and his usefulness would become compromised.[5]

I ran into precisely this kind of duality during my ministry at Antioch Baptist Church in Cleveland during the time that I was aspiring to a seat in Congress. One the one hand, there were members of that congregation and of other congregations in Cleveland who encouraged me to pursue that goal, but many of them were unwilling to get involved in the campaign themselves.

On the other hand, there were people in that congregation and in other Cleveland congregations who told me directly that they would not support me in my pursuit of a political office because they believed politics to be a corrupting activity. In fact, they believed that in order to be effective in political life, one had to be willing to make certain moral compromises and establish certain relationships or alliances with unsavory characters. People told me that they voted against me because they believed that they were acting in my best interest. Moreover, as more than a few members of Antioch said to me after they voted for one of my opponents, "I just didn't want to lose you as my pastor."

A serious and insightful caution about preachers being involved in politics comes from one of my own ministry mentors, Gardner C. Taylor, who for more than forty years was pastor of Concord Baptist Church in Brooklyn, New York, and one of my preaching professors at Union Theological Seminary in Manhattan. In his book coauthored with Samuel DeWitt Proctor, *We Have This Ministry*, Dr. Taylor says,

> A pastor who is elected to public office can exert a real influence for good. But there are some real pros and cons. ... The moment you become identified too closely with any segment of the political undertaking, you lose a certain moral ground and objectivity.[6]

However, having offered that caution, Taylor concludes with two important observations. The first was the affirmation "There would be hope if the people of God would honestly be the Lord's people in public affairs."[7] The second is this observation: "I believe that blacks have a greater stake in the political process than any other group in this society, because the nation's promise to the people is disproportionately unkept to the African American community."[8]

It is possible, as I argued in 1998, that the presence of God's people using politics as a means of grace can actually influence the political process for the better, and we need not assume that they would quickly be corrupted by involvement in that process. As Paul stated in 1 Corinthians 5:6 and again in Galatians 5:9, "A little yeast works through the whole batch of dough." It is just as possible that God's people can have a positive effect on the political process as that the political process can have a negative effect upon them.

THE MAKING OF A POLITICAL CHURCH

In most instances successful black preacher/politicians come from churches that fit into a model defined by political scientist Eric L. McDaniel as being "a political church" or "a politicized congregation." Three things are essential in order to achieve such a designation.

First, there must be a pastor who sees the importance of political engagement as a means of achieving the overall goals of the church. This means that the pastor either embraces Robert McAfee Brown's idea of politics as a means of grace or employs Anthony Pinn's notion of bringing one's religious sensibilities to bear in shaping governmental policies that aid the most disadvantaged persons in society. This can mean that either the pastor personally seeks a political office or openly supports others who do seek such an office.

Second, a substantial portion of the members of that church must be willing to embrace political activity within the life of their congregation as being consistent with their mission as a church. There may never be uniform and unanimous support for a local congregation becoming a "political church," but there does need to be a core of persons who stand with and work with an activist pastor. Together, they can keep political and policy issues front and center in the life of that congregation. It may also be the case that members of a local church can be the catalyst that causes an initially cautious pastor to finally get more involved in political life in particular and public policy matters in general. This can be especially true when a pastor is beginning a new ministry in a community where he or she has not previously resided. Church members who have lived there for a longer period of time and who are familiar with the people, the problems, and the politics of that community can be very useful in encouraging and enabling political involvement for their new pastor.

Third, "there must be a setting that both necessitates and allows political action."[9] Both verbs are important: "necessitates" and "allows." In other words, it is not enough for the pastor and the congregation to be willing to get involved in the political process if their involvement is not embraced by the surrounding community on whose behalf, theoretically, such involvement would be exercised. The assistance of the pastor and of the church must be sought by and embraced from outside its membership, and the members must ask themselves if they are willing to respond to that request when it comes.

That request might be for the pastor of that church to seek an office. When asked whether or not members of the clergy should seek political office, Gardner Taylor responded by, "Yes, when there are no other credible candidates."[10] Sometimes it is necessary for a pastor to get involved in politics as a candidate because he or she may simply be the best person for the job according to the community that is seeking the pastor's involvement. Other times, it might be sufficient for that church to host or sponsor some political forum or candidates' debate.

When Antioch Baptist Church hosted President Bill Clinton in 1994, it was the first time a sitting president had visited a local church in the city of Cleveland. President Clinton wanted to deliver a speech on urban policy from within the context of an inner-city location. He turned to U.S. Representative Louis Stokes of the 11th District of Ohio, which includes the east side of Cleveland, to identify such a location in his district. Congressman Stokes called me to see if we would be willing to host such an event. We were pleased and honored to do so. Thus, a politicized congregation is one in which an invitation to become involved with electoral politics is encouraged by the pastor, embraced by the congregation, and welcomed by the wider community.

Using Eric McDaniel's paradigm as a model, we must understand that all three components of a politicized congregation must be present in order for the full effect of political influence to be felt. The pastor must have a biblical and theological understanding of ministry that can both make room for and, when necessary, make a compelling case for the blending of religion and politics in the life of the church that he or she serves. However, a willing pastor is not enough to make for a politicized congregation; there must be broad and deep consensus within the congregation that political activity by both the pastor and the members and through use of the church facilities is appropriate and consistent with their understanding of the mission of their church.

The third step in becoming a politicized congregation is also crucial: the wider community, whose support will inevitably be needed in the election of any candidate, must see the preacher and the church as valid political players. It is often this third step that has blocked white clergy from emerging as political leaders within their community. The number of white people from other professions who can serve in political positions has never required white clergy to assume that role.

American historian Peter Dobkin Hall reminds us that there was a time when white clergy played a dominant role in the political life of colonial America. However, as he points out,

> By the early decades of the eighteenth century, clerical authority and the status of clergymen in their communities could only be maintained by actions that made clergymen dependent either on the legislature ... or on powerful factions of the congregations, which were usually mercantile. ... Where once clergymen, as the only highly educated trans-local group, had led the colonists, forming their opinions and serving as advisors and sometimes as masters of the magistrates, by the mid-eighteenth century they were struggling to survive.[11]

In short, while the occasional presence of white clergy in politics has been allowed, it has not been necessary for them to serve in that role, since there were adequate numbers of persons available from various other parts of white society who could play that role and fill that need.

As was demonstrated in Part III, things were altogether different for the black preacher. Beginning in the Reconstruction era, the setting in which black people found themselves necessitated and thus allowed black clergy to become what is referred to here as preacher/politicians. There was no other professional group positioned to serve in that capacity. In the present generation, however, it is no longer necessary for black communities to turn solely to their clergy for a significant portion of their political leadership. Black people with backgrounds in law, business, law enforcement, nonprofit sector work, and education have also moved into the ranks of political leadership.

However, it is useful to point to the cautionary note sounded by political scientist Charles Hamilton, in *The Black Preacher in America*, concerning the continuing importance of black preachers and black churches in the political process. Leadership involves more than holding an elective office; it also involves having regular access to masses of people who come together in a space that they own and control for the purpose of frank and unfettered conversation about matters of community concern. Thus, Hamilton states,

> The black lawyer, the black labor leader, the black politician—all these people are growing in number in the black community. But until they develop pervasive, indigenous black organizational structures, they will have to rely heavily on the black preachers for help in reaching and mobilizing the masses.[12]

Now consider the black preacher in light of Hamilton's comments regarding other black professional groups. Only the black preacher can provide regular and extended access to masses of potential voters without having to rent a hall or party center, and without even having to extend a call. Millions of black people show up in churches across this country on a regular basis. Depending upon the disposition of the pastor and the congregation, those gatherings can touch upon many more topics besides spiritual nurture or denominational disciplines. For nearly 150 years, dating back to the Reconstruction era, black churches have also been places where political candidates were screened, where political dialogue was held, and where an occasional preacher/politician emerged.

Little wonder that black churches and the black preachers who preside over them are sought out both during the political seasons and when politicians need a place to gather their constituents in order to address pressing community problems. This explains why every election cycle sees political candidates of all ethnic groups and political parties lining up to be seen in and hoping to be introduced to as many black churches as possible. It is inconceivable that any political season could come and go without the words of Jeff Johnson, spoken as both of us campaigned for Congress in 1998, coming to pass: "You seek as many ministers' blessings as possible. You literally seek each minister."[13]

BALANCING POLITICAL ACTIVISM AND TAX-EXEMPT STATUS

This discussion now moves into the specific ways in which congregations and the clergy who serve them can be actively involved in politics. First, however, there is one issue that must be addressed: the appropriate balance between political activism and the tax-exempt status enjoyed by religious institutions in this country. The separation of church and state prevents the government from any direct involvement in the practices and beliefs of religious institutions.

At the same time, the tax-exempt status granted by the government to all recognized faith groups requires those religious groups to avoid any involvement in what is best described as partisan politics. This means that religious groups cannot offer endorsements of or financial support to any political candidate without running the risk of losing tax-exempt status. In light of the ways in which religious groups can and cannot be involved in politics, as will be noted below, every church must be careful to operate within the rules set up by the U.S. Internal Revenue Service (IRS) that allow churches to operate as tax-exempt organizations.

Churches are not exempt from all forms of taxation. Churches are responsible for income taxes for their employees. Either the church must withhold a required amount of money from the salary of their employees to cover those taxes or employees must sign a form declaring that they do not want any taxes withheld and will pay their own taxes to the IRS, the state, and whatever local taxes are required. There are no exemptions for people who work for a church when it comes to paying income tax.

However, churches are granted tax-exempt status by the IRS under provision 501(c)(3), which declares the church to be a charitable, not-for-profit organization as far as property taxes and sales taxes are concerned. Given how much a church would have to pay annually in property taxes alone if it were not tax-exempt, it is easy to see why this status is so important to churches. In addition to relief from property tax, a 501(c)(3) organization is also given a tax ID number that allows it to purchase whatever goods and services are needed without having to pay sales tax. Taken together, these two tax exemptions have a profound impact on the annual budget of any local church or church-owned entity.

Add to this the fact that the IRS does not require any taxes to be paid by the church on contributions received from members and other donors, and that those who make such contributions can deduct the total amount of such gifts from their income taxes every year. In addition, a separate benefit falls to ordained clergy assigned to church-related entities in the form of a parsonage allowance, which allows them to deduct from their income tax most of the money they spend on providing housing for themselves and their families.

The authority for such tax-exempt status is tied to the Revenue Act of 1896, which set up the current income tax system. That law was upheld by a January 14, 1924, ruling of the U.S. Supreme Court, which interpreted the reason for the tax exemption in *Trinidad v. Sagrada Orden*. The court ruled, "Evidently the exemption is made in recognition of the benefit which the public derives from churches' corporate activity."

The price that religious organizations must pay in order to enjoy that tax-exempt status is to remain neutral and disengaged from partisan political activity. A ban on church intervention in political campaigns became law in 1954 with an amendment to the IRS code section 501(c)(3) drafted by U.S. Senator Lyndon Johnson of Texas. According to the IRS,

> Under the Internal Revenue Code, all section 501(c)(3) organizations are absolutely prohibited from directly or indirectly participating in, or intervening in, any political campaign on behalf of (or in opposition to) any candidate for elective public office. Contributions to political campaign funds or public statements of position (verbal or written) made on behalf of the organization in favor of or in opposition to any candidate for public office clearly violate the prohibition against political campaign activity.

Violating this prohibition may result in denial or revocation of tax-exempt status and the imposition of certain excise taxes.[14]

The code has been interpreted to mean that pastors may campaign as individuals without the imprimatur of the church, and that churches may speak out on public issues as long as they do not devote a substantial part of their activities to attempting to influence legislation. What churches cannot do is endorse candidates for political office or direct church funds toward that end; what pastors cannot do is endorse a candidate in the name of the church or speak on behalf of a particular candidate while functioning in the official capacity as pastor of that congregation.

Churches must be very clear about these regulations, and they must be very careful not to violate them. In 2000 the first known instance of a church losing its tax-exempt status took place, involving the Pierce Creek Church in Binghamton, New York. That church took out newspaper ads in *USA Today* and the *Washington Times* condemning Bill Clinton under the headline "Christians Beware" just four days before the general election of 1992. The problem was not just that the church placed a political ad, but also that the bottom of the ad ran a line appealing for tax-exempt donations to pay for it.[15]

Churches have tried and failed in making the claim that they have a First Amendment right to free speech that should exempt them from the risk of losing tax-exempt status. Both the IRS and various court rulings have determined that churches can have unfettered free speech or tax-exempt status, but not both. Robert Maddox, former executive director of Americans United for Separation of Church and State, puts it this way,

> Non-profit, tax-exempt organizations cannot have it both ways: They cannot enjoy tax advantages and unbridled political activity at the same time. In defense of the Internal Revenue Service, it generally leans over backward to avoid lifting tax-exempt status. But once the exemption is lifted, it is exceedingly difficult to get it back.[16]

Churches and their clergy need to keep their tax-exempt status in mind as they venture into the political arena. What follows in the next chapter are the things that churches and clergy can and cannot do without endangering their tax-exempt status as they function as a political church or a politicized congregation.

Notes

1. John Ragosta, *Religious Freedom: Jefferson's Legacy, America's Creed* (Charlottesville, VA: University of Virginia Press, 2013), 20.
2. Eric Foner, *A Short History of Reconstruction, 1863–1877* (New York: Harper & Row, 1990), 41.
3. Robert McAfee Brown, "Confessions of a Political Neophyte," *Christianity and Crisis*, December 24, 1953, 186.
4. Anthony B. Pinn, *The Black Church in the Post–Civil Rights Era* (Maryknoll, NY: Orbis Books, 2002), 76.
5. Dennis C. Dickerson, *African American Preachers and Politics: The Careys of Chicago* (Jackson: University Press of Mississippi, 2010), 84.
6. Samuel D. Proctor and Gardner C. Taylor, *We Have This Ministry: The Heart of a Pastor's Vocation* (Valley Forge, PA: Judson Press, 1996), 131.
7. Ibid., 130.
8. Ibid., 127.
9. Eric L. McDaniel, *Politics in the Pews: The Political Mobilization of Black Churches* (Ann Arbor: University of Michigan Press, 2008), 10–11.
10. Proctor and Taylor, *We Have This Ministry*, 129.
11. Peter Dobkin Hall, *The Organization of American Culture, 1700–1900: Private Institutions, Elites, and the Origins of American Nationality* (New York: New York University Press, 1984), 28.
12. Charles V. Hamilton, *The Black Preacher in America* (New York: Morrow, 1972), 221–22.
13. Joe Hallett, "Storming the Churches," *Cleveland Plain Dealer*, May 3, 1998, A1.
14. http://www.irs.gov/Charities-&-Non-Profits/Charitable-Organizations/The-Restriction-of-Political-Campaign-Intervention-by-Section-501(c)(3)-Tax-Exempt-Organizations.
15. Julie Foster, "Church Loses Tax-Exempt Status," May 13, 2000 (http://www.wnd.com/2000/05/4497/).
16. Robert L. Maddox, *Separation of Church and State: Guarantor of Religious Freedom* (New York: Crossroad, 1987), 157.

11

THE MARKS OF A POLITICIZED CONGREGATION

Local churches can do a great many things that can move them in the direction of being a politicized congregation. As Robert Maddox has said, "Clearly, churches may take some actions without offending the Constitution or the Internal Revenue Service. . . . Churches can do more than they cannot."[1] There are many more things that individuals, whether pastors or church members, can do that can be discussed and even encouraged at a Sunday morning worship service.

Sadly, most people in our churches equate political involvement almost entirely with the act of voting or casting a ballot. That is too often the case in the black community because it was that simple act of voting that had been denied to so many for so long. It is almost impossible to imagine that less than fifty years ago millions of black people remained disenfranchised (legally disallowed from voting) due solely to the color of their skin. The right to vote had been granted to black males with the adoption of the Fifteenth Amendment to the U.S. Constitution, which says, "The right of citizens of the United States to vote shall not be denied or abridged by the United States or by any State on account of race, color, or previous condition of servitude."

It was on the strength of that amendment that so many black people, including more than one hundred black preacher/politicians, were elected to political office during the Reconstruction era (see chapter 7). However, the ink was not dry on the document before one barrier after another was placed between black people and the voting booth. In certain parts of this country two or three generations of black people born after the Civil War were never able to become registered voters, much less to cast an actual vote. It was the Voting Rights Act of 1965 that outlawed the practices that had prevented blacks from voting and reestablished the right granted ninety-five years earlier with the Fifteenth Amendment. Thus, it is easy to see why so much attention has been focused on the right of individual citizens to vote for the candidate or cause of their choice.

However, there is far more involved in the American political process than casting an individual ballot. A truly politicized church does not just urge its members to vote on Election Day; it also invites them and instructs them on how to be involved in other activities that are an equally important part of the political process. Such instruction includes answering these and other questions:

- How does a person qualify to appear on the ballot?
- How are political campaigns financed?
- What does one have to do in order to be qualified to vote?
- In what ways beyond voting can citizens provide support for their favorite candidates?
- What else can citizens do on Election Day itself after they have cast their vote?
- How can churches make their space and their other resources available so that their members and the surrounding community can learn more about the candidates who are running for various offices?

The topics to be shared in this chapter are informed by my thirty-plus years of involvement as a candidate, an officeholder, a member of the executive committee of the Cuyahoga County Democratic Party, and an active and informed citizen. It is this information, along with the right to vote, that most often determines who wins and who loses on Election Day. Let us now consider several of the most important actions in which a politicized church can freely and legally be involved without any fear of putting at risk its tax-exempt status, and with the increased likelihood that its involvement will make a real difference in the political process.

PUTTING A VALUE ON VOTING

We start with the obvious, which is to urge churches to impress upon their members the importance of the voting process and encourage them to vote in every primary, general, and special election. Documented evidence now exists that persons who belong to politically active churches vote in higher numbers than persons belonging to churches that do not emphasize political involvement in general and regular voting in particular. According to Katherine Tate in *From Protest to Politics*, black people who belong to what she calls "political activist churches" are more likely to vote in every election than black people who belong to less politically engaged congregations. Reflecting on the 1984 and 1988 presidential campaigns of Jesse Jackson, Tate says,

> Blacks who belonged to activist churches were more likely ... to vote regularly, and to participate in campaign activities. ... The percentage of core voters was far higher among Blacks who belonged to churches where political participation was encouraged. ... Far from representing an "anti-political agency," the church continues to serve as a vital link to politics within the Black community.[2]

Black churches must continue to place a value on voting as a way of impacting the political process.

Gardner Taylor is correct to observe, "Blacks have a greater stake in the political process than any other group in this society, because the nation's promise to these people is disproportionately unkept to the African American community."[3] This observation is consistent with the remarks made by Martin Luther King Jr. at the 1963 March on Washington: "It is obvious today that America has defaulted on this promissory note in so far as her citizens of color are concerned. Instead of honoring this sacred obligation, America has given the Negro people a bad check; a check which has come back marked 'insufficient funds.'"[4]

VOTER PARTICIPATION

It is incumbent upon black pastors and black churches to emphasize the importance of voting and to do so in every election cycle and for every elected office, from president of the United States to the local school board. This simple focus on voting is a nonpartisan and totally uncontroversial action. This is not about telling people for whom to vote; it is simply about emphasizing the importance of the vote and also emphasizing the work that was done and the sacrifices that were made by so many to secure the right to vote for all citizens. In his book *Make It Plain: Standing Up and Speaking Out*, Vernon Jordan talks about the power that comes as a result of an energized black electorate. He writes:

> The power of black ballots can be seen in the South today, where hundreds of black people hold elective office and where white politicians can no longer ignore the needs of black voters. In addition to the noticeable improvement in diction forced upon many segregationist politicians, the black vote has put into the governor's mansions of several Deep South states men of pronounced progressive sympathies who are announcing the death of Jim Crow and who herald a new era in race relations for the South.[5]

People today take the right to vote for granted. In doing so, they allow themselves to forget or, worse, to ignore Freedom Summer in Mississippi in 1964, when civil rights workers from across the country went to locations throughout that state to encourage black residents to bolster their courage to attempt to register to vote. It was during that voter-registration effort in 1964 that Andrew Goodman, Michael Schwerner, and James Chaney were kidnapped and murdered, their bodies found two months later buried in a mud embankment near Philadelphia, Mississippi. People who take the right to vote for granted trivialize the events that occurred on the Edmund Pettus Bridge in Selma, Alabama, on March 7, 1965, when a group of nonviolent protesters led by John Lewis and Hosea Williams were beaten by Alabama state troopers, some of them on horseback, simply because they wanted to march to the state capitol in Montgomery to demand the right to become registered voters. At that time, only 2 percent of the black population of Selma (i.e., about three hundred of a potential fifteen thousand) was registered to vote. The subsequent march led by Martin Luther King Jr., which successfully arrived at Montgomery on March 25, 1965, resulted in the passage of the Voting Rights Act.

Today, voter suppression such as existed in the South in 1965 at the hands of power-grasping whites has been replaced by voter apathy on the part of blacks who fail to realize how much power they have when they become active voters. In fact, it seems that voter apathy has become endemic throughout all groups in our society. In my city of Rochester, New York, voter turnout for the primary election for the office of mayor, city council, and school board was a dismal 22.5 percent of the eligible voters. The turnout for the general election that followed was not much better, at 27 percent of registered voters. These are three of the most important jobs in government, and the decision about who would fill them was made by roughly one out of four eligible voters and less than one out of five residents of the city.

These dismal numbers are reflected in towns and cities across the country. The first thing that politically active churches can and should do is remind people of the importance and the responsibility of voting, no matter for whom their vote is cast. In doing so, churches should never refrain from telling the story of the people, black and white, who bled and died to gain that right for those of us who are able to vote today. This activity is entirely within the rules for a 501(c)(3) tax-exempt organization.

EARLY VOTING

The next step that churches can take is to challenge their members to participate in what is called "early voting." There was a time when everybody, across the country or across the county, depending upon the nature of the election, would vote on the same day. Whether it was a primary, a general, or a special election, the date was set and all votes were cast on that one day. That is no longer the case.

Two things have changed regarding the voting process that must be emphasized in churches: early voting and absentee voting. Early voting allows people to go to their local board of elections days and even weeks before the stated election day and cast their ballot. This is not only a way to avoid long lines on Election Day; it is also a way to increase voter turnout because it offers an alternative to those who might find it difficult to get out on Election Day. According to a CNN poll, more than 40 percent of those who voted in the 2012 election took advantage of early voting.[6]

Another form of early voting is absentee voting. Under this format a registered voter contacts the board of elections and requests that an absentee ballot be sent through the mail. The ballot is then filled out and returned to the board at any point before Election Day. Many people who are homebound, who will be out of town on Election Day, or who simply want to avoid standing in line at a polling place see absentee voting as a convenient alternative. Members of the military who are deployed overseas or assigned to posts outside of their normal residence can also cast their ballot via absentee voting.

This opportunity to vote eliminates the uncertainty about inclement weather, the lack of transportation to the polling place, a work schedule that makes it hard or impossible to vote on a single election day, or being physically unable to leave one's home or the hospital or nursing home where one is being housed or treated. Absentee voting takes away many of the excuses that people often use when they do not vote on Election Day.

SOULS TO THE POLLS

One of the most important innovations in the voting process over the last several years is a faith-based, church-based program, first perfected in Ohio, known as "souls to the polls." In this program local churches use vans, buses, or some assemblage of private vehicles to drive voters to the board of elections in their community after the Sunday morning worship service. Persons do not have to worry about how they would otherwise get to their local polling place. They do not have to find a place to park. All they have to do is get on the bus and be driven to the place where they can cast their ballot.

Again, this is a totally nonpartisan operation. No literature is handed out, no campaign personnel are riding along on the bus, and no pressure is applied regarding for whom people should be voting. This program can be used for many weeks prior to Election Day. In 2008 I led my congregation in Cleveland on a "souls to the polls" trip. We did this over two separate Sundays, running multiple trips to and from the church each week until everyone who wanted to share in that form of early voting had been allowed to do so.

Not surprisingly, some attempts to limit this program have been made due to the perceived advantage it gave Democratic candidates in 2008 and again in 2012. It has been stated that early voting in general and "souls to the polls" in particular helped Barack Obama carry Ohio and go on to win the presidency in 2008. There is now a bill in the legislature of Ohio, where "souls to the polls" was most successful, to eliminate voting on the Sunday before Election Day. Other forms of voter suppression and voting restrictions are being offered up by Republican-controlled legislatures in states ranging from Ohio to North Carolina, from Florida to Texas, and others. Since black voters have directly benefited from early voting plans, black churches and black clergy need to keep a close watch on any and all attempts at voter suppression.

VOTING IN PRIMARY ELECTIONS

Churches must remind members that it is not enough to vote in the general election, when the final determination is made about who will occupy any given office. It is just as important, and in some cases even more so, that people vote in the primary elections as well, when it is determined whose names will appear on the ballot. Primary elections are the process by which major political parties place before the eligible voters of their party the names of those who are aspiring for the endorsement and support of that party in that candidate's pursuit of a political office in the general election that will follow. The primary is typically held many months in advance of the general election, and the winner of that election then moves into the general election with the endorsement and the active support of their political party.

Primary elections are very much like intramural sports in college, where persons of the same school compete, but in this case members of the same political party seek the party's endorsement for a given office. The general election is analogous to intercollegiate sports, where persons from different schools (or different political parties) seek to win the ultimate prize.

No candidate can be successful in winning the prize in the general election unless he or she first wins in the primary. Barack Obama did not become president of the United States of America simply because he won the general election against John McCain in 2008 and against Mitt Romney in 2012. He first had to win enough votes in primary elections in every state of the country to qualify to be the nominee of the Democratic Party. In many respects, it was Obama's victory in the 2008 primary election in Iowa that propelled a little-known senator from Illinois into being the eventual nominee of the Democratic Party and then on to become the first African American to be elected President of the United States.

Churches must encourage people to vote in primary as well as general elections.

VOTING IN OFF-YEAR ELECTIONS

Voter turnout is always highest in those four-year cycles when a presidential campaign is underway. As much as 75 percent of eligible voters might turn out to vote in that election. From there, the numbers fall off significantly when only seats in national and state legislatures, governors' offices, or county and local offices are being decided. According to one national political media firm, races where the office of the governor is the highest office on the ballot draw only 49 percent voter turnout. When the top office on the ballot is for the state legislature or for city office, the turnout plummets further to 33 percent.[7]

As was stated earlier, turnout in the primary for the mayor's race in Rochester, New York, was 22.5 percent of eligible voters. However, according to FairVote.org, the voter turnout for the mayor's race in Dallas, Texas, was only 7 percent, and it was only 5 percent in Charlotte, North Carolina. In many cases excellent candidates lose elections not because of their lack of aptitude for the job, but because of voter apathy on Election Day.

People get very excited when the nation is deciding the next occupant of the Oval Office in the White House. They need to understand that it is just as important to have a voice in choosing the person who will occupy the city hall, the local school board, the county executive's office, the State House, and every seat in the U.S. Congress.

Candidates understand the importance of off-year elections, and that is why they campaign just as hard during that cycle as they do in those years when the President of the United States is being elected. Pastors and churches need to be as aggressive in urging people to vote in off-year elections as they are in the elections to determine our nation's next president. As this book is being written there is an off-year election looming in November 2014. It is already feared that voter turnout will be low. That is regrettable, because many important races will be contested in that election, including U.S. Senate races that may well determine which party has control of that legislative body. The answer to that question will have direct bearing on the policies and judicial appointments that will be considered during the remainder of the Obama presidency, as well as on matters ranging from gun control, to reproductive choice for women, to voter suppression tactics in states across the country, to name only a few.

VOTER REGISTRATION

As important as it is for churches to encourage their members to cast their ballot on Election Day, it is equally important for churches to encourage their members to register to vote. Voting is a right, but there is a process involved in being able to exercise that right. Proof that you have reached the age at which voting is allowed, and proof of residence within the town or city where you are planning to cast your ballot, must first be established. You cannot just show up at a polling place on Election Day and request a ballot.

When you register to vote, you will be assigned a location where you will go to vote. Your name will appear on a sign-in page alongside the names of other voters in your precinct or voting district. You will sign alongside your printed name. That book will become the continuing record of all the elections in which you cast a vote. If your name is not listed in that record of registered voters, you will not be allowed to vote. You might be allowed to cast what is known as a provisional ballot if you have registered and there was some confusion about your name being placed on the registry. However, if you have not registered, you will not be allowed to vote.

Who needs to register? First-time voters, especially those who have reached voting age since the last general election, need to become registered. Anyone who has changed his or her home address since last voting in a primary or general election needs to reregister to vote. The same is true for anyone who has legally changed his or her name due to marriage or any other circumstance. If your name today is different from the name that is presently on the voting roll at your polling place, you need to reregister.

My first vote was cast in Illinois in the 1972 election that saw George McGovern running against Richard Nixon for President of the United States. My next vote was cast in New York State in races for governor and mayor. My wife and I then moved to New Jersey and then on to Ohio, where we resided for twenty-four years. Now we once again live and vote in New York State. Every time we have moved, not only did we change our mailing address, but also we had to register again in order to vote in the new state. If for any reason we decide to move to a different location in the city of Rochester, we will have to register to vote again because we will have changed our mailing address. Churches should constantly remind members about the reasons why people need to register to vote.

Voter-registration drives can be held in the church itself or at any church-sponsored event. Members of the church can receive registration forms from their local board of elections, and they can be instructed not only on how the forms must be filled out, but also on who is and is not qualified to vote in any given state. One of the recent practices of voter registration that is now being contested in some states is known as "same-day registration." This would allow a person to register and then vote on the same day rather than having had to be registered or resided in the state for a given period of time before being allowed to cast a ballot. The same forces opposed to early voting and "souls to the polls" are also working to eliminate same-day registration. This is something else for pastors and congregations to watch for in their local communities.

As an election season begins to roll around, churches can begin to put voter registration on the minds of their members. Display signs in the halls asking, "Are You a Registered Voter?" Place announcements in the weekly bulletin or run them on the closed-circuit television screens in the church reminding people about being registered to vote. Someone from the board of elections, the League of Women Voters, the NAACP, or some other nonpartisan group can be invited to address the congregation, not only on the importance of voting, but also on the voter-registration process in that community. A committee comprised of church members can make it their special ministry to coordinate a voter-registration drive in their church. They can sit at a table where people tend to gather, or they can stand by the exits of the church as people come and go from the building. They can, if allowed to do so, make personal appeals to the church membership to be sure that everyone is registered in time to participate in the upcoming election.

VOTER EDUCATION

An educated and informed electorate is essential for an effective democracy. Voters need to be familiar with the candidates whose names will be appearing on their ballot, and they need to understand the nonpartisan issues that will also be awaiting their support.

Churches can play a central role in providing voter education through strategies such as candidates' forums, distribution of leaflets and fliers that provide background information on ballot issues, and even enclosing a sample ballot in the church bulletin so that people can get familiar with it before they cast their vote. In doing these things, churches may be the only place where people can turn that is not stridently partisan, or engaged in political demagoguery, or mired in negative campaign ads.

Most of what passes for campaigning in politics today in the United States is little more than mudslinging and character assassination. Television and radio commercials by most candidates are not intended to inform voters about what a particular candidate will do if elected. Instead, these commercials display shadowy and grainy images of an opponent with a message about how bad that person is and how much harm he or she would cause if elected. These attack ads are not limited to elections involving candidates. They are also used to frame negative public opinion about ballot initiatives and other issues that require the voters to authorize either a new tax or the continuation of an existing tax in order to deliver some public service. Those services can range from social welfare programs, to supporting community colleges, to funding a local school district, to providing improved resources for water supply and sewage treatment.

It is amazing to consider that people go into the voting booth or fill out an absentee ballot without knowing much about the candidates or issues that appear before them. They may be familiar with a few of the people running for a seat in the executive branch of government (president, governor, mayor) or legislative branch of government (congress, state legislature, city council) but have no idea about the city and county judges whose names also appear, and who may have far more of an impact on the lives of their families than any mayor or city council person ever would or ever could.

The church could play a major role in changing all this. Host a candidates' forum and allow persons contesting for any given political seat to come before the community in a debate hosted by and inside the church. Candidates can make a case for their election, answer questions raised by people in the audience, and engage with their opponents for that seat in a moderated discussion about which of them is the best person for that job. This can be done in both the primary and the general election cycles. This can be done at separate times for various offices that are being contested: mayor's office, city council, school board, statewide offices, and positions at the federal level.

During the years that I served Antioch Baptist Church in Cleveland, we played this role on a regular basis. We allowed persons running for statewide or federal office to actually address the congregation on a Sunday morning. I can still see Howard Metzenbaum and John Glenn, both of them U.S. Senators from Ohio, standing before our congregation to make the case for their reelection. We had candidates for governor, attorney general, secretary of state, and state treasurer presented either to speak during the worship service or to meet the congregation at an event after the worship service devoted to that purpose. We hosted events during the week where persons from other churches could come and meet candidates because the churches to which they belonged did not allow candidates to appear or make presentations.

We decided for several reasons not to allow persons running for local or county offices to speak. For one thing, there were just too many such persons who would seek to avail themselves of that opportunity. For another, Antioch has members that reside in five different counties surrounding the city of Cleveland. Allowing all of the candidates from all of those counties to speak would leave us with little time for our primary purpose for gathering on Sunday, which is to hear a word from the Lord, not from a candidate for a judgeship in juvenile court.

Nevertheless, these local and county offices are important positions, and so we would invite them to attend our service, where they could be introduced and acknowledged. In the case of a church that has a reputation for being candidate-friendly, there is no need to invite candidates to come; they will call ahead and ask if they can come to church for that purpose. In addition to being introduced, we allowed those who wished to do so to distribute their campaign literature outside of the church as people were leaving the building.

THE CHURCH AS A VOTING LOCATION

My polling place in Rochester, New York, is inside a church not far from the campus of Colgate Rochester Crozer Divinity School, where I work and reside. The first time my son served as a poll worker on Election Day, it was at a church in Pepper Pike, Ohio, outside of Cleveland. Although Antioch Baptist Church in Cleveland never served as a polling place, many other churches in that city do serve in that role. This practice has occasionally raised the objections of Barry Lynn, clergy, attorney, and executive director of the group Americans United for Separation of Church and State, but there is absolutely nothing illegal or improper about this practice in which thousands of churches across this country are regularly engaged. There is nothing in the IRS regulations that prohibits or even warns against this use of church-owned space.

The voting booths are not set up in the sanctuary. No member of the local church is on hand to distribute information about the ministries of the church while citizens are standing in line waiting for their turn to vote. Church hymns are not being piped in through the sound system in a subtle attempt to evangelize the electorate. The pastor is not standing at the front door to greet people as they enter or to invite them to return on the next Sunday for the worship service.

What does happen when the church serves as a polling place is that for two or three days every year (primary, general, and occasional special elections) the host congregation provides a public service for its surrounding community. In most instances church members do not reside in the community where the church is physically located. Thus, it is likely that very few church members would even be involved in actually voting inside of the very church of which they are also a member. They may well be voting inside of other churches in other sections of the city or in other cities altogether.

Most churches sit empty for most of the week, with very little activity going on outside of Sunday mornings and some midweek evenings for Bible study and choir practices. Church consultant Paul Nixon, in *Fling Open the Doors: Giving the Church Away to the Community*, challenges pastors and churches to be intentional about allowing their church to serve the various needs of its surrounding community. He invites churches to think of themselves as "village churches that exist for and belong to the community. ... They consider it a sacred responsibility to serve the people who live in the community. ... Once the church understands that it belongs to the community, the community itself will figure this out as well."[8]

A similar argument is made by Rick Rusaw and Eric Swanson in *The Externally Focused Church*. They say, "Externally focused churches have concluded that it's really not church if it's not engaged in the life of the community through ministry and service to others."[9] Rather than community ministry simply being something that a church does occasionally, they stress that externally focused churches are always on the lookout to find ways to be of service to their local community. They say that outreach and community service of various types are "embedded in the DNA" of an externally focused church.[10]

There is no reason why the same church that serves as the homeless shelter, the soup kitchen, the HIV/AIDS testing center, the after-school tutoring location, and the home of a prison ministry support group cannot also serve as a polling place on Election Day. All of these are valuable community services in which any externally focused church that has flung open its doors can perform.

WORK AGAINST ALL FORMS OF VOTER SUPPRESSION

Another important role the church can play regarding the voting process is keeping its members aware of the various efforts at voter suppression that have arisen in recent years in states across this country. Since the U.S. Supreme Court ruled in June 2013 that some of the provisions of Section 4 of the 1965 Voting Rights Act dealing with pre-clearance are no longer constitutional, there has been a flood of activity allegedly aimed at deterring voter fraud but is actually intended to lower voter turnout among certain groups of voters. Pre-clearance meant that no state that was listed within the text of the Voting Rights Act as having had a history of attempting to deny black people access to the voting process could make any changes in its voting regulations without getting prior approval (pre-clearance) from a federal district court or from the office of the U.S. Department of Justice and the Attorney General of the United States.

On the very same day when the Supreme Court voted to throw out parts of the Voting Rights Act, legislatures and governors in Texas, Mississippi, North Carolina, South Carolina, Virginia, Pennsylvania, and Florida introduced laws to put restrictions on who was qualified to vote in those states. It was almost a return to the practices of the post-Reconstruction era.

The earlier twentieth-century forms of voter suppression, such as the literacy test and the grandfather clause, are not being proposed. Now it is a push for a government-issued photo ID, which not every citizen has or needs. Senior citizens, college students, persons who use public transportation and do not carry a driver's license, and many other Americans will be unable to vote unless they go out and purchase a state-issued ID card or a U.S. passport. This prerequisite of requiring people to purchase any form of government-issued photo ID card is virtually a return to the poll tax of more than one hundred years ago, when black and poor people were required to pay a fee in order to vote in national elections, thus denying them their constitutional right to vote because of their economic status. Then and now, that inability to pay essentially disenfranchises that part of the population.

There is another way by which many people are being disenfranchised, especially within the African American community, and that is as a result of a felony conviction. According to the American Civil Liberties Union (ACLU), some states (Virginia, Tennessee, Mississippi, Alabama, Wyoming, Nevada, and Arizona) permanently restrict voting rights to persons convicted of a certain set felony offenses. Three states, Florida, Kentucky and Iowa, permanently disenfranchise all persons convicted of any felony offense.[11] The ACLU notes,

> A patchwork of state felony disenfranchisement laws, varying in severity from state to state, prevent approximately 5.85 million Americans with felony (and in several states misdemeanor) convictions from voting. Confusion about and misapplication of these laws de facto disenfranchises countless other Americans.[12]

Civil rights attorney Michelle Alexander, most noted for her book *The New Jim Crow: Mass Incarceration in the Age of Color-Blindness*, draws a compelling link between mass incarceration and the issue of race in America. As a result of the so-called War on Drugs, millions of black and Hispanic men and women have been convicted of misdemeanor and felony drug offenses, and as a result have lost the right to vote in many states. She puts that problem in stunning historical perspective in the introduction to her book:

> Jarvious Cotton cannot vote. Like his father, grandfather, great-grandfather, and great-great-grandfather, he has been denied the right to participate in our electoral democracy. ... Cotton's great-great-grandfather could not vote as a slave. His great-grandfather was beaten to death by the Ku Klux Klan for attempting to vote. His grandfather was prevented from voting by Klan intimidation.

His father was barred from voting by poll taxes and literacy tests. Today, Jarvious Cotton cannot vote because he, like many black men in the United States, has been labeled a felon and is currently on parole.[13]

However, Alexander also draws a connection between the findings of her book and how people of faith can and should respond to this crisis in voter suppression. Writing in "Bearing Witness: A Nation in Chains," which reports on a study by the Samuel DeWitt Proctor Conference, Alexander says,

> During the past 40 years, millions of people have been locked in cages and stripped of basic civil and human rights—the very rights supposedly won in the Civil Rights Movement. ... Unfortunately, many of us, including people of faith, have remained quiet for too long. Much of the silence is rooted in ignorance about the true nature of mass incarceration. But some of the silence can be traced to a lack of courage—a lack of moral courage—as well as a lack of clarity regarding what our moral and spiritual commitments require of us.[14]

This is a clarion call to action, both by Michelle Alexander and by the people involved in the Samuel DeWitt Proctor Conference for people of faith in general, and also in this book for politically active churches to work against this particular form of voter suppression.

Other new forms of voter suppression include reducing the number of days for early voting so that people cannot take advantage of that option. Others are attempting to eliminate Sunday voting, which has clearly increased voter turnout among African American voters.

Another obvious form of voter suppression in the 2012 election was reducing the number of voting machines in some districts so that people would have to stand in long lines for hours to cast their ballot. At his 2013 State of the Union Address, President Obama introduced Desilene Victor, a 102-year-old woman from Florida who stood in line for three hours on a Sunday to cast her ballot. The lines could have been eliminated if more voting machines had been delivered, but the goal of the local board of election was to suppress the vote in that part of North Miami.

In 2013 I had the opportunity to participate in a panel discussion about voter suppression and the Voting Rights Act that was hosted by Asbury First United Methodist Church of Rochester in partnership with the local chapter of the League of Women Voters. My assignment was to give an overview of the voter-suppression practices that existed before the Voting Rights Act. Also on that panel was a representative for U.S. Representative Louise Slaughter, who talked about efforts underway in Congress to restore those parts of the Voting Rights Act stripped away by the U.S. Supreme Court. There were also two members of the local board of elections, a Republican and a Democrat, who talked about the voting process is Monroe County and in New York State.

The event was held on a Tuesday evening in the social hall of the church. One of the ministers of the church provided a greeting. The League of Women Voters provided some light refreshments. An audience of fifty or so people gathered for a lively exchange on this important topic. The next morning a story in the local newspaper made note of the fact that the event was held at the church, and it reported to the wider community on the major points that had been made.[15] Not only did the church provide a valuable public service, but also the church received very positive news coverage in the local paper, raising its profile as an externally focused church.

There is no reason why this kind of public service cannot be offered by churches across this country working in partnership with the League of Women Voters, the local branch of the NAACP, or the county board of elections, all of which are highly regarded nonpartisan groups. Churches not only need to encourage people to vote, but also to work to protect the right to vote in the face of concerted attempts at these new efforts at voter suppression.

VOTER ENDORSEMENT OF CANDIDACY

Most people think about voting as choosing one person from all the names that appear on the ballot. What they may not appreciate is how those names happen to appear on that ballot in the first place. Many would-be political careers have never taken off because those candidates could not secure enough signatures to qualify for inclusion on the ballot.

In order for a person's name to appear on the ballot for any elective office, he or she must secure a certain number of signatures from persons who live within the community, the county, or the country in which that office operates. Whether the office is for the local school board, a seat on the city council, an election to a judicial position, or a state- or federal-level office, all candidates must first qualify to appear on the ballot by getting signatures from citizens that essentially serve as endorsements of their candidacy. Those petitions are then turned in at the local board of elections, which will determine if an adequate number of valid signatures have been secured.

The number of signatures needed will, of course, vary, depending upon the office being sought. When I ran for the school board in Shaker Heights, Ohio, in 1992, I needed to secure signatures from just fifty registered voters who lived in that community. When I ran for the U.S. House of Representatives in 1998, I needed fifteen hundred signatures from legal residents of my congressional district. When I ran for the U.S. Senate in 2000, again I needed fifteen hundred signatures, but they had to be secured from people living in at least ten different counties in Ohio. Anyone desiring to run for the office of President of the United States must secure signatures from at least ten counties in every state in which they will be campaigning in a primary election.

It is possible to run for an office as a write-in candidate, which means that voters would literally have to write your name on their ballot as a preference over all the names that are pre-printed on that form. However, the most desirable way to run for public office is to secure the needed signatures and have your name printed on the official ballot. But where can candidates go to obtain the necessary number of signatures? They can stand on street corners and solicit people as they pass by. They can attend some public gathering and invite people whom they may not know to sign their petition of candidacy. Or they can go to their own faith community or to several other churches, synagogues, mosques, or temples in their community. They can get the permission of the leading clergy to make a personal appeal—not for a vote, but for a signature. That being done, it is possible that the signatures needed could be secured in one day.

In most cases, candidates would do well to secure at least 20 percent more signatures than they actually need to qualify for a spot on the ballot, because every signature will be examined by the board of elections to make sure that each person who signed is both a lawful resident and a registered voter in the voting district in question. I have known of many instances in which a candidate got the fifteen hundred signatures needed to run for Congress or for a statewide office, but upon review by the board of elections, 10 to 15 percent of those signatures were deemed invalid for one reason or another. It may be that a signer did not live in the voting district in question. It may be that a signer moved since they last voted, and his or her current address did not match the address on file with the board of elections. It may be that the signer is not even a registered voter.

Therefore, a church can play two distinct roles in this part of the electoral process. First, churches can educate their members about the rules and regulations governing who is qualified to sign a particular candidate's petition. When I ran for federal office as a resident of a district in Cuyahoga County, some members of Antioch Baptist Church lived in Lake, Lorain, Portage, Summit, and Geauga Counties. I was their pastor, and they may have wanted to support my candidacy by signing my petition, but their signatures would have been invalidated by the board of elections. When I ran for the school board in Shaker Heights, some members of the church lived in Cuyahoga County, but they did not live in Shaker Heights. If they had signed that petition, their signatures would have been deemed invalid. A candidate who does not get enough valid signatures by a given deadline will not appear on the ballot. Churches can help a candidate in that initial part of the electoral process by being sure that members are educated about their qualifications by residence and voter registration to sign a petition for candidacy.

The second way a church can help is to be willing to allow for the distribution of such petitions at church functions. Can a potential candidate stand outside of the church at the end of service and gather signatures from those willing to offer their support? Can potential candidates walk through the crowd at a church picnic, at a reception in the social hall, at the end of a church business meeting, before or after a choir practice or the meeting of a church auxiliary? All of these actions are legal and in no way jeopardize a church's tax-exempt status. The question is simply whether any given church is willing to engage in the political process at that level.

Be sure to inform members of the congregation that signing a person's petition does not obligate you to vote for that candidate on election day. Supporting him or her in getting on the ballot simply allows that person an opportunity to make a case for why he or she should subsequently be elected. It may be that the candidate does not make a strong enough case ultimately to win your vote. Bear in mind that most people who get the requisite number of signatures to appear on the ballot are defeated on election day. However, failure to get an adequate number of valid signatures for the position in question will prohibit a person from even being able to state the case for election.

Notes

1. Robert L. Maddox, *Separation of Church and State: Guarantor of Religious Freedom* (New York: Crossroad, 1987), 158–60.
2. Katherine Tate, *From Protest to Politics: The New Black Voters in American Elections* (Cambridge, MA: Harvard University Press, 1994), 95, 100, 106.
3. Samuel D. Proctor and Gardner C. Taylor, *We Have This Ministry: The Heart of a Pastor's Vocation* (Valley Forge, PA: Judson Press, 1996), 127.
4. James Melvin Washington, ed., *A Testament of Hope: The Essential Writings of Martin Luther King, Jr.* (San Francisco: Harper & Row, 1986), 217.
5. Vernon E. Jordan, Jr., *Make It Plain: Standing Up and Speaking Out* (New York: Public Affairs, 2008), 19.
6. Allison Brennan, "Early Voting Surge Suggests Democratic Push Pays Off in Iowa," October 19, 2012 (http://www.cnn.com/2012/10/18/politics/early-voting-status-check/).
7. Ken Kurson, "Stoking Turnout in Off-Year Elections," *Campaigns & Elections Magazine*, October 14, 2011 (http://www.campaignsandelections.com/magazine/us-edition/262202/stoking-turnout-in-offyear-elections.thtml).
8. Paul Nixon, *Fling Open the Doors: Giving the Church Away to the Community* (Nashville: Abingdon Press, 2002), 22.
9. Rick Rusaw and Eric Swanson, *The Externally Focused Church* (Loveland, CO: Group Publishing, 2004), 24.
10. Ibid., 25.
11. ACLU.org, "Map of State Criminal Disfranchisement Laws" (https://www.aclu.org/maps/map-state-criminal-disfranchisement-laws).
12. Ibid.
13. Michelle Alexander, *The New Jim Crow: Mass Incarceration in the Age of Colorblindness* (New York: New Press: 2012), 1.
14. Michelle Alexander, in "Bearing Witness: A Nation in Chains" (Report of the Samuel DeWitt Proctor Conference; Chicago, 2014), 5.
15. "Voting Rights Act Is Aired," *Democrat & Chronicle*, September 24, 2013, B3.

12

POLITICAL CHURCHES AND CAMPAIGN FINANCE LAWS

The next area in which churches can be involved in politics, but where they need to be sure to know and adhere to Internal Revenue Service (IRS) regulations, involves campaign finance laws and the rules that govern making contributions to political candidates. Money is the lifeblood of American politics. People in public office spend an enormous amount of time raising money to fund their campaigns either for election or reelection. The U.S. Supreme Court includes financial support of political candidates as one of the protected forms of free speech. While every candidate for every office is as busy soliciting our financial support as they are soliciting our votes on Election Day, churches must help their members to fully understand the ways they can and cannot provide financial support for political candidates, at least as far as their church-based activities are concerned.

INDIVIDUAL CONTRIBUTIONS TO POLITICAL CANDIDATES

Individual church members can make contributions up to the maximum amount allowed by law in both the primary and general elections. Pastors and members of the clergy can also make individual financial gifts to political candidates. In 2008 and again in 2012 I made monthly contributions in support of the election of Barack Obama. I placed a credit card on file with his online fundraising operation, and with a monthly click of a button my contribution was sent and received. I made the maximum contribution in both the primary and the general elections in 2008 and again in 2012. Obama's was the first and remains the only campaign that I supported at that level. However, since I was operating as a private citizen, my actions were entirely within the law.

When we decided to have campaign events inside Antioch Baptist Church in Cleveland, especially where we intended to do some fundraising during that event, we decided to enter into a lease arrangement with the campaign in question for a very small amount, sometimes just $1. Then the event was being sponsored by the campaign of the candidate in space that they had leased from us. We never made a secret of the fact that we operated this way, and we were never questioned, investigated, or contacted by the IRS concerning that practice. If funds were raised, they were immediately turned over to the campaign. Clear instructions were given to make checks out to the candidate's campaign committee and not to Antioch Baptist Church. It would have been a violation of IRS regulations for a check to be issued by the church in support of any candidate.

When I served as pastor at Antioch, we made that mistake once in 1992 when Harvey Gantt, who was then the mayor of Charlotte, North Carolina, ran for a seat in the U.S. Senate from that state. We were excited about the fact that an African American was running for the Senate, even though he had no connection to our church. We were especially attracted to his campaign because it offered the possibility of removing from office Senator Jesse Helms, who was one of the remaining Southern senators openly hostile to civil rights programs and legislation. With the consent of the church leadership, we took up an offering to assist in the costs of his statewide campaign. We combined those funds into a single check that was issued from the church's account.

Several days after the check had been sent to North Carolina, we received a letter from the Harvey Gantt campaign with our uncashed and unendorsed check enclosed. The campaign managers reminded us that they were unable to receive corporate checks, including checks from churches. They thanked us for our support, but they had to decline our financial assistance in that form. Rather than returning the money to those who had made the initial donation to Harvey Gantt, we voted as a congregation to place those funds in our benevolence budget and use it to support local programs that served people in our community. We never repeated the mistake of making a financial contribution to a political campaign in the name of Antioch Baptist Church.

During my pastorate at Antioch we did allow candidates for political office to distribute contribution envelopes that could be used to support their campaign. I would regularly remind church members of the importance of being financially supportive of the candidates of their choice, especially when so much money is now entering the political process from political action committees, which are not constrained by the same IRS regulations as local churches or private citizens.

CAMPAIGN FINANCE REFORM EFFORTS

Beyond individual donations, supporting campaign finance reform becomes a key strategy to remove the inappropriate and excessive influence of money, and especially the disproportionate influence of very wealthy donors such as the Koch brothers or George Soros, on the political process. Pastors and churches can get involved in letter-writing campaigns to Congressional representatives to vote for campaign finance reforms that can take away the influence of money that places an enormous disadvantage on candidates who are not independently wealthy or backed by others with huge financial resources.

When I ran for the U.S. Senate in 2000, I was interviewed in Washington, DC by then-Senator Robert Torricelli of New Jersey, who was serving as chair of the Senate Democratic Campaign Committee, the group that seeks out and screens viable candidates for election to the Senate. His first question to me was "How much money can you raise?" His first question was not why I wanted to run, or what my campaign themes would be. He understood that none of that would matter if I could not generate enough resources to mount a viable, statewide campaign that would include enough money to open campaign offices and run television ads in the Cleveland, Columbus, Cincinnati, Dayton, Toledo, Youngstown, and Zanesville markets. He estimated that I would need to raise between $3 million and $4 million in order to win in both the primary and the general election and thus gain a seat in the U.S. Senate. My campaign ended up raising $450,000 and garnering more than

250,000 votes in the Democratic primary, in which I placed second. He was correct in his estimate, because in the general election both candidates spent more than $3 million each, most of it on television ads and campaign literature.

In 1990 Andrew Young was ending his second term as mayor of Atlanta and announced his intention to run for the office of governor of Georgia. In order to raise the money needed to run a competitive campaign for the office, he came to Cleveland, Ohio, among other urban centers in Northern states, to do fundraising. Young was not independently wealthy, nor was he tied in to the major corporate donors and business leaders who were helping to fund the campaigns of his primary opponents. A proven political leader and a battle-tested civil rights icon, Young was unsuccessful in his quest for state governor because he was unable to "buy the office" through raising and spending massive amounts of money in the process, which is how so many people end up in political positions these days.

As long as money remains the main ingredient for success on Election Day, most African American candidates will operate at a disadvantage in their quest for public office. If they are not personally wealthy and willing to invest their own money in their campaign, or if they are not well connected to a core group of wealthy donors willing to invest in their campaign, they will be hard pressed to win against better-funded opponents. This reality does not make for a strong democracy. According to PolitiFact.com, more than 47 percent of the members of the U.S. Congress are millionaires. Sheila Krumholz of the Center for Responsive Politics writes,

> The vast majority of members of Congress are quite comfortable, financially, while many of their own constituents suffer from economic hardships. Few Americans enjoy the same financial cushions maintained by most members of Congress—or the same access to market-altering information that could yield personal, financial gains.[1]

In light of these factors, pastors and congregations can help in two specific ways. First, as discussed above, individuals can make financial contributions to the candidates and causes of their choosing within the boundaries of all existing IRS regulations. Second, they can raise their voices at the local church level, in ministers' conferences, and in state and national church gatherings to call for meaningful campaign finance reform. That can mean anything from the public financing of political campaigns to limiting the amount that a candidate can receive from individuals or political action committees. What does it say about the influence of money in the political process in the United States when more than $2 billion was spent in the campaign between Barack Obama and Mitt Romney? This is not government of, by, and for the people. This is government of, by, and for the rich and well-connected. Black churches and black communities have a vested interest in campaign finance reform; it levels the playing field and allows more minority candidates to get elected.

OTHER FORMS OF CANDIDATE SUPPORT—BEYOND VOTING

There are a great many ways by which citizens can demonstrate their public support for the candidates of their choice beyond simply casting a vote. Each of these strategies is just as important as what happens in the privacy of the voting booth. Churches can play an important role by making their members aware of these opportunities and encouraging their involvement. Everything mentioned here is completely within the limits of any and all IRS concerns about churches as tax-exempt agencies.

DISPLAYING CAMPAIGN SIGNS

One of the easiest ways to indicate support for the candidates or causes of your choice is by agreeing to display a campaign sign that bears the name of your candidate. These displays may include plastic yard signs to be placed in the ground in front of your home and the homes of your neighbors who are willing to follow your example. These signs are an indication to anyone who walks or drives by your home of your support for a given candidate. It may be that your public indication of support can influence others who are still trying to make up their mind about whom they will vote for in the upcoming election.

Candidates can bring these signs to the church, where they can be distributed. We did that at Antioch Baptist Church in Cleveland without ever being challenged by the IRS or by any other candidate who, for whatever reason, never thought to ask us to help distribute campaign materials. Materials usually can be picked up at the campaign office of a given candidate. If they are the endorsed candidate of a major political party, those signs can also be picked up at party headquarters. It is just as likely that residents will receive a phone call from a candidate's campaign committee asking if a sign can be delivered and placed in their yard by someone affiliated with that campaign. The value of this form of candidate support cannot be overstated; it is a virtual "24/7" advertisement on behalf of a candidate appealing for the vote of everyone who sees that sign.

BUMPER STICKERS

A second way to aid the campaign of your favorite candidate is to attach a sticker on the rear bumper of your car or truck. The bumper sticker will likely carry only the candidate's name or campaign slogan. For a long time many people refrained from doing this because the stickers were difficult to remove after the campaign season was over. However, stickers today are either magnetic or otherwise made to be easily removed after the election is over. Unlike a yard sign, which is fixed in the ground and visible only to those who pass by your house, a bumper sticker on your vehicle goes wherever you go and announces your voting preference all along the way.

These campaign bumper stickers can also be distributed at a local church by any campaign that requests permission to do so. Members are free to take whichever stickers support the candidate of their choice. Arrange the stickers on a table in a lobby where church members can see them and pick one up if they choose to do so. This practice does not amount to the endorsement of any particular candidate by the church if all candidates are allowed to place materials on that table. However, it is clearly an endorsement by a private citizen when someone agrees to affix that sticker to the bumper of his or her vehicle.

BUTTONS, CAPS, AND SHIRTS

Campaigns are more and more likely to prepare various items that supporters can actually wear to signal support for their favorite candidate. These items include lapel pins or button badges that carry the name or slogan of a particular candidate or campaign. Baseball-style caps have also become popular, although these are often used as a fundraiser for the campaign, thus providing the candidate with added revenue while providing campaign supporters with another way to announce their support both through purchasing and then wearing the cap. The same is true for shirts, sweatshirts, or any other item of clothing sold by the campaign.

It would not be wise for churches to get in the business of selling campaign paraphernalia, but it is perfectly acceptable for church members to come to church events and go to other locations proudly wearing these items that declare their support for a given candidate.

VOLUNTEERING ON ELECTION DAY

One of the most important things church members can do to aid and assist in the political process is to volunteer their time on Election Day in one of several ways. First, they can volunteer to work as a poll worker to assist other voters in getting signed in and steered through the voting process. These persons tend to work all day, typically from 7:00 a.m. to 7 p.m., sitting inside the polling place. Some are observers looking for any signs of fraud on the part of voters or campaign workers. Others are there to sit at tables and make sure that the process goes smoothly.

Another option is to provide support to the volunteers at the polls. For more than twenty years my wife made it her mission and ministry to deliver food to poll workers on every Election Day. Her delivery included bagels, muffins, coffee, and juices in the morning, and then a deli tray or deli salads with more juice or sodas for lunch or a mid-afternoon snack. This was her way of supporting the poll workers, and they were always grateful for what she brought. In fact, whenever she was out of town or unavailable to do this, she made sure that I picked up the slack and carried on the work that she had begun. We did this not only at the polling place where we voted, but also at the polling place in a different community where our son had been assigned as a poll worker by the county board of elections.

There is not a polling place or a poll worker in America who would not appreciate this act of support for such service. If there are church members serving as poll workers, others in that church can take it upon themselves to do something similar at the polling places where their church members have been assigned. This can be orchestrated easily by the church office as a purely nonpartisan expression of support for poll workers, not candidates.

Volunteering to drive people who lack transportation to their polling place is something else that can be done on Election Day. Like supporting poll workers, such volunteer-based transportation is nonpartisan in nature and supports the political process rather than the campaign of a particular candidate. If a person is unable to get to the polling place because of a lack of access to transportation, the availability of a ride to the voting location can be a great service. Many political campaigns will pay persons to do this on their behalf, but the church can simply provide to the local Democratic or Republican Party county office a list of names of volunteers who can be called if transportation is needed.

It is very rewarding to hear the expressions of gratitude from persons, most of them members of your church, who might not have been unable to vote had you not been willing and available to drive them to and from the polls. Churches often provide this service for its members who need transportation to a doctor's appointment or to the grocery store. Why not offer a similar service on election day?

CAMPAIGN COMMITTEE WORKERS

Political campaigns are most closely identified with the name and the face of the candidate who is seeking a particular political office. It can be absolutely guaranteed that a candidate will lose in the election if he or she has not been able to assemble a loyal and devoted campaign committee to assist in the process. Whether the candidate is running to become President of the United States or a member of a local school board, he or she will need the help of campaign workers to reach that goal. In every campaign in which I was involved church members from Antioch and other churches formed the core of my campaign committee.

When I ran for a seat from Ohio in the U.S. Congress in 1998, my campaign chairman was Rev. Dr. Otis Moss Jr., who was pastor of Olivet Institutional Baptist Church in Cleveland. My campaign treasurer was Rev. Dr. William Myers, who was pastor of New Mt. Zion Baptist Church also in Cleveland and professor of New Testament at nearby Ashland Theological Seminary. The person who ran the campaign and coordinated all of our activities was Rev. Sam Tidmore, also of Olivet. The driver who took me to various campaign events was a deacon of a local church. Dorthea Alexander,

Eva Bekes, and Edrice Clark, all members of Antioch, ran the campaign office every day for two months.

When I ran for the U.S. Senate in 2000, my legal counsel was Gladys Harrison, who was then a member of Mt. Olive Baptist Church in Cleveland, and my driver and campaign coordinator was Lang Dunbar, a lifelong member of Antioch. Much to my surprise and delight, they got acquainted during the campaign, got engaged a few weeks after the campaign, and are now in their fourteenth year of marriage. I lost that election, but it proved to be a winning experience for them!

Campaigns need people to hand out literature, make phone calls, write and answer letters, coordinate fundraising events, and accompany the candidate to various events across the voting district, whether that involves a single county, an entire state, or a whole nation. This includes campaign gatherings in the homes of persons who are willing to invite their neighbors to come to meet a candidate.

This is grassroots campaigning at its best when a candidate sits down with a dozen or so potential voters and makes a case to get their vote. Individual church members can volunteer to host such events for the candidate of their choosing. Or they can volunteer to accompany the candidate and assist in things such as answering the door, working at a sign-in table, preparing name tags, staffing a refreshment table, receiving financial contributions to the campaign, and handing out campaign materials such as the yard signs and bumper stickers mentioned earlier.

HONORING ARTICLE 6: NO RELIGIOUS TEST

No matter what a church or an individual church member decides to do about political involvement, I both caution and encourage people to avoid one thing at all costs. Do not require a candidate to agree with you on every aspect of your religious dogma or denominational doctrine as a precondition for receiving your vote. Not only is it unlikely that you will ever find a person who agrees with you in all of those areas, but also expecting or requiring a candidate to do so is clearly a violation of Article 6, Section 3 of the U.S. Constitution, which says in part, "no religious test shall ever be required as a qualification to any office or public trust under the United States."

Congregations may want to be sure that their pastor believes in the divinity of Jesus or in the authority of the Bible in ways that match their own beliefs. However, political candidates are exempt from having to share those religious views, and furthermore, they should also be exempt from having to answer such questions in the first place. Nothing but trouble resides in an election where church members are being directed to vote only for candidates who share their views on some religious or biblically based view on a social issue, without regard for the ways in which that practice becomes "a religious test." Remember that it is not only the government that should never impose a religious test on a political candidate. The electorate also should not exclude someone because of their religious views or affiliations.

In a secular society that places great value on religious liberty, no one religious group ought to attempt to impose its doctrinal or ethical views on the whole of society by only electing people to political office who agree with them on those religious and ethical dogmas. What a group cannot win in the court of public opinion, it ought not to try to impose through a backdoor political maneuver. As Robert Maddox, former executive director of Americans United for Separation of Church and State, says, "Churches should not seek to impose their distinctive dogmas on the general population, or to see their theological doctrines imbedded in the civil law."[2]

This is precisely why so many people in the United States want to keep churches and clergy outside of the political process, fearing that they want to transform society in their own biblical and theological image. This is why many parents in Shaker Heights did not want to support my first campaign for election to the local school board. With images of Jerry Falwell and Pat Robertson dancing in their heads, they were suspicious that what I was really up to was a plan to impose a school-sponsored Christmas pageant on Jewish students, or school prayer in Jesus' name on Muslim students, or Bible-based curriculum on atheist students.

This is part of what makes the national debate about abortion and same-sex marriage so complicated. No one can object if people seek to make the case that they personally oppose those matters on religious grounds. If that is the case, then people can have an honest and open conversation about whether or not the biblical verses being invoked actually mean what opponents of abortion or same-sex marriage are asserting. This is what religious liberty is all about.

However, it is another matter altogether when religious groups try to use the electoral process to impose their views upon the entire country, including those who do not share membership or agreement with those who are trying to impose their views on others.

What is most troublesome about trying to use politics to reinforce religion is that, more often than not, the religious issues in question have been narrowly defined, with many other issues left off the table. For instance, many people who strongly oppose same-sex marriage or abortion do not seem to hold equally strong views about mass incarceration, the human and financial costs of war, the staggering number of persons in this country living at or below the poverty line, or the ease with which guns or drugs can be acquired in a society being torn apart by both.

As author and educator Bill McKibben writes, "America is simultaneously the most professedly Christian of the developed nations and the least Christian in its behavior."[3] He notes that more than 85 percent of all Americans identify themselves as Christians, and yet this country leads all developed nations in the murder rate, the use of capital punishment, the number of persons incarcerated, the percentage of marriages ending in divorce, the rate of teen pregnancy, and the number of children living in poverty.[4]

The solution to these realities is not to elect more Southern Baptists, or more United Methodists, or more Christians or Muslims or Jews of any type. The solution is first of all to get over our "national fixation with abortion and human sexuality so we can focus on these other embarrassments in our national life."[5] Churches, mosques, synagogues, temples, and other places of religious gathering should be outraged over these realities in our society. However, being sure that a candidate for school board or the White House agrees with me on the meaning of a particular verse of Scripture is not how our system of government is designed.

THE SEPARATION OF CHURCH AND STATE IS STILL BEING DEBATED

In 2013 an issue of *The Christian Century* carried a story with the headline "Evangelical Body Supports Politicking in the Pulpit." The article begins with these words: "Bucking popular opinion and a decades-old IRS policy, a group of conservative evangelicals is urging that pastors be allowed to endorse political candidates in church without risking their congregation's tax-exempt status."[6]

The leader of the group known as Commission on Accountability and Policy for Religious Organizations asserted that "members of the clergy should be able to say whatever they believe is appropriate" in their religious contexts.[7] That effort ran into swift opposition, first from Americans United for Separation of Church and State, whose executive director, Barry Lynn, stated that the "proposal [by the Evangelical Council for Financial Accountability] would reduce America's houses of worship to mere cogs in political machines."[8] It was also opposed by the Interfaith Alliance, whose president, C. Welton Gaddy, observed,

> The rights of the clergy to preach about the most pressing issues of the day and to provide moral guidance to their congregations are not in danger and must be protected. But those rights are very different from standing at the pulpit—shrouded in your faith—to announce that your congregation should vote for one candidate or party over another.[9]

I repeat here a warning from John Bennett, which was first raised in chapter 1:

> The churches in America should not use their members as political pressure groups to get special ecclesiastical privileges for themselves as against other religious bodies. They should not seek legislation ... which interferes with the religious liberty of minorities and they should be thankful that the courts stand guard at this point. No church, no matter how powerful, should bring pressure on the state to enact laws which are based upon principles that depend for their validity on its own doctrine or ethos. ... It is wrong to seek to make the ethos of one part of the community the basis of law.[10]

WILLIAM REHNQUIST AND SEPARATION OF CHURCH AND STATE

We should note that the issue of separation of church and state was the basis of a remarkable dissent written by Justice William Rehnquist in the 1985 *Wallace v. Jaffree* case. The issue in the case was whether some relaxing of the prohibition against school prayer should be allowed. The majority of the court ruled against that practice again, as they did in *Engel v. Vitale*, viewing such prayer as a breach of the wall of separation between church and state.

Writing for the majority, Justice John Paul Stevens noted that the practice lacked any secular purpose and thus did not pass the three-part test, based on the 1971 U.S. Supreme Court ruling in *Lemon v. Kurtzman*, of government entanglement in religion.[11]

William Rehnquist, who had not yet been appointed Chief Justice of the court, took strong exception to the idea that the state had to be neutral on the matter of religion. He said,

> Any decision based on *Everson v. Board of Education* was wrong; the Constitution does not impose a wall of separation between church and state. ... The establishment clause of the First Amendment merely forbids state establishment of a national church or preference of one sect over others.[12]

Thus, government funding of some religious programs, including school vouchers to attend parochial schools, was something that Rehnquist regularly endorsed. He based his decision upon this opinion, which is wholly different from how most people historically have understood the concept. He wrote, "There is simply no historical foundation for the proposition that the Framers intended to build the 'wall of separation' between church and state that was constitutionalized in *Everson*," adding that the wall concept itself is "in no way based on either the language or intent of the drafters."[13]

The many recent challenges to the separation of church and state notwithstanding, the principle remains firmly in place in American life in general. The principle remains firmly in place more particularly in the way in which limits are placed upon the ways government can intervene in or interfere with the free exercise of religion and also upon religious groups that try to use political office to advance or fund their doctrinal and parochial agendas. More importantly for this study, at no point in any of these rulings, whether by the majority or the minority of the U.S. Supreme Court, was there even a hint that the involvement of members of the clergy in electoral politics was a violation of the separation of church and state.

PART IV: QUESTIONS FOR DISCUSSION AND REFLECTION

1. What does it mean to belong to a political or politicized church? In what ways, if any, does your local church function as a politicized congregation?

2. What is the relationship between the IRS and political activity by religious organizations?
3. What things does the IRS prohibit churches from doing in the realm of politics?
4. What are some common objections to religious leaders being involved in politics?
5. What is your personal response or reaction to those objections?
6. What verses from the writings of the apostle Paul can be used to respond to the criticism of clergy being involved in politics?
7. What is the one thing every citizen must do in order to be eligible to vote in this country?
8. How can churches assist in the process of registering voters? What forms of assistance with voter registration are employed by your local church?
9. What are some of the different ways church members may legally be involved in a political campaign?
10. What does Article 6, Section 3 of the U.S. Constitution say, and why is it important?
11. What group is urging that all restrictions be dropped regarding clergy openly endorsing candidates from the pulpit? Do you agree that such restrictions should be dropped? Why or why not?
12. Would you support the idea of your church being used as a polling place? Why or why not?

PART IV: THINGS TO REMEMBER

1. What amendment to the U.S. Constitution guaranteed to former slaves the right to vote? In what year was that amendment adopted?
2. What types of voter suppression were used to prohibit black people from voting?
3. What act of Congress was passed, and in what year, to restore those voting rights?
4. What major civil rights demonstration set the stage for the passage of that act?
5. True or false: It is unconstitutional or against IRS regulations for a church to serve as a polling place on election day.

6. True or false: The IRS prohibits candidates from visiting or even speaking during a worship service.
7. What are religious bodies not allowed to do as far as campaign finance laws are concerned?
8. Name one thing that all candidates must do in order for their name to appear on the ballot.
9. What group has argued that existing laws covering separation of church and state be even more vigorously enforced?
10. Which U.S. Supreme Court Justice challenged the validity of the separation of church and state as a principle intended by the founders of this nation, and why?
11. What did Pierce Creek Church of Binghamton, New York, do that endangered its tax-exempt status?

Notes

1. Quoted by Tom Shine, "47% of Congress Are Millionaires—A Status Shared by Only 1% of Americans," *ABC News*, November 16, 2011 (http://abcnews.go.com/blogs/politics/2011/11/47-of-congress-members-millionaires-a-status-shared-by-only-1-of-americans/).
2. Robert L. Maddox, *Separation of Church and State: Guarantor of Religious Freedom* (New York: Crossroad, 1987), 160.
3. Bill McKibben, "The Christian Paradox: How a Faithful Nation Gets Jesus Wrong," *Harper's Magazine*, August 2005, 32.
4. Ibid.
5. Marvin A. McMickle, *Where Have All the Prophets Gone? Reclaiming Prophetic Preaching in America* (Cleveland: Pilgrim Press, 2006), 41.
6. John Dart, "Evangelical Body Supports Politicking in the Pulpit," *The Christian Century*, August 29, 2013, 15.
7. Ibid.
8. Ibid.
9. Ibid.
10. John Bennett, *Christians and the State* (New York: Scribner, 1958), 207.
11. Kermit L. Hall, ed., *The Oxford Companion to the Supreme Court of the United States* (New York: Oxford University Press, 2005), 1062.
12. Ibid.
13. Justice Rehnquist's dissent in *Wallace v. Jaffree* (1985), U.S. Supreme Court (http://www.belcherfoundation.org/wallace_v_jaffree_dissent.htm).

A CONCLUDING WORD
Calling All Interested Persons!

Imagine that the pastor or a group of members within a local church decides to host a Politics 101 workshop, at which time the facilitators want to share with their church membership all of the ideas and political practices described in chapters 11 and 12. Persons who belong to that church can lead such an effort simply by following the topics set forth in the preceding pages. They could invite someone in from the League of Women Voters, the county board of elections, the local Democratic and Republican Party, or the political action committee of the local NAACP to lead such a discussion. No actual candidate has to be involved, because the objective is not necessarily to support a particular political campaign. The objective is to aid that congregation in becoming a political or politicized church. Not one suggestion listed here is in conflict with any IRS provision for a 501(c)(3) organization. These things have been employed by other churches across the country without raising any concerns about endangering their tax-exempt status.

What these suggested actions do is allow for increased involvement of private citizens in the electoral process that will eventually and inevitably have great impact upon every aspect of their lives. What these steps also do is serve as a reminder that the actual act of casting a vote on election day is the final step in a much longer and far more complex process that no one candidate can navigate alone. It may be that only a single name will appear on the ballot. However, all the work that went into getting that name on the ballot and bringing that name to the attention of the electorate is what politics in a democracy is all about.

I hope that with increasing frequency the name on the ballot will be that of a black preacher/politician. That is a tradition of clergy leadership in the black community that I hope will be restored in some instances and sustained in others. However, no black preacher/politician can get elected by his or her own efforts. That is where the active involvement of politicized churches and politically engaged church members is needed.

I have argued in this book that there are no legal or constitutional prohibitions regarding a member of the clergy serving in a political office. It has been demonstrated that the idea of the separation of church and state does not even appear in the U.S. Constitution, and that what the Constitution does seek to do is limit the reach of government into the life of the church, not limit the involvement of clergy in the life of government. This book has argued that black preacher/politicians were the result of the social forces in this country that defined and limited the opportunities available to black people from its formation until the end of the Civil War (1776–1865) and from the Post-Reconstruction era until the climax of the Civil Rights movement (1877–1968).

If black people had been able to pursue the career goals and opportunities that were available to white people in this country during this same period of time, there might never have been a need for black preachers to serve as political leaders. In the case of white society, their clergy were never needed as political leaders because there was an ample supply of other candidates emerging from other professions such as business, education, the military, and the nonprofit sector.

However, from the moment that slavery ended in this country, black preachers have been serving as political as well as spiritual leaders for their communities because there was such a shortage of other persons who could serve in that political role. Although there was never a time when the majority of black officeholders were members of the clergy, it is also true that there has never been a time when some members of the clergy have not served in a political office at some level of government. Black people from other professions have come to the fore in political life, and that is a good thing. Nevertheless, the door should always remain open to members of the clergy who seek to serve as black preacher/politicians. That is a historic model of leadership in the black church that I hope is never lost.

I have argued, especially in Part IV, that more black churches need to be politicized so that they can function effectively and legally within the sphere of electoral politics. There are a great many things that churches can do when it comes to politics that are in no way in conflict with their tax-exempt status. Given the important role that the church continues to play in the black communities of this country, it is crucial that churches see the necessity of helping their members become better informed regarding the candidates, officeholders, and policy issues that will impact their lives in significant ways.

All that being said, it is my earnest hope that more and more black preachers will consider the history of the black preacher/politician and then decide to explore that role as an aspect of their ministry. It is my hope that an increasing number of black preachers will bring their religious sensibilities into the political arena, where they can aid in shaping public policies that enrich the lives of people all across this country. Politics can be a means of grace, and it is my hope that more and more black preachers will consider the fact that the black preacher/politician is a legitimate model of leadership in the church that can be traced back as least as far as the Reconstruction era (1865–1877). Finally, it is my hope that when a black preacher does seek to be involved in electoral politics, he or she will not be discouraged or assumed to be disqualified based upon the issue of the separation of church and state. As long as political office is used to serve the common good and never used to advance a narrow doctrinal or denominational agenda, and as long as religious liberty is respected and IRS regulations are observed, there is no reason why a member of the clergy should not seek and serve in a political office.

RECOMMENDED BIBLIOGRAPHY

Barry, John M., *Roger Williams and the Creation of the American Soul: Church, State, and the Birth of Liberty*, Viking Press: NY, 2012.

Corbett, Michael and Julia Mitchell Corbett, *Politics and Religion in the United States*, Garland Publishing: NY, 1999.

Crawford, Sue E.S. and Laura R. Olson, *Christian Clergy in American Politics*, Johns Hopkins Press: Baltimore, MD, 2001.

Dickerson, Dennis C., *African American Preachers and Politics: The Careys of Chicago*, University Press of Mississippi: Jackson, MS, 2010.

Hamilton, Charles V., *Adam Clayton Powell Jr: The Political Biography of an American Dilemma*, Atheneum: NY, 1991.

——— *The Black Preacher in America*, Morrow: NY, 1972.

Haygood, Wil, *King of the Cats: The Life and Times of Adam Clayton Powell, Jr.*, Houghton Mifflin: NY, 1993.

Henry, Carl F., *The Christian Mindset in a Secular Society: Promoting Evangelical Renewal and National Righteousness*, Multnomah Press: Portland, OR, 1984.

Litwack, Leon and August Meier, eds., *Black Leaders of the Nineteenth Century*, University of Illinois Press: Urbana, IL, 1991.

Logan, Rayford W., *The Betrayal of the Negro: From Rutherford B. Hayes to Woodrow Wilson*, Collier Books: NY, 1965.

Maddox, Robert L., *Separation of Church and State: Guarantor of Religious Freedom*, Crossroad Books: NY, 1987.

McMickle, Marvin A., *An Encyclopedia of African American Christian Heritage*, Judson Press: Valley Forge, PA, 2002.

216 PULPIT & POLITICS

Meyerson, Michael I., *Endowed by Our Creator: The Birth of Religious Freedom in America*, Yale University Press: New Haven, CT, 2012.

Morris, Aldon D., *The Origins of the Civil Rights Movement: Black Communities Organizing for Change*, Free Press: NY, 1984.

Paris, Peter J., *Black Religious Leaders: Conflict in Unity: Insights from Martin Luther King, Jr., Malcolm X, Joseph H. Jackson, and Adam Clayton Powell, Jr.*, Westminster/John Knox Press, Louisville, KY, 1991.

Pinn, Anthony B., *The Black Church in the Post–Civil Rights Era*, Orbis: Maryknoll: NY, 2002.

Quarles, Benjamin, *Black Abolitionists*, Da Capo Press: NY, 1969.

Ragosta, John, *Religious Freedom: Jefferson's Legacy, America's Creed*, University of Virginia Press: Charlottesville, VA, 2013.

Smith, R. Drew and Fredrick C. Harris, eds., *Black Churches and Politics: Clergy Influence, Organizational Partnerships, and Civic Empowerment*, Rowman & Littlefield: New York, 2005.

Tate, Katherine, *From Protest to Politics: The New Black Voters in American Elections*, Harvard University Press: Cambridge, MA, 1994.

Taylor, Mark Lewis, *Religion, Politics, and the Christian Right: Post-9/11 Powers and American Empire*, Fortress Press: Minneapolis, MN, 2005.

Wallis, Jim, *God's Politics: Why the Right Gets It Wrong and the Left Doesn't Get It*, Harper: San Francisco, CA, 2005.

Woodson, Carter G., *The History of the Negro Church*, The Associated Publishers: Washington, DC, 1921.